ON READING
FRENCH VERSE

ON READING
FRENCH VERSE

A Study
of Poetic Form

ROY LEWIS

CLARENDON PRESS · OXFORD
1982

Oxford University Press, Walton Street, Oxford OX2 6DP

London Glasgow New York Toronto
Delhi Bombay Calcutta Madras Karachi
Kuala Lumpur Singapore Hong Kong Tokyo
Nairobi Dar es Salaam Cape Town
Melbourne Auckland

and associate companies in
Beirut Berlin Ibadan Mexico City Nicosia

Published in the United States by
Oxford University Press, New York

British Library Cataloguing in Publication Data

Lewis, Roy
On reading French Verse
1. French poetry
I. Title
841'.009   PQ413
ISBN 0-19-815775-4

Printed in Great Britain by
The Thetford Press Limited, Thetford, Norfolk

ACKNOWLEDGEMENTS

I wish in particular to thank Professor R.C. Knight of Swansea not only for his interest in this book, but for his encouragement and guidance, as well as for many acts of personal friendship, over many years. Also Professor L.J. Austin of Cambridge to whom I am much indebted for his scholarly judgement and his moral support. And to these I add the advisers of the Oxford University Press. All the above gave me the benefit of detailed and meticulous commentary on the typescript from which I learnt much. For the contents of this book I am of course responsible, but I hope they will feel that it has benefited from their advice. I would also like to acknowledge the contribution made by students in tutorials and seminars, some of whose suggestions have undoubtedly found their way into this book. I hope it may in some small degree serve to communicate their enthusiasm to others. And I must also place on record my debt to one particular A–Level candidate who produced a commentary on a poem by Verlaine which was so outstandingly bad as to convince me of the need for a work of this kind directed to the needs of the student whose native language is not French.

R. A. L

CONTENTS

HOW TO USE THIS BOOK

Very little has been written on the work of the French poets, while much has been written on their lives, their thoughts, and their theories. Anyone who has taught and studied French literature in schools or universities will know that it is possible for a student not only to qualify at A–Level but to graduate and even carry out advanced research without ever having heard a French poem adequately read. By adequate reading I mean a rendering which befits a work of art. And yet the prime claim which poets have on our attention is that they are artists in words. If we compare the study of poetry with that of music, we note that in the latter field anyone who has pretensions to be more than an amateur must learn a notation, study a technique, and practise a craft. He must be able to assess the merits of varying interpretations of a work, which requires an understanding of its potential. No such demands are made of the student of poetry. It is taken for granted that he can read. But familiarity with the reading and writing of prose does not qualify one either to read or to write verse. This involves entirely different techniques. It is simply not possible to study an art unless one studies also the craft which is its medium of expression. Failure to appreciate this point has led to a widespread, if often unavowed, belief in English-speaking academic circles that French is simply not a 'poetic language', and that, with the possible exception of a few outstanding individuals, French poetry represents a minor achievement. It has already been dropped as an essential requirement from the curricula of many A–level examining boards, being considered either relatively unimportant or too difficult. To teach in this field is indeed difficult, but where the attempt is made the response is often enthusiastic. However much importance may be attached to the teaching of a language as a means of day-to-day communication, the student of literature must acquire a love of the language and an awareness of its imaginative potential. It is not possible to know a language as a literary medium unless one knows its poetry.

This book is not a treatise on versification, of which a number exist by authorities of greater competence than the present writer. It is a personal attempt to assess those features of verse which make it a suitable medium of expression for great poets. It is less concerned with the statement of rules—though of necessity this is part of the field covered—than with consideration of their *raison d'être* and with examination of the way in which they are actually applied. It would be pretentious to attempt a study of French poetry as such. My aim is very limited. I have not discussed poets or even poems. But every conclusion reached in the following pages is based on the examination of specific stanzas or, for the most part, lines from the work of poets whom the student is likely to be called on to read. The selection has been limited largely but not entirely to the nineteenth century, and to poems which any serious student of the subject is likely at one time or the other to read. I have not hesitated to include some which would now be frowned on as hackneyed, because I think their qualities, like those of French verse in general, are little known and little understood. The limits of my field are such that this book is no more than one of many possible starting-points to the appreciation of French poetry. Its aim is clearly stated in the title. It is concerned simply with reading verse.

Its approach is deliberately, in some respects, controversial. If the reader disagrees fundamentally with my findings, I hope he will, in due course, sit down and write a better book.

This book is addressed in general to the student of French verse: but those aspects of it which may, I hope, be of value to the A–Level student are unlikely to be of much interest to the advanced reader, and vice versa. I might therefore say that it should be read with discernment, which simply means skipped and pillaged to meet individual interests and requirements. What may for one reader be an unduly meticulous examination of a familiar point may perhaps raise issues of interest and controversy to another. The A–Level student will certainly need his teacher's advice as to which pages to consult. Some of the more general remarks on the nature and function of verse may throw light on the subject he is studying. He will certainly benefit from knowledge of the exact terminology he is called on to use. Many years' experience of examining at A–Level have left me in no doubt at all that, when called on to round off a commentary on a poem with a section under the heading *Versification*, most students flounder helplessly and lose marks as a result. Having also had the experience of teaching sixth-formers, I am fully aware of the difficulties encountered by the teacher who endeavours to arouse the interest of students whose knowledge of the language is inadequate. One cannot appreciate a line of verse if one has to open one's dictionary twice, or even once, to get through it. Translation should be disposed of quickly, and poetry should never be regarded as a means of increasing vocabulary. I think the teacher should translate, and the student should read, sufficiently often to be able to do it easily and well. Only so can any feeling for French verse be developed. Even from the purely practical point of view of passing examinations, the student who displays sensitivity to verse will get better marks than the one who retails clichés. Anyone who has marked a thousand or so examination scripts will know the feeling of relief, even of gratitude, with which one welcomes the answer which demonstrates that the student has actually thought about the poem on the paper before him. I hope the teacher will find in the following pages material which will help him convince the student that poetry is a worthwhile activity.

While much that is in this book will be irrelevant to the needs of the sixth-former and even to the university student in his earlier stages, I believe that some of the terms which I have used in the discussion of verse will be of value at every level, because they direct attention to meaningful features and make possible some awareness of form. This in turn makes it possible correctly to memorize lines and to quote them. Obviously incorrect quotation, or inability to quote, always undermines the examiner's confidence in a candidate. Some feeling for phonetic patterning, or for the correct placing of the caesura and the internal rhythm of a line, is a valuable aid to memory. Many of the technical terms here used have been devised especially for this study (or rather for the years of practical teaching on which it is based) simply because no equivalent exists, and I have personally found them helpful in describing and examining verse. But I must add the warning, which I have repeated elsewhere, that the student who uses them in an examination answer must be able to explain their meaning, or at least refer to their source, so that the examiner may know what he has in mind.

The greater part of this book is intended for university students, and it is in this field that the principles it incorporates have been most extensively tried out. The serious student will be able to read it for himself, and select what he thinks important. Its intention is to supplement lectures on individual poets and their works, and it should be of some value in the preparation of commentaries and tutorials. The book ends with two commentaries on poems which are intended to illustrate the relevance of the issues here discussed to the wider field of poetry. Of course, they are not model answers, but rather examples of exploration. The ordinary commentary is of more modest proportions and intent, but I think it can be based on similar principles, though applied with much greater selectivity. It is a matter of experience that many students find it difficult to compose even half a dozen lines of meaningful comment on the poet's handling of verse and sound. I hope to convince them that the problem is not what to say but what to leave out.

It would be impertinent of me to attempt to assess any value which the more advanced reader will find in this book. I would only say that it is a serious study in what is in many respects an unfamiliar field, and that a good deal in it is intended specifically for the consideration of the advanced reader. I hope that he will at some times find it enlightening, and at others provocative. He will of course excuse the inclusion of a certain amount of very elementary material, which is there because most students find some difficulty even in simple matters such as syllable-count; and if basic matters are not understood, the remainder of the book would be worthless.

Since I am dealing largely with the sound of verse, I have had recourse on occasions to phonetic transcript. The symbols used are not those of the International Phonetic Association, but have been chosen to be immediately comprehensible to all and to suggest clearly features such as the distinction between open and closed vowels, vowels and semi-consonants, and others which are directly relevant to French verse. Since the phonetic script is used only in association with normal orthography, it should present little difficulty. But the student should bear in mind that this system is not in general use, and that if he chooses to employ it in, for instance, an examination answer, he should indicate its source.

I hope that, at whatever level this book is approached, the reader will find some material which will stimulate his own thought, and a measure of practical assistance in the intelligent and sensitive reading of French verse.

TERMINOLOGY AND SYMBOLS USED
IN THE TEXT

The generally accepted terminology for the discussion of French verse has been used wherever appropriate in the following pages. However, in many cases this terminology is incomplete or inexact. I have therefore proposed precise definitions for certain terms (e.g. caesura, *enjambement, rime riche*); and whether or not he accepts these definitions, the student who uses such terms in writing on French verse is advised to specify exactly what he means by them, since common usage is often ambiguous. In a number of cases I have proposed new terms where no adequate ones at present exist. In the glossary (which also serves as an index) at the end of the book, I have indicated such terms by the use of an asterisk. The student will appreciate that such terms will be understood only by readers of this book; if therefore he finds them useful—as I hope may be the case —in writing on French verse, he should either define them for the convenience of his reader or indicate their source. It is intended that the glossary should serve as a summary of many of the points raised in the text.

PHONETIC TRANSCRIPTION

In order to draw attention to the language of verse, I have made some use of phonetic transcription. Where this is done, the phonetic transcript is always placed in square brackets after the normal spelling, so that no difficulty should be encountered in interpreting it. Thus *père* is represented as [pèr] and *beau* as [bó]. Since it is a phonetic transcript, it represents only sound and takes no account of spelling: *sept* appears as [sèt], *fils* as [fís]. Each symbol represents only one sound. Thus [g] is always as heard in *gloire* [glwár] or *gonfler* [gò flé] and not as in *rouge* [rúj] or *gens* [jà], this sound being represented by [j]. The ambiguous symbol [c] is never used, the appropriate sound being represented as either [k] or [s]. I have not used international phonetic script, since this is too remote from normal spelling for my limited purpose, which is the representation of the sound of verse, and it does not clearly indicate relationships and differences which are important in the study of verse. The system adopted brings out the following distinctions:

    (*a*)   oral vowels carry an acute accent when they are closed: e.g. *agir* [á jír], *écouter* [é kú té], *saut* [só]. A grave accent is used when they are open: *hâte* [àt], *elle* [èl], *sotte* [sòt]. For the sake of consistency, an acute accent is used on the vowels [í] and [ú]—the latter of which represents the vowel written as *ou*: e.g. *bouche* [búdɥ]—even though these vowels have no open form. The symbol [ü] represents the closed vowel heard in *du* [dü] or *plume* [plüm]. The closed vowel heard in *peu* [pœ́] and the open one of *peuple* [pœ̀ pl] are distinguished by their accents. The neutral [e] heard in *de* or *regarder* is represented by [ĕ], as in [dĕ], [rĕ gár dé]. When used without an accent, symbols such as [a] or [e] represent the vowel without specifying whether it is closed or open, oral or nasal.

(*b*) Nasal vowels are indicated by italics, and as they are always open carry a grave accent. Thus: *grand* [grà], *sonder* [sò dé], *lundi* [lœ̀ dí]. The vowel which is variously spelt as *in*, *ein*, *ain*, *aim* and occasionally as *en* is represented by [ë]. Thus: *vin* [vë], *pain* [pë], *quinze* [këz], *examen* [ĕg zá më]. This is of course an open vowel even though it does not carry a grave accent. The purpose of the diaeresis is to avoid confusion with the vowel written as *en* in words such as *entendre* [à tàdr].

(*c*) Unless otherwise indicated, vowels are short. A naturally long vowel (i.e. one long in normal usage) is indicated by a full stop. Thus: *grande* [grà.d], *l'âme* [là.m], *rose* [ró.z]. A vowel which is slightly lengthened in verse by a following neutral [e] is indicated by a raised full stop, thus: *calmĕ* [ká˙lmĕ], *belle* [bè˙lĕ].

(*d*) Semi-consonants are marked by the breve [˘]. These are:

  1. The very short [i] (called *yod*) which is heard in *ciel* [sy̆èl], *tiens* [ty̆ë] and *soleil* [sò lèy̆]. This sound is indicated by [y̆].

  2. The very short [ü] heard in *nuit* [nŭi], *pluie* [plŭi], *nuance* [nŭà.s] is represented by [ŭ].

  3. The very short [u] heard in *oui* [w̆í], *ouest* [w̆èst], *souhaiter* [sw̆è té] is represented by [w̆].

The palatalized [n] heard in *cogner* is represented as in [kò ny̆é].

(*e*) In the phonetic transcript, syllables are normally separated, thus: *majestueusement* [má jè stü œ̈ zĕ mà]. This is done purely to facilitate scansion. There is no separation of words, and liaison is shown where appropriate, as in *nous avons* [nu zá vò]. Phrases are sometimes separated by stress-bars [|] which may be doubled for a major stress. A pause—usually between lines—is indicated as either [] or [], according to its effective length.

SCANSION, STRESS AND PITCH

When quotations are given in normal orthography, vowel-length is indicated by placing a full stop after a naturally long vowel and a raised dot after a vowel lengthened by a following neutral [e]. All other vowels are short. In cases where diaeresis occurs, a colon may be placed between the two adjacent vowels so as to facilitate scan-

sion, thus: inflexi:on, silenci:eux. A breve [˘] is used to indicate a
neutral [e] which is sounded in verse but would be mute in normal
prose usage. Syllables may be indicated by placing a dot beneath the
sounded vowel, this dot being doubled for a subsidiary stress and
trebled for a major stress. Thus:

Les sillons de l'espa|ce où fermen.tĕnt les mon.des [.]
 · · ··   · · ···   · · ·· · · ···

The caesura of the alexandrine is indicated by an upright stress-bar;
but if the major stress of the line is displaced, this is shown by a
sloping bar as in:

Derriè.rĕ la mura.ille immen./sĕ du brouilla.rd [;]
 · ·· · · · ··   · ···   · · · ···

(These stress-bars are also used when rhythm is indicated by num-
bers. Thus the rhythm of the above lines would be shown as 3:3| 3:3
and 2:4:2/4 respectively. Enjambement on the line-ending is shown
by an added hyphen, as in, for instance, 1:5| 4:2 − . A pattern such
as 3:3:3/3 − would show enjambement on both the caesura and the
line-ending.)

Since the melodic pattern of a line depends very much on personal
interpretation, it is indicated only when it is the subject of special
comment. The terms *neutral*, *middle* and *high pitch* are used to
represent a rising sequence, or, reversed, a falling one; while *low
pitch* describes the fall of the voice at a full stop. These voice-levels
may be represented by placing words or their phonetic equivalents
in a specific relationship to the square brackets which enclose them.
Thus 'Moi, je ne crois pas cela [.]' may be shown as [^{Moi} | je ne
crois pas ce $_{\text{la}}$] or with corresponding phonetic symbols. The same
pitch-sequence may be represented by dots as [$_{...}$ | · · · $_{··}$ · $_{...}$].

The punctuation which terminates any line quoted is always
given, since this modifies its melodic form. Such punctuation is
placed between square brackets in order to separate it from the
punctuation of the text of the book (since, for instance, a quotation
ending in a full stop will frequently not be the end of the sentence in
which it is quoted). In the case of an open-ended line, square
brackets without punctuation are used, thus: [ ].

LINE REFERENCES

Where a poem is quoted at length, individual lines are numbered for
purposes of reference. A reference to any such line in the text is

given as a number enclosed between square brackets, thus: 'The caesura in [6] is displaced ...'. This avoids superfluous quotation and over-use of the word 'line'. Stanzas are represented by roman numerals enclosed in square brackets: thus 'in [V]' means 'in the fifth stanza'. In the case of alexandrines, the first hemistich is referred to as [A], the second as [B]: thus [6B] identifies the second hemistich of the sixth line.

Quotations are numbered consecutively as they occur throughout the book, these numbers being in bold type without brackets. They are also listed alphabetically in the Index. References to the Index are made by italic numbers.

RIME-SCHEMES

The usual practice is followed of indicating rime-schemes by lower-case italic letters, the same letter being used for the proposal and answer of each rime. It is not normally necessary to show the gender of rimes, but when this is to be done upper-case letters are used for feminine rimes. Thus a rime-scheme may be shown as *aBBa CddC* etc. A short line may be shown by the use of square brackets. Thus the rime-scheme of Lamartine's *Le Lac* is *AbA[b]*. A repeated word is shown by the symbol [']. So the rime-scheme of Baudelaire's *Le Balcon* is *AbAbA'* cDcDc' etc.

Chapter One
POETRY AND VERSE

A POEM is an object made out of language.

We might say the same of any work of literature, but only in the case of poetry are we likely to find the statement worth thinking about. We learn a poem by heart, word for word, with its rimes, its rhythms, its images; but we should gain nothing by treating a short story in this manner. We know that a novel can be turned into a film, in which case much that was previously expressed in words must now be indicated by the photographic image, and by gesture and action and scene. The film does not replace the novel, yet it does reflect it, which suggests that the words of the original narrative can be successfully interpreted in another medium. But no one could make a film of a poem. When we listen to a poem being read, we hear a particular combination of thought, imagination, and sound, and each feature is an essential part of the whole. Language is the chosen vehicle for all three, and forms the substance of the poem just as marble may be that of a statue and paint that of a picture.

Alone among literary forms, the poem cannot be translated from one language to another. Attempts are frequently made to translate poems, partly because poets find the effort both challenging and rewarding, and also because it is felt to be better for us to have an imperfect reproduction of the poetry of unfamiliar languages than none at all. A poem translated is merely a paraphrase or a reminiscence of the original; or sometimes, when the translator is a poet in his own right, a new poem. The original may well contain important intellectual and imaginative statements which can be perfectly well expressed in another language, but the relationship between these ideas and images and the language in which they were first expressed cannot be reproduced, since no two languages sound alike and each appeals to the mind and emotions in its own way.

Mankind has always believed that some of the most significant of human statements have been made by its poets. These statements take the form of communicated experience, and go far beyond the limits of 'prose meaning'. Also, mankind has always regarded poetry as a source of intellectual and sensuous pleasure. The nursery rime and the *Iliad* may differ widely in form and significance, but both were composed to give pleasure and would have little function if they lost the capacity to do so. It is true that most students make the acquaintance of great poetry through an academic system which lays stress not only on 'prose meaning' but also on historical and biographical facts related to the composition of the work and to psychological and philosophical suppositions which may be deduced from it, for these are things which can be reproduced in an examination paper or thesis or discussed in a book. Such information can be useful and may occasionally be necessary for the appreciation of poetry, but can never be a substitute for the delight which is to be obtained from reading it. If the student should find himself reading a poem with no other object than to be able to write an essay about it or its author, then he is obviously engaged in a highly artificial exercise. Academic discipline of this kind may be valuable if it makes us read, but only on condition that we learn to enjoy what we read.

French poetry must be read in French, and for this the familiarity with the language which the student gains in his academic studies may well be insufficient. Since a great deal of French poetry is written in the form of regular riming verse, he must be acquainted with the rules of French versification. Some of these rules have a specific function, some are merely conventional, others derive from the nature of the language itself and from the particular demands of the poetic vision. Even more important, he will need to read creatively. As they appear on the printed page the words no more constitute a poem than the notes on a stave constitute a song. They have to be brought to life. The substance out of which poetry is shaped by the imagination is not merely language but, more specifically, speech. The student must therefore be able to hear and reproduce the sounds and rhythms of spoken French as closely as possible. Finally, and most important of all, he must be able to take an active pleasure in well-written imaginative language. Naturally, this requires a certain innate capacity, but the capacity is more widespread than is generally imagined; if it were not so, poetry and song would not have played so important a part in the cultural life of peoples of all ages and countries. In our own time at least what is most generally lacking is practice. The student's training encourages him to read with his intelligence. But the enjoyment of poetry requires him to be sensitive to sounds, rhythms, and images, and such sensitivity comes only with practice.

In the following poem by Henri de Régnier, which exists to give imaginative pleasure, the poet is 'playing' in at least two senses. He imagines himself playing a melody on a flute cut from a reed, and he is at the same time playing with rhythms and sounds of language to create the atmosphere of a musical dream in which all the sounds of nature are in harmony with him.

1   Un petit roseau m'a suffi
       Pour faire frémir l'herbe haute
       Et tout le pré
       Et les doux saules
       Et le ruisseau qui chante aussi;
       Un petit roseau m'a suffi
       A faire chanter la forêt.

       Ceux qui passent l'ont entendu
       Au fond du soir, en leurs pensées,
       Dans le silence et dans le vent,
       Clair ou perdu,
       Proche ou lointain ...
       Ceux qui passent en leurs pensées
       En écoutant, au fond d'eux-mêmes,
       L'entendront encore et l'entendent
       Toujours qui chante.

       Il m'a suffi
       De ce petit roseau cueilli
       A la fontaine où vint l'Amour
       Mirer, un jour,
       Sa face grave
       Et qui pleurait,
       Pour faire pleurer ceux qui passent
       Et trembler l'herbe et frémir l'eau;
       Et j'ai, du souffle d'un roseau,
       Fait chanter toute la forêt.

This poem is written in lines of four and eight syllables, though, unless he has made some prior study of the subject, it is highly unlikely that the student will be able to read them correctly so as to bring out this rhythm. The lines are meant to dance, but it requires a certain elementary skill and experience to make them do so. It also requires experience to hear the abundant use of assonance which strikes the practised ear. But even on first hearing most readers would agree that the poem has imaginative appeal. This appeal is lyrical: i.e. it is associated with that instinct which, in moments of extreme joy or seriousness, makes us want to sing. This is only one of the sources of poetry. Imagination ranges over the whole field of human experience. There is a sense in which the epic, the religious, or the philosophical poem results from the urge to express the imaginative interpretation of life in the form of a song; but poetry may also tell a story or exteriorize emotional or intellectual experience. It always transforms human experience into verbal forms which the reader reinterprets in his own mind, and derives aesthetic pleasure from so doing. A prime error which often leads the student away from the appreciation of the poem itself is the too literally accepted half-truth that a poem 'expresses feeling'. What is important is that it has the capacity to make the reader feel— and think and imagine.

The feeling which the poem creates in the reader is not the same as that which gave rise to it in the poet's own experience. The type of transformation which is brought about depends upon the temperament and vision of the poet. Musset's lines

2   Les plus désespérés sont les chants les plus beaux,
        Et j'en sais d'immortels qui sont de purs sanglots [.]

demonstrate a typically Romantic conversion of sorrow into an object of beauty. Baudelaire wrote a considerable body of poetry on a theme which we may loosely describe as 'boredom', but what the poems express is something far different from the state of mind which gave rise to them. In a sense, they are an antidote to that feeling. Verlaine's life was a disaster and its aimlessness is perfectly depicted in his stanza

3   Et je m'en vais
        Au vent mauvais
            Qui m'emporte,
        Deçà, delà,
        Pareil à la
            Feuille morte [.]

but what the mirror reflects, in the beauty of its form, is not futility and waste but the enduring skill and imagination of the artist. Verlaine is saying 'My life is as futile, as aimless, as ephemeral as a dead leaf.' But the poem itself says 'I have another life which is beauty and immortality,' and it will continue to say this as long as the French language lasts. The poem is also saying, or doing, something else. It is enabling us to share that life, to pass with it into a world of sensuous delight. Verlaine is not just making a statement about himself or about life. He is practising a chemistry of the imagination.

We see the same kind of transformation effected, though on entirely different material, in Leconte de Lisle's poem *Solvet Saeclum*. The title is taken from a traditional Christian hymn, the *Dies Irae*, which foretells the destruction of the earth at the second coming of Christ. Since Leconte de Lisle's poem also deals with the end of the world his use of the quotation is appropriate; but it is at the same time ironical, for the poet has no religious faith. He describes the final annihilation of humanity and of human values in a gigantic cosmic collision. He sees man as heading not towards wisdom or happiness but towards extinction.

4   ... Et ce ne sera point, sous les cieux magnifiques,
Le bonheur reconquis des paradis antiques,
Ni l'entretien d'Adam et d'Ève sur les fleurs,
Ni le divin sommeil après tant de douleurs;
Ce sera quand le Globe et tout ce qui l'habite,
Bloc stérile arraché de son immense orbite,
Stupide, aveugle, plein d'un dernier hurlement,
Plus lourd, plus éperdu de moment en moment,
Contre quelque univers immobile en sa force
Défoncera sa vieille et misérable écorce,
Et, laissant ruisseler, par mille trous béants,
Sa flamme intérieure avec ses océans,
Ira fertiliser de ses restes immondes
Les sillons de l'espace où fermentent les mondes.

The statement which the poem makes is one which, while not verifiable, is scientifically possible. It is a description of something which, if it ever happens, man will not see, since he will not be there to see it. It is a work of imagination, man conceiving his own non-existence, his own insignificance. On one level it casts doubt on all human values. At the same time it demonstrates man's uniqueness, for only man could conceive such a picture; and it also asserts his value, for apart from this the 'incident' it describes would be truly trivial. The poem may say that it *is* trivial, but by its language, indeed by its existence as a poem, it convinces us otherwise. The poet conjures up the futility of man and the vast meaninglessness of the universe; but his powerfully-constructed image is a demonstration of human lucidity. Whatever may come in the future, the present is enriched by this vision which broadens our imaginative horizons. If we read the poem simply or mainly as a scientific or a philosophical hypothesis, we miss the point. The poet doubtless believed what he said, but he also believed in poetry. As in the case of the stanza by Verlaine, the impact of this thing made out of language and imagination is complex, and its meaning is vastly extended by the form in which it is expressed.

Every poem is an image of some aspect of reality, some thought or emotion, some experience. But a 'realistic' of 'factual' poem would be an absurdity. Poetic form necessarily implies the wish to communicate something more than mere information. Obviously, war in the Dark Ages was not as described in the *Chanson de*

Roland. This epic is not a record but a spectacle to inspire, astonish, and entertain men who set store by values and achievements such as it portrays. So, on a more sophisticated level, are the plays of Corneille and Racine. They present not a mirror of the age but an imaginary world, parallel to their own but, according to the concepts of the time, complete and significant, in which man's potential for good or evil could be contemplated in its purity. In different ages poets have represented different values. In nineteenth-century commercial and industrial society they sought to revalue man's relationship with the natural world, to restore a lost innocence, to assert human joys and sorrows in the face of the indifference of science and technology. We call such poets Romantics. Others, the Parnassians, sought to use words as a sculptor uses stone, as a jeweller uses gems, to create things of beauty in a setting of social ugliness. Symbolists used them to evoke new sensations, new visions, a new awareness of human experience. In our own century poets have explored the subconscious, put man back into his cosmic setting, endeavoured to restore to ordinary things some of the lustre which, through over-familiarity, they had lost. In all ages they have made images of the great commonplaces of life—love, grief, death —which make them meaningful to us. They have also laughed, criticized, attacked, complained. And all this has been the work of an imagination which commented on reality by making something different from it.

Since a poem is an act of the imagination, it only comes to life when we ourselves respond to it imaginatively. Reading a poem is unlike any other form of reading in which we are ever likely to engage. It has nothing to do with dramatization or reading 'with feeling'—since the latter process usually means counterfeiting a feeling which is not ours but is put on for the occasion. Good reading consists in bringing out, for the imagination to respond to, all that is in the words; we do not have to pretend to be the poet, but simply to read his words as if they were our own. This may seem very easy, but it is not. Poetry is written to be read aloud, or, as a second best, to be articulated mentally in such a way as to enable us to respond to its sound; and this is not a very familiar activity. Normally we either speak or read, but do not mix the activities. Further, poetry is usually expressed through verse, and in verse the language is arranged in rhythms and combinations which, although related to those of ordinary speech, are by no means identical with them.

Let us consider the following sonnet by Baudelaire.

5   Je te donne ces vers afin que si mon nom
       Aborde heureusement aux époques lointaines,
       Et fait rêver un soir les cervelles humaines,
       Vaisseau favorisé par un grand aquilon,

Ta mémoire, pareille aux fables incertaines,
Fatigue le lecteur ainsi qu'un tympanon,
Et par un fraternel et mystique chaînon,
Reste comme pendue à mes rimes hautaines;

Être maudit à qui, de l'abîme profond
Jusqu'au plus haut du ciel, rien, hors moi, ne répond!
– O toi qui, comme une ombre à la trace éphémère,

Foules d'un pied léger et d'un regard serein
Les stupides mortels qui t'ont jugée amère,
Statue aux yeux de jais, grand ange au front d'airain!

It may help, in reading this poem, to know that it is addressed to the poet's mistress, Jeanne Duval, and that she was a woman of formidable if unconventional beauty and of poor reputation. Also the fact that she was a half-caste has a bearing on the last line with its reference to eyes of jade and forehead of brass. However, the first readers of *Les Fleurs du mal* were expected to appreciate the poem without this knowledge, so we need not make too much of it. Baudelaire's relations with the real Jeanne Duval were lamentable. But she was his inspiration, and he transformed her into one of the great figures of French literary myth. Today she exists only as Baudelaire saw her; and the hope he here expresses that her survival will be permanently linked with his 'rimes hautaines' has been fulfilled. But clearly what is interesting in the poem is not the simple declaration of intent. The poem is a series of word-images, cadences, and sound-combinations which transform the perishable Jeanne Duval into an immortal and enable us, in reading them, to partake in the process of transformation. To read it effectively, all one need do is to savour its language.

In another poem, this one addressed to a cat, Baudelaire speaks of the effect upon him of a line of verse as if it were a magic potion:

6   Cette voix, qui perle et qui filtre
       Dans mon fonds le plus ténébreux,
       Me remplit comme un vers nombreux
       Et me réjouit comme un philtre.

Elsewhere he speaks of the creative power of riming. As he walks through Paris he carries on a duel with words, a hunt for relationships between sound, meaning, and the outside world.

7   Je vais m'exercer seul à ma fantasque escrime,
       Flairant dans tous les coins les hasards de la rime,
       Trébuchant sur les mots comme sur les pavés,
       Heurtant parfois des vers depuis longtemps rêvés.

Verse and poetry, although often associated together, are by no means identical concepts. The term poetry applies to rhythmic language which gives pleasure through its appeal to the imagination. The only element of this definition which applies necessarily to verse is rhythm. Regular verse is the arrangement of language so that its rhythms form regular, recognizable, and satisfying patterns. Our concern in this book will be with verse as a medium for poetry. The examples we shall consider will be taken from major French poets, but we shall be more concerned with the structure of their work than with their vision, and also more concerned with what they have in common than with what differentiates them. The aim is to learn to read French verse with discernment and pleasure.

Language, as we shall consider it, is like money. The term 'money' may refer to actual notes and coins, which are metallic or crisp and may be handled (briefly, so far as most of us are concerned) with a certain physical satisfaction. The nineteenth-century miser, who lived before the days of cupro-nickel or indeed of paper money, hoarded his gold and derived physical satisfaction from contemplating and touching it. There is something of the nineteenth-century miser in the poet's approach to language: he handles words lovingly, enjoys them for their own sake, and does not spend them casually. But money is also an abstraction, a system which makes possible the exchange of goods. Language too is a vehicle of meaning which permits the exchange of ideas and experience. Verse, when handled by a great poet, is the product of both aspects of language, and derives its power from a principle which is applicable to both. This principle is the creation of patterns, stimulating to the imagination, by the rhythmic association of the similar with the dissimilar.

We have already seen, in the poems from which we have quoted, that a poet's subject is not simply what his words say if taken at face value. The poetic experience transforms the subject. The poet evokes something which we can recognize as being situated in 'real life', but in his hands, without ceasing to be real, it becomes something new which is his creation. This is the association of the similar—in this case similarity with what we think of as 'the real world'—with the dissimilar, the world of the poet's imagination. The result is a kind of harmony between two notes which are not the same but belong to the same scale, so that one is called up by the other to complement it. Rime is another application of the same principle. Two rime words cannot be the same—they must differ either in sound or in meaning or in both—yet what makes them a rime is their similarity. Two quite different words, which are what they are because of the chance development of language, are associated together in a way which satisfies the mind. Two consecutive alexandrines may have the same metrical rhythm but will differ in the natural cadence of the language, as well as in meaning and intonation. And simile and metaphor, which form one of the main resources of poetry, imply necessarily the association of similar and dissimilar: and since so much French verse is rhetorical, one clause will generally be balanced against the other to give an equilibrium of similarity and contrast.

Rhythm combines the expected with the unexpected in a pattern satisfying to the mind. We have it in many forms in verse: rhythms of metre, of the natural cadence of language, of the recurrence of rime and, in lyrical verse, of stanza-divisions. We also have it in the recurrence of themes, of images, of phrases, and of phonetic patterns. But why should rhythm give us satisfaction? That the repetition of sound—for instance, the beat of a drum—can give pleasure is a fact—though it can equally well drive us mad. Our reaction is not under the control of reason. In spite of ourselves our mind associates itself with the recurring beat and moves rhythmically with it. We anticipate its recurrence and respond when it does recur. When we dance we make rhythmic movements for the sheer pleasure of doing so. Rhythm produces emotional elation and induces a kind of hypnosis. But to be pleasurable or even bearable rhythm must involve variation, since we cannot free ourselves from its grip and we find it intolerable over a long period to be compelled to anticipate the invariable.

The rhythms of verse are not so overpowering as those of music, but even so, excessive or inadequate rhythmic effects can ruin a poem for us. False rhythm produces a sense of frustration: too strong a rhythm destroys awareness of sense and reduces the verse to a level of obtrusive triviality. In good verse one type of rhythm is balanced against another. Pope's line

> The sound must seem an echo of the sense

is strongly rhythmic, and the rhythm is that of metre. He is in fact making a statement with which, as a proposition, we might disagree: but because of its rhythm we accept it as an aphorism, and it has a quality of inevitability, of necessity, which goes beyond reason. Rhythm is here reinforced by alliteration, since three stressed words—*sound, seem*, and *sense*—all begin with [s]. But one stressed word—*echo*—does not. If Pope had written

> The sound must seem subservient to the sense

the result would have been excessive and the sound would dominate the meaning. In the line as Pope wrote it the pattern in [s] is slightly modified in that the sound occurs also in unstressed positions, in *must* and *sense*. So the stress-pattern and the alliterative one, while working together, do not exactly correspond. We have the similar with the dissimilar.

The way in which rhythm goes beyond sound into the realms of imagery and ideas is well exemplified by a stanza from Hugo's *Paroles sur la dune*:

8   Ne verrai-je plus rien de tout ce que j'aimais?
        Au dedans de moi le soir tombe.
    O terre, dont la brume efface les sommets,
        Suis-je le spectre, et toi la tombe?

So far as metre is concerned, we have a clearly defined stanza of four lines having alternately twelve and eight syllables, with the lines of similar length riming together. But the inner rhythm of the two alexandrines is not identical. In the first case the main internal stress falls on *rien*, the sixth syllable; in the second it falls on *terre*, which is the second syllable. And of the octosyllabic lines, the first is stressed on the fifth syllable, the second on the fourth. Moreover, the phonetic patterning sets up counter-rhythms. Thus the alliterative sequence in [s] overruns the line-ending:

```
        ..... efface les sommets,
                    s     s
        Suis-je le spectre ...[?]
         s    j    s
```

and is encased in a pattern in [t]:

```
        O terre ...
         t
                    .... et toi la tombe [?]
                          t       t
```

Further, it may be noted that the two question marks raise the pitch of the line-endings, and so further modify the basic pattern of the stanza.

In terms of sense, the stanza brings together two images: an exterior and an interior twilight. The poet is standing (alone, since he is a Romantic) among the mountains as night falls. And night is also falling in his soul. The word *tombe* (= falls) and the identical *tombe* (= tomb) with which it rimes provide a link between the two ideas; and offer, incidentally, an example of a type of rime which would be considered very weak in English verse because the two words lack contrast in sound, but is felt to be rich in French. The image of *brume* applies both to the physical landscape (mist on the mountains) and to the poet's thoughts, since mist obscures sight and in this case is associated with the opening question:

Ne verrai-je plus rien ... [?]

Thus the stanza possesses certain rhythms generated by contrast and association of sound—in metre and line-length, rime and phonetic patterning—and also a number of contrasted and associated images. This is a demonstration of the functioning of verse form.

Poetry is the most complex use of language known to man, and the apparent simplicity of lyric verse is always an illusion. In art there is no merit in simplicity, unless by this we mean the avoidance of unnecessary complication. The student will rarely find signs of effort in the work of the poets he studies. Metre, rhythm, and rime do in fact present even the greatest of poets with difficulties (only the occasional line or stanza materializes unbidden as if from outer space) but the difficulty of the medium serves as a challenge and an inspiration. The demands of verse are not merely restrictive. If they were, the poet who uses free verse would be able to express himself more effectively than the traditional poet: but there is no evidence that this is the case. For the poet is not trying to force into a predetermined mould ideas or emotions which already exist in his mind. It is in the process of handling his chosen medium—rhythmical language—that the poet's meaning becomes enriched and clarified and his vision gains permanence and communicability. Words and imagination are fused into enduring form.

This raises the question of how we read aloud what the poet has written. In the case of light verse there is no problem. But when verse is the medium of poetic vision, the need to express this adequately presents us with problems which we do not face in our everyday use of language. We regularly use language in speech, and we regularly read it silently to ourselves. But we rarely read aloud from the printed page, and when we do so it is usually to communicate the meaningful content of the words. In reading poetry we must convey also the quality of the sound and its relationship to meaning; and we must also communicate, to ourselves and perhaps to others, the substance and the form of a vision which is in some respects out of the ordinary. How do we do this? The printed page does not serve as a very adequate guide.

No transcript of human speech can tell us how a language really sounds, since it omits the most vital factor in all human communication, which is tone of voice. If needs be we can communicate without meaningful words, as we do when we express extreme emotion or talk to a baby or an animal. (In the latter cases, the words may be meaningful to us, but not to the hearer.) Our interpretation of statements such as 'I'm sure you're right' or 'I love you' will depend upon the voice which utters them, which we regard as the key to the real meaning of the speaker. Conviction, urgency, irony, doubt, uncertainty, and many other nuances of meaning are conveyed by means largely independent of syntax and grammar. The word 'Non' may represent a simple flat denial or indignant protest or resigned despair. Or it may be a question. In French almost any simple statement, if pronounced with a rising tone, may become a question. Symbols such as the question mark or the exclamation mark help us to interpret the meaning of the written language and to avoid ambiguity, and indeed punctuation is the only means we have by which we can represent sound-groups essential to syntax and emotional qualities which modify or reinforce the literal sense of the words. They are hardly adequate. Even so, the student should pay careful attention to a poet's punctuation. Failure to do so often results in interpretations which falsify what the poet has written.

The more familiar the student is with the basic rhythms and intonation of the spoken language the more satisfying will be his rendering of French verse, provided that he is aware of those respects in which the language of verse differs from that of prose. The nature of this difference has varied from age to age. Interpretations of verse which were acceptable once might sound quite absurd today. Before the invention of printing the reading of verse was not the solitary activity that it so often is for us, and the poet or his interpreter was conscious of his role as a public performer. He declaimed his verse, perhaps (as in the case of the *chanson de geste*) to a musical accompaniment. His voice had to carry. The manner of delivery would be nearer to a chant than to the tones of ordinary conversation. Lyric verse, even if not written to be sung, derives from the tradition of the song. Although the verse-reader is no longer an entertainer in the generally accepted sense, we should still as far as possible read poetry aloud in groups. To learn to love it one must read it to others, and listen to others reading it to us—for other people's interpretation will often throw new light on it. Quite apart from considerations of diction, this is important in that it changes one's attitude to the work. If one reads poetry silently with the book on one's knee, one has the impression of listening to the poet. But if one reads his work aloud to others, one participates actively in his creation. The student who has had this experience is less likely to write, in a commentary on a poem, 'Hugo says ...', for he will be aware that the poem belongs not just to Hugo but to himself and to mankind. The expression 'The poet says ...' or even 'The poem says ...' may often more adequately express this awareness that we are reading the work not just of an individual in a particular situation but of an artist speaking through our voice.

The kind of regular verse we are studying in this book has tangible, complex, and permanent form. To read it requires study and rehearsal, as does the performance of music or of a play. It would be absurd to suppose that what is perhaps the greatest of the arts would yield up its magic to the casual reader. The belief that it will is sometimes rationalized by the claim that study and preparation destroy the spontaneity of the work; for, it is argued, poetry is the outpouring of emotion and demands from us nothing but receptivity. But poetry is not spontaneous. Poets may work for months, sometimes for years, to perfect their lines, as we may often see by comparing one edition of their works with the next. All art has in it necessarily an element of the artificial. Men and women do not naturally speak in alexandrines or in rime; they do not often talk to lakes or to the moon; and if they despair of life they are more likely to commit suicide than to sit down, as Baudelaire did when he wrote *Le Voyage*, to produce thirty-six impeccable stanzas with due regard for the rules of metre. The 'naturalness' of a poem is an illusion, even though it is one which some poets, proud of their genius rather than their craft, have done their best to foster.

In reading, we aim to recreate that illusion of naturalness. The listener should not think of our performance as studied. When we hear the accomplished singer or pianist we do not think of the hours of rehearsal that lie behind his performance. Our own preparation will not be as thorough as theirs, but even so it should be carefully done. We should be aware of the possibilities of the lines we are reading, and the way in which we read them should have been decided thoughtfully, taking into account sense, rhythm, and melody.

Tastes change. We no longer chant verse. But we shall normally not be satisfied with the casualness of ordinary speech. Nor shall we violate the metre in the interest of 'dramatic', 'realistic', or simply whimsical renderings. Nor shall we reel off the lines in a sing-song tone which makes each one sound the same. Our rhythms and our intonation must of course be French, not English. We must be conscious of the sense-groups within the line, and of the stress which falls on the rime-word. And we must also bring out the melody which results from modulation of pitch. If we listen to the ordinary French speaker, we note that his voice rises and falls in a manner characteristic of the language, and that there is a considerable variation of stress. So marked is this that we can tell if someone is speaking French (or any other language with which we are familiar) even if we are not close enough to distinguish individual words, since no two languages 'sound alike'. Characteristics of this kind are likely to be more strongly brought out in reading regular verse than in ordinary usage, because rhythm is the foundation of verse, and language the very substance out of which it is made. Almost all verse implies some kind of appeal to the emotions, and variations of pitch and stress are the means through which emotion is expressed and awakened. Therefore, while avoiding any exaggeration which would distract and irritate the hearer, we may assume that these features will play an important part in our reading. Also, as is the case in public speaking, the reading of verse is likely to involve a greater volume of sound than does casual speech, for we shall savour the quality of the language, and respond to it to some extent as if it were music. In fact, we shall recognize that lines and stanzas have their 'melody', deriving partly from the language itself, partly from the poet's statement and the response it evokes, and partly from the way in which he uses his metre.

We cannot fix the melodic line of verse as we can fix, on paper or in the memory, a musical tune. We may not always give a line the same intonation when we read it. The poet's words will suggest a limited number of possibilities from which we must choose. Whatever melodic line we use must be relevant to the line, appropriate to its theme, and consistent with good French usage. So it will be well to consider some of the principles underlying our choice.

The pitch at which the majority of syllables in a sentence or line are pronounced may be described as *neutral*. This pitch may be represented symbolically by a dot between two square brackets, thus: [.]. The only occasion when the voice will fall below this level is when we wish to express finality, and this effect is usually represented on the printed page by a full stop. At the end of a sentence the voice normally descends from neutral to *low pitch*, and we indicate this level by placing the dot below the brackets: [.]. Thus a simple statement such as 'Je l'ai vu' followed by a full stop would have a melodic line which we represent as [. . .], or, in phonetic transcript, [jĕ lé ᵥü]. But a question—'Vous l'avez vu?'— or an exclamation—'Vous l'avez vu!'—will involve a sharp rise of pitch on the final syllable: and we would represent such a phrase as [. . . ·] or [vú lá vé ⱽü]. This last syllable we describe as being at *middle pitch*. Any stress in the interior of a sentence, such as occurs at the end of a sense-group, will produce a change in pitch, whether or not it is marked by punctuation. Thus the sentence 'Je l'ai vu de temps en temps' has the melodic line [jĕ lé ᵛᵘ dĕ tà zà ₜₐ̀]. Although we cannot represent this in our phonetic transcript, we shall note that in practice neutral represents a somewhat variable pitch: the voice does not rise or fall suddenly, but rather the first part of this sentence represents an upward slope and the latter part a downward one, the slope becoming most steep as we pass to the stressed syllable. The type of sentence represented here, in which the voice rises towards the middle and falls towards the end, is very common in French, and is indeed normal when there is no particular emotional stress on the final syllable.

Outside a zoo we see a sign with the heading 'Le Jardin zoologique'. This we read as [lĕ jár ᵈë̈ˊ zó ò lò ⱼˈᵢ″ₖ]. Underneath is a statement which begins 'Le Jardin zoologique est ouvert...' Now if this was a complete sentence, it would have the melodic line [lĕ jár dë̈″zó ò lò ʲíʺ kè tú ᵥè̀″.ᵣ]. Instead of falling to low pitch, the final syllable of *zoologique* has continued the upward slope to reach *high pitch*, which we represent by placing the sound above the square brackets, as in [˙]. Following this, the word *ouvert* which closes the sentence falls to low pitch. The distinction here is that the terminal stress of *zoologique* is stronger than that of *jardin*, since it rounds off a more substantial sense-group. But we will assume that the sentence does not end there. What the sign says is 'Le Jardin zoologique est ouvert tous les jours.' This changes the melodic line. We now have:

[lĕ jár ᵈë̈ | zó ò lò ʲⁱ | kè tú ᵥè̀ˊ.ᵣ | tú lè ⱼᵤ″.ᵣ]

And, if the full sentence was 'Le Jardin zoologique est ouvert tous les jours sauf le mardi', the melodic line would become:

[lĕ jár ᵈë̈ˊ | zó ò lò ʲⁱˊ | kè tú ᵥè̀ˊ.ᵣ | tù lè ⱼúˊ.ᵣ | só flĕ már ᵈᵢ]

The main interior stress reaches the highest pitch. Thus if we wished to put particular emphasis on the fact that the zoo was open *tous les jours*, we could take the final syllable of this phrase to high pitch: and indeed we could do the same with the word *ouvert*. Thus we see that the sentence as a whole has a recognizable slope upwards and downwards, but that its precise shape depends on where the intermediate stresses fall and how strong they are. And in certain cases, as we have seen, a sentence will end with an upward slope. Thus if it ended in an exclamation mark we would have something like

[lĕ jár ᵈë̈ˊ | zó ò lò ʲⁱˊ | kè tú ᵥè̀ˊ.ᵣ | tù lè ⱼúˊ.ᵣ | só flĕ már ᵈⁱ]

This sentence indicates the general principles which govern the melodic form of a line of verse, and most clearly in the case of a long line such as the alexandrine. This line, which we shall discuss more fully in our next chapter, has a certain number of interior stresses, one of them, generally on the sixth syllable, being particularly strong. The voice will tend to slope upwards towards this, and then to fall, unless its sense requires otherwise. An alexandrine which ends in a comma will normally close at neutral pitch. Here is a typical example, in which we indicate degree of stress by doubling (..) or trebling (...) the dots indicating syllables:

9   Les plus richĕs cités, les plus grands paysa.ges [,]

$$[\quad . \quad . \quad .. \mid . \quad .^{...} \mid \cdot \quad \cdot \quad .. \mid . \, . \, ... \,]$$

(Here the dot after the last sounded vowel indicates that the vowel is long. This is put in simply as guidance in reading, and of course does not appear in the poem.)

If the line ends in a full stop, the feeling of finality is much greater, and the voice drops to low pitch.

10   De plonger dans un ciel au reflet alléchant [.]

[dĕ plò jé| dà zæ̀ sÿè | ló rĕ flè| á lé ฺchà]

In quoting a line of verse, the terminal punctuation should always be added, as this affects its melodic line. Both the above lines give an impression of completeness, and for this reason they may be described as *stable*. If a stable line ends with a comma, it is complete only in a metrical sense and, syntactically, in that it is rounded off with a grammatical phrase, although the sentence in fact continues on to the next line. Such a line ends at neutral pitch. The full stop is both stable and completely final, and so the concluding syllable falls to low pitch. If, however, a line ends without punctuation, then it is *unstable*. An unstable line or phrase is one which does not leave the mind satisfied, but rather gives the impression of incompleteness. Such a line does not fall to neutral or low pitch: its final syllable rises, generally to middle. Consider the following:

11   Les plus ri˙chĕs cités, les plus grands paysa.ges,
       Jamais ne contenaient l'attrait mystérieux
       De ceux que le hasa.rd fait avec les nua.ges [,]

Here the first and third lines are stable and end at neutral; but at the end of the second the voice will tend to rise in order to lead on to the third line. Lines such as this which end without punctuation are known as 'run-on lines'.

But not only run-on lines are unstable. Those which end with a question mark, an exclamation mark, or a colon are usually unstable too. (But not always a semicolon, since this may be the equivalent of a full stop or comma, and produce a stable line.) The reason these punctuation marks produce an unstable line is that they create in the mind the demand for some kind of response, which weakens the sense of finality. If I say 'Je l'ai vu [.]', I am merely making a statement. If, on the other hand, I protest strongly 'Mais moi, je l'ai vu!' I obviously demand a response from the person I am speaking to, and the sense of what I have said is not complete until he agrees with me. Let us now complete Baudelaire's stanza:

> Les plus ri˙chĕs cités, les plus grands paysa.ges,
> Jamais ne contenaient l'attrait mystérieux
> De ceux que le hasa.rd fait avec les nua.ges
> Et toujou.rs le dési.r nous rendait soucieux [!]

If with the last line the voice were to fall to low pitch, we would simply have a statement. But if it rises, in response to the exclamation mark, we have a statement strongly tinged with emotion. The effect of the question mark can be clearly heard if we compare Verlaine's

12   Toujours vois-tu mon â.me en rê.vĕ?—Non [.]

in which the voice rises on *rêve* but falls with total finality on the line-ending, with Mallarmé's

13   Est-il de ce destin rien qui demeu.rĕ, non [?]

in which the voice rises at the line-ending and the line is clearly unstable.

Terminal punctuation, with its effect of creating unstable lines, is often of the greatest importance in the reading of classical tragedy. The following short speech from Racine offers a typical example:

14   Que ces vains ornĕments, que ces voi˙lĕs me pè.sent!
Quelle importu˙nĕ main, en formant tous ces nœuds
A pris soin sur mon front d'assembler mes cheveux?
Tout m'affli.ge et me nuit et conspi.re à me nui.re [.]

Here the first, second and the third lines are clearly unstable and will end at high or middle pitch. The last line is stable and must end at low.

Verlaine's stanza

> **15**   Tout suffocant
> Et blê˙mĕ, quand
>   So˙nnĕ l'heu.re,
> Je me souviens
> Des jours anciens
>   Et je pleu.re [.]

must be read with strict observance of its punctuation, as otherwise its lightness and the delicate balance of its rhythm will be lost. The run-on lines are all unstable and end at middle or high pitch: the two short lines are stable, [3] ending at neutral and [6] at low pitch. The fact that the lines are run-on does not mean that there is no pause between them. It means that the pause will be shorter than if there were punctuation, but it must be clearly heard: otherwise we are not reproducing what the poet has written. It is the fact that when we reach the line-ending the sense is still unfinished, that makes the line unstable: therefore our reading must make it clear that line and sense-group do not coincide. We must also be careful with vowel-length. The raised dots indicate vowels which would normally be short but, in the verse, are somewhat lengthened (for reasons explained on p. 31). These lengthened vowels are likely to be slightly shorter than vowels which are naturally long.

In each of the couplets following Verlaine makes a strong contrast between the first line, which expresses romantic illusion and so is unstable, and the second which expresses disillusioned finality, and is stable.

> **16**   – Ton cœur bat-il toujou.rs à mon seul nom?
> Toujours vois-tu mon â.me en rê.vĕ?–Non.
>
> – Ah! les beaux jou.rs de bonheur indici˙ble
> Où nous joignions nos bou˙chĕs! –C'est possi˙ble.
>
> – Qu'il était bleu, le ciel, et grand, l'espoi.r!
> L'espoir a fui, vaincu, vers le ciel noi.r [.]

Of course, lines do not always begin at neutral pitch. If the initial word is stressed, it will be at middle or even high pitch. This is apparent when we read 'Ah!' at the beginning of [3] in the above example. There are in fact many variations possible, some of which we shall consider later in other contexts. What we have considered here is the effect of the normal stress of the language on verse. But when we are dealing with poetry—that is, with the imaginative use of verse to convey vision or emotion—the substance of the poet's words and thought will govern the melody of the line, and this will involve personal interpretation by the reader: though it will not, normally, involve violation of the principles here stated. These principles are valid as far as they go, but the reading of verse is not a mechanical process, and it requires imagination. In the line

17   L'espoir a fui, vaincu, vers le ciel noi.r [.]

we may, for instance, feel it appropriate that *fui* should reach high pitch and that *vaincu* should have a falling slope and come down to neutral.

[lè ˢᵖʷᵃ́ʳ ᵃ́ ᶠᵘ̆ⁱ | ᵛë̈ kü | vèr lĕ sÿ̈èl ₙwá.ᵣ]

Likewise, in Baudelaire's

18   Bientôt nous plongerons dans les froi˙dĕs ténè˙bres [;]

although the word *plongerons* bears strong stress (which would normally lead it to high pitch at the middle of the line) its sense suggests a downward slope of the voice. It would also be perfectly appropriate that *ténèbres* should descend to low pitch, and this is a possible interpretation of the semicolon. However, so far as the latter point is concerned, it seems likely that Baudelaire's purpose in using a semicolon instead of a full stop was to avoid this degree of finality and to lead on naturally to the line following, and so the reading we adopt might well be:

[bÿ̈ë ᵗᵒ́ | ⁿᵘ́ plò jĕ ᵣò | dà lè frwá˙ dĕ té ⁿè˙br]

Therefore, in fixing the melody of a line, there are two principles at work. One is the variation of stress which is characteristic of the French language. The other is the interpretation of this stress in the light of the meaning and emotional quality of the words. The latter leaves vast scope for personal choice, and for this reason, in our representation of lines in this book, we shall not attempt to fix their melodic form. The reader will do this for himself in the light of the points which we have raised. Any composer, in setting words to music, will follow the same principles; nevertheless, a twentieth-century composer would not necessarily arrive at the same results as a composer of nineteenth-century drawing room ballads. For us, the most convincing reading may not necessarily be that which the poet himself might have imagined. Even so, our reading must be a meaningful interpretation and not the result of carelessness or insensitivity.

With respect to this point (and indeed to many others that will be raised in the course of this book), it may be felt that we are making the reading of verse unnecessarily difficult, and that it is really not practicable to approach every poem we read with the meticulous care here suggested. To this very sensible objection there are two answers. The first is that the habit of good reading, once acquired, will be applied without too much conscious thought to any poem: to enjoy a poem it must in any case be read more than once, and provided the principles are understood it is no more difficult to read it well than to read it badly. It simply calls for a heightened degree of interest, which any poem of quality will demand. Also, it must be recognized that the number of poems that we get to know *thoroughly* will, for most of us, be relatively small. It is likely that we shall never get beyond a casual acquaintance with many of the poems that we read. But some poets are likely to appeal to us particularly, and among their works are poems of which we shall wish to realize the full potential. We cannot prepare every poem as if we were going to give a concert recital. But we should make a very real effort to get to know the poems which most appeal to us. If a poem is worth liking, it is also worth knowing properly. The student who indulges in fulsome praise of, for instance, Verlaine, and at the same time so misquotes him as to show that he is not only unfamiliar with his work but has absolutely no sensitivity to the nature of his achievement, merely demonstrates that so far as poetry is concerned his education has been wasted. One does not enjoy poetry because the critics say it is good, or because it happens to be included in a reputable anthology. One enjoys it because one has learnt to read it with pleasure. At one level or another, verse appeals to almost everyone. But the appreciation of poetry, like most of life's more significant pleasures, does demand a certain initiation and certain skills. The object of the following chapters is to provide information and to raise questions, from among which the reader will select those which he finds most helpful in recreating the poet's achievement from the words on the printed page.

Chapter Two

SCANSION

As SOON as we open it, we recognize a book of verse by the layout of the pages, for it is printed in discontinuous lines. This is not mere whim or convention. Each line represents a rhythmic unit, and the blank which follows it represents a pause in speech. Verse, whether regular or free, can only be said to exist when it is divided into units of this kind. The French word *vers* means 'a line', and not, as its English equivalent does, a stanza (which in French is called a *strophe*). It is usual to begin each line with a capital letter in order to mark it out more clearly as a metrical unit, but this is not strictly speaking necessary, and in recent times the convention is often ignored in order to produce a freer flow of language. It is possible to write rhythmic language without using discontinuous lines, and the result may be poetry, as in the case of Rimbaud's *Illuminations*, but it is not classed as verse. Verse always involves a kind of rhythm which, whether free or fixed, is not that of prose, and the line is the unit of that rhythm. In free verse, lines will be of irregular length, but they are still heard as rhythmic units. In regular (or isometric) verse, which is what we are concerned with in this book, all the lines are of equal length; or, if they vary, they do so in a way which forms a recognizable pattern.

However, the term *length* does not refer either to the time which it takes to read the line, or to the amount of space it occupies on the printed page. We may read a line quickly or slowly, but this does not alter its length. Most of the lines indexed at the end of this book contain twelve syllables and are therefore of equal length, but they do not appear so to the eye: one need only compare, for instance, *31* and *32* in the Index to realize how great may be the difference in apparent length between the lines which are in fact equal. In the two examples we quote below:

19   Ellĕ gouvernera | la Flan.dre ou la Sardai˙gne [,]

and

20   Vient, passe et disparaît | majestueu.sĕment [.]

the upright stress-bar in both cases represents the middle of the line, even though it does not appear to do so. The point is that the length of a line is measured in syllables; and since, for instance, both *à* and *chambre* may count as a single syllable in verse, it is clear that syllables are not really equal units at all. What they have in common is that they contain one sounded vowel, and one only. That vowel may be long or short; and the syllable may also contain one, two, or more consonants, but such differences are beside the point. In fact, although we are obliged by custom to say that a line of French verse consists of so many syllables, it is really simpler for the student to remember that its length depends upon the number of its sounded vowels. These we can indicate by placing a dot under each one:

> Ellĕ gouvernera | la Flandre ou la Sardaigne [,]
> .   .   .   .   . | .   .   .   .   .   .
> Vient, passe et disparaît | majestueusĕment [.]
> .   .   .   .   .   . | .   .   .   .   .   .

We now see that each half of these lines contains six sounded vowels, and hence six syllables. Unless the reader already has some familiarity with French versification, it will not be immediately apparent to him why we have placed the dots where they are (for instance, placing one under the second syllable of *elle* but not under that of *Flandre*); but that is a matter to which we shall return. Our point for the moment is simply that the French ear hears the length of a line of verse in terms of the number of sounded vowels it contains, and nothing else.

One of the effects of writing in discontinuous lines is to encourage us to read more slowly. We approach much prose with the object of assimilating what it says as rapidly as possible, and the words are mere symbols designed to convey meaning. In verse the words exist as real things, and we savour their sound and associations. For us today, this is easier to do in the case of a short lyric than it is in that of a longer poem. Life no longer moves at the leisurely pace it had when Hugo penned his more massive works; nor can we ever think ourselves back to the dependence on the spoken word which was characteristic of all ages until very recent times. Practically all the poets whose works are quoted in this book wrote in an age when pictures were few and much more depended on direct human speech than is the case today. But verse still demands of us, today as it did in earlier times, that we give it our full attention, and listen to it not only with our mind but with all our senses. The use of a device such as rime on the line-ending helps to make us conscious of the sound of words, but if we read well we respond sensuously to the language as a whole. The texture of verse is made up not only of sound but also of the silences which serve to group syllables into rhythmic units. The space which follows the line must always be rendered as a pause in reading. Lines may often be 'run on' in terms of their meaning, but rarely if ever in terms of their sound. Common sense tells us that not all such pauses will be of equal duration: those which correspond to a syntactical break will be longer than those which do not. But each line must be heard as a single unit. In principle, there should be no pauses within the line, although this is not invariably the case in practice. We draw breath only at the line-endings, and the rhythm of the lines is consequently a rhythm of human breathing. It is in this respect that the reading of verse differs most systematically from any other kind of reading. The difference must not be exaggerated. Nothing sounds so stilted and, indeed, trivial, as a verse-reading in which the metrical pauses are so monotonously self-conscious as to amount to a mere mannerism. The pause must be functional, and nothing more.

On the printed page, and in writing generally, language is broken up into words. This is done purely to facilitate comprehension. We do not adopt the same practice in speech, since the spoken language has other resources—mainly intonation and stress—which are scarcely represented in print but enable the ear to disentangle meaning. Every student of French who is more familiar with the written language than with the spoken knows the difficulty of comprehension which arises from the French-speaker's habit of running his words together. We do the same thing in our native language but are unaware of the fact. In French, as in other languages, the flow of speech is divided not into words but into meaningful groups of words. The end of any such group in French is marked by a stress on the last syllable, and occasionally—very occasionally, with some people—by a pause. In verse, phrases are generally so grouped that the natural pause falls on the line-ending, which means that on the whole syntax and metre run together, as they do in Racine's

21   Capti.vĕ, toujours triste, importune à moi-mê˙me,
      Pouvez-vous souhaiter qu'Androma˙quĕ vous ai˙me [?]

Here the punctuation in the interior of the line simply represents a stress, whereas the blank at the line-ending represents both a stress and a pause. It may be noted that in French stress always falls on a vowel, not on a consonant, so that it is the [i] of *captive* and *triste* which is stressed.

In English verse, metre depends on the arrangement of words in *feet*, which correspond in some respects to a bar of music. Each foot contains one stressed syllable and one or more unstressed ones; and their regularity is such that we can tell within a few seconds whether a passage being read aloud is verse or not. This effect is possible in English because most words carry a stress on a fixed syllable, or are at least capable of carrying such a stress. The line

> And snówy súmmits óld in stóry [:]

derives its rhythm from the fact that three of the words used have a stress on the first syllable, and that *old* is capable of stress. In this example the beat runs with perfect regularity throughout the line. But in Blake's stanza

> And did the countenance divine
> Shine forth upon our clouded hills?
> And was Jerusalem builded here
> Among those dark Satanic mills [?]

we note in the third line not only a variation in rhythm but the introduction of an extra syllable: there are nine when we would expect eight. Stevenson's

> Home is the sailor, home from sea
> And the hunter home from the hill [.]

is often misquoted so as to read '... home from the sea ...', and the introduction of the superfluous definite article, although it weakens the idiomatic force of the language, does not disturb the metre. We all know that many lines of irregular length are introduced among the decasyllabics which Shakespeare uses in his dramatic works. It may therefore come as a surprise to the English-speaking reader to realize that nowhere in the plays of Racine (or for that matter in the poems of Hugo or Baudelaire) is there a single line with an incorrect number of syllables. In English, we require only that the stress shall recur with a reasonable degree of regularity. In French, it is syllable-count that is the basis of metre.

The reason for this is that individual French words do not bear stress as do words in English. In English, the words *concert* and *telephone* bear a strong stress on the first syllable. Their French equivalents, *concert* and *téléphone*, bear no such stress: when read in isolation, all syllables sound equal. In French stress falls not on individual words but on the final syllable of meaningful groups of words. When we say *Je suis allé au conce.rt*, we stress the final syllable of *concert*. If we add a further phrase—*Je suis allé au conce.rt avec des amis*—this syllable still retains some stress, but the main stress now passes to the final syllable of *amis*. *Conce.rt* has a sort of intermediary or subsidiary stress on its last syllable. But in *concert de musique ancienne* it may well have no stress at all, since it no longer concludes a sense-group. Stress falls on the final syllable of *ancienne*. In the same way the final syllable of *téléphone* bears stress when we say: *Je vous donnerai un coup de téléphone*, but not in an expression such as *téléphone automatique*.

In verse, as in ordinary speech, stress falls on the final syllable of a sense-group, and since such groups are likely to be of unequal length, the internal stresses of one line are likely to occur in positions which differ from those of the next. This means that French verse has nothing equivalent to the English foot. When Baudelaire describes oncoming night in the line

22   Et, comme un long linceul traînant à l'Orient [,]

he uses a sequence of sense-groups which we may break up as follows:

Et	– 1 syllable
comme un long linceul	– 5 syllables
traînant	– 2 syllables
à l'Orient	– 4 syllables

which gives us a twelve-syllable line having the rhythm 1:5 | 2:4. Each of the sense-groups represented by these numbers carries a stress on its last syllable, and it is this which gives the line its rhythm and its form. The essential feature of the line is the total number of syllables, which is twelve. However the phrases within the line may be arranged, the final stress must occur at regular syllabic intervals, and so the total number of syllables must not vary: and the total number of syllables, as we have seen, depends upon the number of sounded vowels. Since he is not working in regular feet as the English poet does, the French poet cannot afford to be approximate in his line-length, for that is what, to the French ear, gives regularity to his metre. It is by no means unknown for English-speaking students to write in a commentary: 'The poem consists of alexandrines of ten, eleven, twelve and thirteen syllables ...' but this is quite impossible. An alexandrine always contains twelve syllables, neither more nor less. A decasyllable has ten. An octosyllabic line has eight—always. The total number of syllables in the line is fixed by metre.

The word *pied* is sometimes found in books on French versification, but it is not equivalent to the English *foot*. It simply means 'syllable'. And since a syllable is best called a syllable, the word *pied* will not be used here. The reader will judge the length of the line by listening for the regular beat that occurs on the line-ending, and will know that the total number of syllables (or sounded vowels) which comes between these recurring beats will be exactly that required by metre, even though the subsidiary stresses may vary.

The French-speaking reader, trained to hear the rhythms of his language, will respond without difficulty to the number of syllables in a sense-group, and so will recognize the regularity of the terminal beat. The foreigner must learn by practice. When Verlaine writes

23   Que ton ve.rs soit la bonne aventu.re
         Éparse au vent crispé du matin
         Qui va fleurant la men.the et le thym [...]

he is using a nine-syllable line, which is somewhat unusual, since in French metres the number of syllables is rarely odd. When we read [1], we recognize at once that there is an internal stress on *vers*, which is the third syllable. So the line divides 3:6. We may hear its length more clearly if we put a slight stress on *bonne*, and then read the line with the rhythm 3|3:3:

[kĕ tò ᵛè·ʳ | swá lá ᵇò | ná và ᵗü·ʳ]
. .   ..

In [2] *éparse* forms a sense-group with a stress on its second syllable: and this leaves seven syllables to complete the line. But there will also be a slight stress at the end of the phrase *au vent crispé*—not a major one, since *du matin* follows on without any marked break, but nevertheless audible. This gives a rhythm of 2 | 4:3 which we can easily hear:

[ᵉ pár | só ᵛà kri ˢpé | dü má ᵗë]
. ...

And [3] *Qui va fleurant* is heard as a stress-group with four syllables; there is some stress on *la menthe* (two syllables) and a strong final stress on *thym* which completes three more syllables: so the rhythm is 4 | 2:3, again making a total of nine.

[kí vá flœ ʳà | lá ᵐà· | té lĕ ᵗë]
. . . .

In each of these cases, with a little practice, we shall quite easily hear the total number of syllables in the line, made up as it is of shorter stress-groups. The pitch in lines such as these is capable of considerable variation: nevertheless, in reading we should associate each group with whatever melodic line sounds to us most satisfactory, so that the pitch-slopes correspond to the syllable-count and reinforce our awareness of line-length.

In these lines, as in all lines, the fact that one vowel is long and another short does not in any way affect scansion: in many lines there may be two or three long vowels, and although they affect our reading, they do not affect syllable-count. All vowels are scanned as equal, provided they are sounded.

Two points should be noted. French spelling, as every student knows, is only loosely related to sound, and sounded vowels are represented in a variety of different ways, often involving more than one symbol. Thus both *eaux* and *hauts* represent the vowel [ó], while the vowels of *saine* and *scène* are both [è]. However many letters are used in groups of this kind, they represent only one vowel; and therefore in our phonetic transcript, we write them with one symbol. So when we speak of the number of sounded vowels in a line, we are in no way concerned with the number of letters used to write them. [á] is a vowel in the word *sa*, but not in *eau*, where it is merely part of the group which represents [ó]. There are no diphthongs in French, and combinations of letters such as *ou* which look as if they represent a diphthong in fact represent a pure vowel written as [u] in our transcript. And the second point we should note concerns the nature of syllables. In French, but not in English, a syllable always begins with a consonant if one is available, and there may often be liaison between two words by which the final consonant of the first attaches itself to the opening vowel of the second. Since syllables are pronounced without any apparent break, this may seem an unimportant point, but in fact it is one of the characteristic features of French which is immediately apparent in ordinary speech. The word *château* is pronounced [ʃà tó] and not [ʃàt ó]. 'Sortez!' does not sound like *sorte* with -*ez* added: the final [t] belongs to the second syllable, and we hear [sòr té]. And we pronounce 'Va-t-en!' as [vá tà], not as [vát à]. The same principle applies when two words are joined by liaison. When we say 'C'est impossible!' we hear the [t] of the verb attach itself to the adjective: [sè të pò sibl]. The principle applies also when we read verse. Note the phonetic representation of

24   Éparse au vent crispé du matin [ ]
    [é pár só và krí spé dü má të]

in which the final -*se* of *éparse* has attached itself to the vowel following. The only syllable in this line which does not begin with a consonant is the first; and the reason in this case is that there is no consonant available. But the word *et* in

25   Qui va fleurant la men.the et le thym [...]

will necessarily attract the final [t] of *menthe*, and so the syllable is heard as beginning with a consonant:

[kí vá flœ̀ rà lá mà té lĕ tё̈]

The need for a final sounded consonant to attach itself to a vowel following is in no way affected by punctuation, since, as we have seen, punctuation within a line does not normally represent a pause. When we read Baudelaire's line

26   Sois sa.ge, ô ma Douleu.r, et tiens-toi plus tranqui˙lle [;]

the punctuation is indicated by a slight lengthening of the vowel, and there is no break in the sequence of sound. As a result, the preceding consonant attaches itself to *ô* and *et*:

[swá sá.. jó má dú lœ̀.. ré tÿё̈ twá plü trà ki˙l]

Where the degree of interruption represented by the punctuation is more extreme, it will produce a more marked lengthening of the vowel:

27   Et des vallons sans on.de! – Et c'est là qu'est mon cœu.r!
        é dè vá lò sà zò...   dé sè là kè   mò̀ kœ̀.. r [!]
        .   .   . .

Most syllables consist of consonant + vowel, whether or not both of these belong to the same word. But occasionally a syllable may end in a consonant. This happens with the word *char* in

28   Et le char vaporeux de la reinĕ des o.mbres [ ]

because the word following begins with a consonant, so the [r] of *char* has no vowel to which to attach itself. So we write

é lĕ chá.r vá pò rœ̀ dĕ lá rè nĕ dé zò.br [ ]
. .   ..

And in the line which we have quoted from Lamartine (27) the final syllable [kœ.r] must end in a consonant, since liaison hardly ever takes place across a line-ending. It may also happen that a syllable begins with two consonants. This is because certain phonemes—[s], [l], and [r]—attach themselves to others to form small consonantal groupings which cannot be broken up. Thus *semble* is written [sà˙blĕ], with both the [b] and the [l] passing to the second syllable since they form a single consonantal group. Likewise *tout près* [tú prè], *sanglot* [sà gló], *oiseau splendide* [wá zó splà did].

A word such as *semble* is not always represented as two syllables. It may be only one—[sàbl]. And in the lines we have quoted, we have sometimes given *e* the value of a full syllable (in which case we often write it as *ĕ*) while on other occasions we have ignored it. An *e* which in ordinary usage is written without an accent may be either neutral (in which case it is sounded) or mute (in which case it is not). But unfortunately usage in verse does not precisely follow that of everyday speech.

The *neutral* [e] is the vowel heard in words such as *je, que, le, ne,* and in the interior of some words such as *véritablĕment*. It is the commonest of phonemes in the French language, and it differs from others in that many circumstances it is liable to disappear altogether. In the case of the short words we have just quoted, the neutral [e] disappears when it occurs before another vowel, and in that case it is replaced by an apostrophe: so we write *j'aime, qu'il, l'arbre, vous n'avez*. But with most words no apostrophe is used. We write *elle est* and not *ell' est*. And at the end of longer words the neutral [e] regularly becomes mute, and yet we continue to write it just as if it was pronounced. We write *cette semaine* but we say [sèt smèn]; we write '*Ce n'est pas vrai*' and we say [snè pà vrè]. In other words, neutral [e] is an unstable sound which is prone to be dropped in ordinary speech. It is so unstable that it can never be stressed. When it occurs in a position which requires stress, it changes its sound. In *mener* it is unstressed: but in *il mène* the [e] has acquired stress and is no longer sounded as neutral. For similar reasons, the stressed form of *me* is *moi*, and of *te* is *toi*. Neutral [e], then, is a weak sound. The tendency to lose or to change it has been at work for a long time, and was already well established in the spoken language four centuries ago. It is one of the chief factors which has caused French to diverge so widely from other Romance languages such as Spanish or Italian, which have retained pure vowels on the word-ending where French changed them first into neutral and subsequently into mute [e]s. Thus the Spanish *cosa* has two syllables, but its modern French equivalent *chose* has only one.

But in verse the position is more fluid, and the neutral [e] is often heard in circumstances in which in ordinary speech it would have become mute. This does not mean that the matter is left to the reader's discretion. It means rather that verse usage tends to be a little archaic. In the Middle Ages the neutral [e] was never mute, and only by degrees did it fall out of use, and then only in certain circumstances. In verse, the process has not gone as far as it has in ordinary speech. There are three reasons for this. The language of verse, in France as elsewhere, is more resistant to change than that of ordinary speech. In practising their craft, poets are extremely conscious of the sound of words and so tend to preserve their form, whereas the man in the street will lose the odd syllable here and there without being conscious of the fact. Moreover, the poetic tradition carries with it large bodies of work inherited from earlier ages, in which the number of syllables cannot be changed without destroying the rhythm and metre. And thirdly, the poet has found it convenient to retain the right to use the neutral [e] as a counted syllable under certain circumstances, so that he may for instance decide for himself whether *semble* has one syllable or two. And as a result of all these factors, what has happened in regular verse is that the tendency to mute the neutral [e] has been arrested at an earlier stage than it has reached in modern French. In certain situations where it was completely unstable it has disappeared in verse as in normal usage, but it has remained in other circumstances where adjacent consonants make it possible to pronounce it without too much artificiality.

In verse as in ordinary speech it is mute when it is immediately followed by another vowel or by a non-aspirate *h*. One cannot say *je aime* or *le homme*, and expressions such as *belle époque* or *notre amour* must be pronounced [bè lé pòk] and [nò trá mu.r] even though we do not write *bell'* or *notr'*. So verse like prose sometimes indicates the loss of the neutral [e] by putting in an apostrophe and sometimes it does not. When followed by a vowel a neutral [e] becomes mute, whether this is shown or not. Verse differs from prose usage only in cases where it is not followed by a vowel. In ordinary speech, we lose the [ĕ] of *cette semaine* even though it is followed by a consonant. We say [sèt smèn]. But in verse we would say [sè tĕ sĕ mèn]. In the same way, in everyday French *Cette femme-là* has only three syllables—[sèt fám lá]. But the neutral [e]s are followed by consonants, and so in verse they must be sounded, giving five syllables: [sè tĕ fá mĕ là]. Only if a line is so spoken is correct scansion possible. In fact, one often hears French readers ignore this rule, through ignorance or carelessness, or because they think it unnatural to sound the [e]: however, when verse is read properly, we must give it the number of syllables the poet intended, otherwise we cannot possibly get the metre right. Words such as *chose* [ʧò.z], *suivre* [sǔi.vr], and *tremble* [tràbl] are monosyllables when followed by a word beginning with a vowel, for the vowel causes the final [e] to be elided. But when followed by a consonant the [e] is pronounced, and these words have two syllables: [ʧò.zě], [sǔi. vrě], [trà.blě]. In verse as in ordinary speech an aspirate *h* counts as a consonant, so we say *le héros* [lě é ró] without eliding the neutral [e]; but any other *h* is ignored: so that *l'horizon* is pronounced as if the noun began with a vowel. Since these rules are invariable, it is always possible to say with certainty whether a final neutral [e] should or should not be pronounced in a line of verse.

When [ě] occurs at the end of the rime-word, it is always mute and is ignored in scansion. This means that if we say a line has ten or twelve syllables, it must have this number of syllables without the final mute [e]. The reason is that in French a line of verse must always end on a stressed syllable, and as we have seen, neutral [e] cannot bear stress and so can never occur either in this position or in any other position in the line where stress is required. Rime-words which end in a mute [e], or a syllable containing a mute [e], are called *feminine*: and although this mute [e] is not heard, its presence is recognized by a lengthening of the stressed vowel of every feminine rime, if that vowel is not already long. The precise length of the vowel is in practice at the reader's discretion, but the naturally long vowel (which is about twice as long as a short one) should in general be heard as longer than a vowel which has been lengthened by a following mute [e]. Thus the vowel of *chose* [ʧò.z] will be longer than that of *a ˙rbre* [á ˙ rbr] on the line-ending, since the vowel of the latter word is naturally short even in a stressed position, and is here lengthened only by the feminine rime. In our phonetic transcript we indicate this fact by raising the lengthening dot above the line.

The principle of lengthening is also applied to any stressed syllable within the line if it is followed by a neutral [e]. When we read

29   Cellě que j'aime à présent est en Chi ˙ ne [,]

we must sound the neutral [e] of *celle* since it is followed by a consonant, and it is to indicate this that we have written the breve [˘] over it. So important is it that the reader should acquire the habit of hearing the correct number of syllables in a line that, in this book, a breve will normally be printed over a neutral [e] which is sounded in verse but would not be sounded in normal usage. So in **29** *celle* appears as *cellě*, and the reader may find it useful himself to add this symbol as required when he is writing out a line of verse. The breve does not appear on the final *e* of *aime*, since this is elided; nor on that of *Chine*, since this is a feminine rime and its final syllable is mute. Both the neutral [e] and the feminine rime result in a lengthening of the stressed vowel, and so we represent the line as

Ce ̇ llĕ que j'aime à présent est en Chi ̇ ne [.]

In *Chi ̇ ne* the lengthened vowel indicates a feminine rime, and the final [e] is mute. In *ce ̇ llĕ* the final [ĕ] is sounded. In the interior of the line it is this neutral [e] following a stress which causes the vowel to be lengthened. This may be compared with the word *j'aime* where there is no lengthening, both because it is unstressed and because the final [e] is mute. The lengthening in the case of *ce ̇ llĕ* is simply to make the reading more natural. In ordinary speech this word would have only one syllable, but in verse it has two. It would sound artificial if we gave the second syllable the same value as the first. Therefore we lengthen the stressed syllable and shorten the neutral [e], giving the word its full value of two syllables, but in a ratio which we can represent as $1\frac{1}{2} + \frac{1}{2}$, rather than the normal $1 + 1$. This is unlikely to happen with words such as *unĕ* or *commĕ* in unstressed positions, but this is at the reader's discretion. In reading

30   Ca ̇ lmĕ commĕ la me.r en sa sérénité [,]

we must sound the neutral [e] of both *calme* and *comme*: to read these words as *calm' comm'* would produce a staccato effect which is certainly not the poet's intention. And since *ca ̇ lmĕ* is stressed, the neutral [e] will lengthen its vowel, which would normally be short. There is no stress on *commĕ*, and it seems to me difficult to lengthen the vowel. The word will be read as two equal syllables; and this produces a satisfactory effect, since the vowels of the important words *calmĕ* and *mer* stand out by reason of their length among the other vowels of the line, which are all short. But, in the interior of a line, even a stressed syllable will not be lengthened if the [e] that follows it is elided. In the case of a neutral [e], the reason for lengthening the preceding stressed syllable is to compensate for the fact that we pronounce the [ĕ] as a half-syllable rather than as a full one. But when the [e] is elided it is not counted at all in scansion, and so no compensation is called for. So the [a] of *arbre* is short in the line

31   J'irai là-bas où l'arbre et l'ho ̇ mmĕ, pleins de sè.ve [,]

since it is unstressed and its final [e] is elided. However, in

32   Où les serpents géants dévorés de punai.ses
           Choient, des arbrĕs tordus, avec de noi.rs parfums [!]
              ..   .   .

the vowel length of *arbrĕs* is more difficult to decide, since the [a] is unstressed, but even so may perhaps be lengthened by the following neutral [e]. This will certainly be the case where [a] is lengthened by a combination of stress and neutral [e] in

33   L'om.brĕ des a˙rbrĕs dans la riviè.re embrumé˙e [ ]
           .   .   .   .

It will be noted that here we are speaking only of short vowels which are lengthened by a neutral [e]. If a vowel is naturally long, it remains so regardless of whether or not it is followed by a neutral [e], so the elision of the final vowel of *riviè.re* does not affect the length of the stressed vowel. (If the reader feels that at this stage he would like to know the circumstances in which vowels in French are 'naturally long', he will find the matter treated more fully in the concluding chapter of this book (page 170 et seq.); but since such vowels will be indicated in our quotations, it is really not necessary to pursue this rather technical point at the moment.)

Here are some examples of the use of the neutral [e] in verse:

34   Le Mon.de est rétréci par notre expéri:en.ce [.]
           .   ..   .

35   Ce li.vre où l'espéran.ce est permi.se aux mourants [,]
           .   ..   .

36   Dans ce morne horizon se sont évanou:is [!]
           .   .   ..

In 34 both the long vowels are naturally long; and even if it were not that on the line ending would be lengthened, as the rime is feminine. The final [e] of both *monde* and *notre* is elided: that of *expérience* is mute since it always must be when it ends the rime-word. So the line is pronounced:

      [lĕ mò. dè ré tré si pár nò trèk spé ri *à*.s]
       .   ..   .

In 35 all the stressed vowels are naturally long except for that on the line ending: this is short, and is not lengthened since the rime is not feminine. The neutral [e] of *livre, espérance,* and *permise* is elided, and the line is read:

[sĕ lí. vrú lè spé rà. sè pèr mí. zó mú rà]

  . ..   .

In **36** the final [e] of *morne* is elided since the *h* of *horizon* is not aspirate; and although *morne* bears some stress the vowel is not lengthened since there is no neutral [e] to be compensated for.

[dà sĕ mòr nò rí zò sĕ sò té vá nú í]

  . . ..

Where there is punctuation, the division of a line into its main sense-groups presents no difficulty, and it is this which governs the placing of stresses. But often there is no punctuation to guide us. This matter will be discussed more fully as we proceed. But the reader should bear in mind from the beginning that the French custom of placing the stress on the final syllable of a sense-group is quite different from anything we hear in English. Words in English have their own stress, which more often than not falls on the root of the word: i.e. that part of it which has the most meaningful and imaginative force. This we hear in words as various as *giving, sensuous,* and *radiant,* in which the final syllable is a grammatical termination which receives no stress. But in French it is precisely this syllable which does receive the stress. We must therefore resist the tendency to put the stress on the root of words such as *chanter, écoutant, entendront*; for if these words receive stress at all, it falls on the last syllable. Failure to recognize this point often makes it difficult for the foreigner to hear the rhythm of verse that he is reading. Note the stresses in Baudelaire's lines:

37   Mon enfant, ma sœu.r,

             . . ..

       Son.ge à la douceu.r

      ..   . .

     D'aller là-bas vivre ensem.ble [;]

      . . .   .

Whereas the English word *infant* is stressed on its first syllable, the French *enfant* here has stress on the second syllable. *Douceur* is an abstract noun derived from *douce*, which is by far the most emotionally powerful part of the word; nevertheless, it is the termination, not the root, which receives metrical stress. And in the third line *vivre* receives no stress at all, and its final syllable is elided. Whenever we distribute stresses in a line of French verse, we must follow the principle that metrical stress falls on the last syllable of the sense-group, even if this is merely a grammatical suffix. We have already noted that [té] is the only syllable stressed in the second half of **30**; and in

38   Et, sans daigner savoi.r comment il a péri [,]

we find that stresses throughout fall on syllables that have no imaginative force at all—*ET, savOIR, commENT, pérI.*

If we apply these principles to reading the poem by Henri de Régnier which we quoted in the first chapter, and which is quoted again below for ease of reference, its rhythm will become clear, and in the case of the reader unfamiliar with French verse techniques the result should sound quite different from his first attempt. To indicate the way in which it should be read it is not necessary to transpose it into phonetic symbols. The principles adopted will be those we have used up to this point, and it may be useful to summarize them briefly. Since the length of a line depends on the number of its sounded vowels, each such vowel is indicated by placing a dot beneath it. A vowel without a dot is elided and does not count in scansion; within a line this produces liaison between two words, and on the line-ending the [e] of the feminine rime is mute always. The stressed syllable on the line-ending is shown by a triple dot. Within the longer lines there is a minor stress, which is shown by a double dot. All vowels are short unless shown to be long. A 'naturally long' vowel (i.e. one which would be long in standard prose usage) has a full stop placed after it; other vowels which are lengthened in verse as a result of a following neutral [e] are shown by a raised dot. The reader will note that in French only a stressed vowel can be long: all unstressed ones must be short, and so are many stressed ones. In the second line the final syllable of *frémir* [fré mi.r] is long and stressed, but in [24] it is unstressed and therefore short. In [5] the [à] of *chante* is short since it bears no stress: in [16] it is stressed and long. In [15] *entendront* contains no long vowels; but *entendent* [à tà.d] on the line-ending does, by reason of stress. This does not mean that stress automatically lengthens a vowel, since many stressed vowels are short. It means that lack of stress shortens any vowel; and when we speak of a vowel in a particular word as long, we mean only that it will be so if stressed.

I have not attempted to give any guidance as to the melodic form of these lines. The reader will recall what has been said about the effect of phrasing upon pitch, and the difference between stable and unstable lines (page 16). The short lines, he will note, have four syllables, and the long ones eight; but the latter are divided by a subsidiary stress into groupings such as 6:2, 5:3 etc. according to the natural syntactical rhythm of the phrases. The pause at the line-ending will be comparatively slight when there is no punctuation, and longer when there is punctuation.

39	Un petit roseau m'a suffi	5:3
	Pour faiˇrĕ frémi.r l'heˈrbĕ hauˈte	5:3
	Et tout le pré	4
4	Et les doux sauˈles	4
	Et le ruisseau qui chante aussi;	4:4
	Un petit roseau m'a suffi	5:3
	A faiˇrĕ chanter la forêt.	5:3
8	Ceux qui paˈssĕnt l'ont entendu	3:5
	Au fond du soi.r, en leur penséˈes,	4:4
	Dans le silen.ce et dans le vent	4:4
	Clair ou perdu	4
12	Proche ou lointain…	4
	Ceux qui paˈssĕnt en leurs penséˈes	3:5
	En écoutant, au fond d'eux-mêˈmes,	4:4
	L'entendront enco.re et l'enten.dent	5:3
16	Toujou.rs qui chan.te.	2:2
	Il m'a suffi	4
	De ce petit roseau cueilli	6:2
	A la fontaine où vint l'amou.r	4:4

20	Mirer, un jou.r	2:2
	Sa fa · cĕ gra.ve	4
	Et qui pleurait,	4
	Pour fai · rĕ pleurer ceux qui pa · ssent,	5:3
24	Et trembler l'herbe et frémir l'eau;	4:4
	Et j'ai, du sou · fflĕ d'un roseau,	2:6
	Fait chanter tou · tĕ la forêt [.]	3:5

All the lines which the student is called on to read will be correct in terms of syllable-count, and in the great majority of cases the application of the rules we have set out will make this clear. While he is familiarizing himself with verse techniques, he will have from time to time to scan lines and count syllables; and if the count comes out wrong, he may assume that he has made a mistake and must count again. There are certain special circumstances which may bring about an apparent irregularity in the number of syllables, and these, although not common, should be noted.

First, the *-ent* ending of the third person plural verb. In ordinary speech this is silent, and in verse it counts as a neutral [e]. This is how we read it in [8] and [13] of our poem. On the line-ending, as in [15] and [23], it produces a feminine rime and lengthens the stressed syllable, though the ending itself of course is silent. Within the line, *-ent* differs from the simple neutral [e] in that it can never be elided: the [t] at the end of the syllable prevents that. If followed by a vowel, this [t] is heard in liaison with it; as in [13] which is pronounced

[sœ̀ kí pá sĕ *tà* lœ̀r *pà* sé ·]

In Lamartine's description of two streams running through the undergrowth:

40 Ils mê · lĕnt un moment leur on.de et leur murmu.rĕ,

Et non loin de leur source ils se pe · rdĕnt sans nom [.]

the *-ent* is heard as a neutral [e] in both lines. In the first, the [t] makes liaison with the vowel following; in the second it is silent,

being followed by a consonant. Like any other neutral [e], this third
person plural ending lengthens a stressed syllable preceding it, if it is
not already long.

However, in the verb-ending *-aient* which is heard in the Imperfect and the Conditional, the neutral [e] is absorbed into the
vowel *-ai-* which precedes it, and is not heard as a separate syllable.
Thus *étaient* is scanned as [é tè], exactly as if it was *était*. This is
apparent in Vigny's line

41   Mais les enfants du Loup se jou:aient en silen.ce [,]
      . . . .

where the [t] makes liaison with *en*, but otherwise the *-ent* is
unheard. It is considered a non-existent syllable. This Imperfect
plural ending occurs only very rarely in the rime-word of any line,
but when it does it is ignored and produces a masculine rime; unlike
the normal *-ent* which, although it is not actually heard on the
line-ending, nevertheless produces a feminine rime. In the same
poem from which we have just quoted, Vigny gives an example of
such a rime:

42   J'aperçois tout à coup deux yeux qui flamboyaient [,]
      . . ..

and it is clear in the context that this rime is masculine.

The neutral [e] is likewise absorbed into the preceding vowel in
the Future and Conditional of verbs in which the stem ends in a
vowel. *Avouer* and *remuer* have the stem *avou-* and *remu-*; and
when grammatical endings are added to form the Future and Conditional we have forms such as *avouera, avouerait; remuera, remuerait*.
In verse, the neutral [e] is swallowed up by the vowel which goes
before it, and does not count as a syllable: so *avouera* is scanned and
read as *avou'ra*, and *remuerait* as *remu'rait*. In fact, the spelling
avoûrait will normally be found in verse.

Apart from these verb forms, a neutral [e] is not absorbed into a
vowel which precedes it; and this has the odd effect that a word such
as *pensée* can only be used in the interior of a line if the word
following begins with a vowel which will cause elision of the final
[e]: otherwise it would be heard as [pà sé ĕ] which is an awkward and
unacceptable sequence of sound. And the plural *pensées* can
never be used in the interior of a line, since the [s] makes elision
impossible: but it is perfectly acceptable on the line-ending, where
the feminine termination just disappears. Such restrictions (of which
there are others in French) do not directly concern the reader, but

they do limit the freedom of the poet. Occasionally he may ignore them, as Leconte de Lisle does when he writes

43   L'eau bleu˘ĕ qu'il pourchasse et dissipe en bué˘es [,]

but normally a poet will re-cast his sentence rather than demand of his reader that he pronounce such strange forms as [blœ˘ĕ]. A clash of vowels in French verse is known as *hiatus*, and since the seventeenth-century poets have been required to avoid it. In fact, *hiatus* occurs quite frequently in the interior of words in French, and in this position is perfectly acceptable. The word [bü é] in **43** offers an example; and so does *jouaient* [ju è] in **41**. But the principle has been firmly held that no two words should be placed together if the first ends and the second begins with a sounded vowel. This rule does correspond to a general tendency in the language. It is to avoid such a clash that one says *Je t'écoute* instead of *Je te écoute*, and *a-t-il* instead of *a-il*? Likewise, the [n] which is silent in *ton père* is heard in *ton ami*, again to avoid hiatus. Liaison of this kind is a characteristic feature of French. However, it is by no means a rigid principle, and the largely successful attempt to make it an obligatory feature of verse was an unnecessary attempt to legislate on what is essentially a matter of taste. In fact, even classical theorists accepted hiatus provided an unsounded consonant came between the sounded vowels. The Romantics allowed themselves still greater freedom in the matter. But the fact remains that in general hiatus between words is avoided in French verse.

But there is one special type of hiatus within the word which deserves attention because it may affect syllable-count: indeed, if a line appears to have one syllable too few or too many, the trouble may usually be traced to *diaeresis* or *synaeresis*. These words describe two possible responses to the situation in which any one of the three vowels [i], [ü] or [u] immediately precedes another vowel. What usually happens is that the first vowel changes into a semi-consonant, and this avoids hiatus. [i] becomes the sound which we write in phonetic transcript as [ỹ] and is called *yod* by phoneticians. It is what we hear in words such as *hier* [ỹèr] or *sensation* [sὰ sá sỹò] in which it is not heard as a full vowel and so will not count as a syllable in a line of verse. In ordinary speech, *lion* and *ciel* are monosyllables, pronounced [lỹò] and [sỹèl]. In the same way, [ü] can change into the semi-consonant [ŭ] when it combines with another vowel: so both *lui* [lŭi] and *nuance* [nŭὰ.s] are monosyllables, with the [ŭ] not heard or counted as a vowel. And [u] shortens into the semi-consonant [w] which is heard in *oui* [wí] *ouest* [wèst], *fouet* [fwè] and *souhaiter* [swè té]. This process, by which two vowels combine to form one, is known as *synaeresis*.

But it may sometimes happen that [i], [ü] or [u] remain separate from the vowel which follows, in which case the result is two syllables, not one. This effect is called *diaeresis*. The choice was not in theory left to the poet, but was based largely on the etymology of the word: however, this is a matter which need not concern the reader, and it must be admitted that poets were sometimes inconsistent. The reader must follow whatever usage the poet has adopted, and this must be judged from the syllable count. If we refer back to **34** we will recall that we read *expérience* as a four-syllable word, which means giving the value of a full vowel to the [i]. And in **36**:

44　　　Dans ce morne horizon se sont évanou:is [!]
　　　　　·　　·　··　　　·· · ···　·　·· · · · ···

the rime-word has four syllables, of which [u] is one. Therefore in this case we have diaeresis: the vowel has not been contracted. When Chenier writes

45　　　Nouer le tri ̆ plĕ fouet, le fouet de la vengean.ce [,]
　　　　　· ··　·　·　·　···　·　··　·　·　·　　···

he uses synaeresis in *fouet* [fw̆è] and diaeresis in *nouer* [nú:é]. And the last line of a well-known sonnet by Verlaine contains a most unusual example of diaeresis, for it requires us to pronounce the word *inflexion* as four syllables—[ë flèk sí ò]—which we certainly would not do in normal usage:

46　　　Et pour sa voix, lointaine, et calme, et grave, elle a
　　　　　　L'inflexi:on des voix chè.rĕs qui se sont tues [.]
　　　　　　·　·· · ··　　·　··　·　·· · · ·　···

Only if we are aware of the possibility of diaeresis can we give this line its full twelve syllables. A convenient way of remembering the difference between synaeresis and diaeresis is to recall that the word diaeresis itself contains an example of diaeresis: i.e. its first two vowels do not merge together but are sounded separately. In our examples, we indicate the occurrence of diaeresis by placing a colon between the two adjacent vowels.

Most of the lines we shall consider in this book are alexandrines: i.e. they have twelve syllables. We shall consider the alexandrine in greater detail in the next chapter. However, the principles of scansion which we have discussed are applicable to lines of any length. Despite the predominance of the alexandrine, French poets frequently use lines of ten or eight syllables: six too is not uncommon, and shorter lines occur, sometimes mingled with longer ones. The reader unfamiliar with French metres will find it easier to grasp the shorter ones, and may well prefer to practise first with these. Even with comparatively short lines there will usually be an interior (subsidiary) stress which must be correctly placed in order to fix the rhythm. In the following stanzas, Gautier uses lines of six syllables, but only two syllables in the third line: while the position of the subsidiary stress in the longer lines varies:

47   Les dieux eux-mê ˙ mĕs meu.rent,
      · · · ·· · ···

     Mais les ve.rs souvĕrains
     · · ·· · · ···

       Demeu.rent
       · ···

     Plus fo.rts que les airains.
     · ·· · · · ···

     Scu ˙ lptĕ, li ˙ mĕ, cisè ˙ le;
     ·· · · ·· · · ···

     Que ton rê.vĕ flottant
     · · ·· · · ···

       Se sce ˙ lle
       · ···

     Dans le bloc résistant!
     · · ·· ·· ···

Short lines are a particularly useful means of training one's ear to hear French rhythms: for after all, the longer lines also consist of a number of shorter phrases joined together, and one cannot appreciate the alexandrine unless one is capable of assessing both the length and the pitch of the segments of which it is composed. In his delightful song-like poem *Colombine* Verlaine constructs his stanzas out of what are in effect two twelve-syllable lines divided up 5:5:2|5:5:2. The proper reading of a series of unstable lines such as these requires not only that we read the correct number of syllables, but also that we interpret their pitch correctly. Here are the two opening stanzas, which introduce some of the characters of traditional Italian comedy—Harlequin, Pierrot and others—as the poet had seen them represented in the paintings of Watteau:

48   Léandrĕ le sot   lé *à* ˙ drĕ lĕ só
      Pierrot qui d'un saut   pÿè ró kí *dæ* só
         De puce   dĕ pü ˙ s

Franchit le buisson	frà ɗí lĕ bŭi sò
Cassandrĕ sous son	ká sà˙drĕ sú sò
Capuce	ká pü˙s
Arlĕquin aussi	ár lĕ kë ó sí
Cet aigrĕfin si	sè tè grĕ fë sí
Fantasque	fà tá˙sk
Aux costu˙mĕs fous	ó kò stü˙mĕ fú
Ses yeux luisant sous	sè zŷœ lŭi zà su
Son ma˙sque [,]	sò ma˙sk [,]

When he has got the rhythm right, the reader may then experiment with pitch. He will note how skilfully the line-endings are arranged in certain cases to run counter to the stress groups, producing highly unstable lines. Verlaine uses this effect to represent the leap of a flea:

$$[\text{pŷè}^{\text{ró}} \mid \text{kí dœ}^{\text{só}} {}^{\text{dĕ}} \text{pü.s}]$$

and throughout he maintains an effect of extreme lightness.

Syllabic rhythm and variations in pitch will be much more strongly heard in verse than is the case in ordinary speech. The reader must not depart too far from normal usage (though this is a matter of taste and interpretation) but he will certainly wish to use rhythms of greater flexibility and power than are necessary for casual communication. The poet gives to his work a certain quality of timelessness and often of dignity, charm, or magic which justifies a more thoughtful and imaginative use of words than we adopt when dealing with more ephemeral material. It was to satisfy such needs that the French metres in all their variety evolved.

Chapter Three
THE ALEXANDRINE

AMONG the various metres available to the French poet, the twelve-syllable alexandrine holds a position of pre-eminence. In the seventeenth century, in Corneille's time, it became the accepted metre for use in stage-plays, particularly in classical tragedy, where it held the field unchallenged through the century following. It was sometimes used, too, in comedy: but comedy generally had a contemporary setting, and the demands of realism encouraged the use of prose. In the nineteenth century it was extensively used by lyric poets, and in it was written much of the greatest and most enduring of French verse. It proved itself astonishingly durable, surviving all changes of emphasis and literary theory, and poets as different as Lamartine and Mallarmé, Hugo and Verlaine, Musset and Baudelaire, adapted it to their needs. It is not, as is sometimes claimed, necessarily a solemn line, though it lends itself well to serious verse. Molière used it to comic effect and so did on occasions La Fontaine, Musset, Verlaine, and Rimbaud. It was the medium of Lamartine's musical reveries, of Hugo's resonant philosophizing and rhetoric, but also of Mallarmé's light and dream-like *Après-midi d'un faune*. It seems to be capable of almost anything, although, when they aspire to pure song and lyricism, poets may prefer a shorter line. The alexandrine is the longest line in normal use in the French language.

It appears to have taken its name from the twelfth-century *Roman d'Alexandre*, the earliest surviving work in this metre. It was not widely used in the Middle Ages, when the ten-syllable line was considered better suited to heroic narrative and still shorter lines for lyric verse. At that time the erosion of the neutral [ĕ] was not far advanced, and ten syllables would have a fuller sound than they have in the modern language. It may not be coincidence that the rise of the twelve-syllable alexandrine closely followed the completion of the process which weakened many unstressed syllables and reduced them to a mere feature of rhythm, for the lengthening of the line helped to compensate for this loss. Its triumph in the seventeenth-century theatre was due to the fact that its length lent itself so well to the cadences of rhetoric as well as to the complexities of psychological analysis. At the height of nineteenth-century Romanticism in France, rhetoric remained the normal manner of self-expression for the poet, though whether we should say that this explains the survival of the verse-form, or rather that the verse-form so dominated the literary tradition as to ensure the survival of rhetoric, is a matter for conjecture.

Both the strength and the weakness of the alexandrine lie in the fact that, more closely than any other metre, it reflects the rhythms of speech. This gives it great flexibility and variety, but also makes it a natural medium for versifiers of pretentious prose. If the alexandrine can be used to express everything, then inevitably it will be used to express much that is not poetry. It has in fact been the medium of much mediocre verse. But even so, in one age after another, the greatest poets have come back to it, and each has found in it new possibilities.

The English-speaking reader, unfamiliar with French verse, will take more readily to the shorter line, for that offers something rather more closely akin to the type of rhythm he is accustomed to, that of the metrical foot with its recurring group of stressed and unstressed syllables and its line-length clearly reinforced by rime. The stresses of the alexandrine strike him first and foremost as a feature of syntax, resulting from the grouping of words in such a way as to make a (generally rhetorical) statement, and he may be only dimly aware of the metrical rhythm they compose. As he stumbles through the alexandrine, he may feel that it is a prosaic and pedestrian form. It seems to him monotonous because he is incapable of reproducing its rhythms.

So let us begin with a shorter line: one of six syllables. It is not difficult to 'feel' a length of six syllables, particularly since each line will contain a subsidiary stress. This means that we hear not an unbroken run of syllables but a grouping such as 4:2, 3:3, or 2:4. If the first stress-group contains four syllables, it must be followed by one of two syllables; and so on. We can get into this kind of rhythm fairly easily.

	Bientôt nous plongĕrons	2:4
	· ·· · · ···	
	Dans les froi˙dĕs ténè˙bres;	3:3
	· · ·· · · ···	
	Adieu, vivĕ clarté	2:4
	· ·· · · · ···	
4	De nos étés trop cou.rts!	4:2
	· · · ·· · ···	

	J'entends déjà tomber	4:2
	· · · · ·· · ···	
	Avec des chocs funè ˙bres,	4:2
	· · · · ·· · ···	
	Le bois retentissant	2:4
	· ·· ·· · · ···	
8	Sur le pavé des cou.rs [.]	4:2
	· · · ·· · ···	

The reader will note first that the fixed stresses on the line-ending, which occur at six-syllable intervals, are very much stronger than the mobile stresses, which occur at irregular intervals: but this irregularity serves to vary the rhythm and make it more interesting. There is nothing in the poem itself to indicate where the subsidiary stresses fall, yet the reader will have no doubt as to why we have placed them where we have. In each case, the sense suggests it. Only in [5] could we seriously hesitate. Why not stress *entends*, and give the line the rhythm 2:4? This is certainly possible, and the placing of the subsidiary stresses is always at the discretion of the reader: though in practice, more often than not, only one position will give a satisfactory reading. In this particular case, I think *déjà* echoes the theme introduced by *bientôt* and *adieu*: the poet is lamenting the speed at which summer is departing and winter approaching. So we stress *déjà*. But that is a personal choice. Another feature of rhythm that the reader will note is that the fixed stresses on alternate line-endings are stronger and followed by a firmer pause than is the case with the other lines: there is a distinct break in sense after *ténèbres, cours, funèbres*, and *courts*, and a greater sense of continuity after the other lines.

This six-syllable metre is too obtrusive to carry a serious theme for long. It would be suitable for a light song. But the lines tend to isolate the phrases more than is necessary. Let us, then, re-write them, joining each pair of lines together, so that the strong stresses come at the line-endings and the lighter stresses in the middle of the line, with the subsidiary stresses, of course, still in their various positions. Now the rhythm becomes gentler, slower, and more flowing. For convenience, we will indicate the middle of the line by an upright stress-bar. The syllable it follows still carries stress, but there is no longer any pause: the voice follows the natural rhythms without a break through the twelve syllables.

49   Bientôt nous plongĕrons | dans les froi˙dĕs ténè˙bres;   2:4|3:3

Adieu, vi˙vĕ clarté | de nos étés trop cou.rts!   2:4|4:2

J'entends déjà tomber | avec des chocs funè˙bres   4:2|4:2

Le bois retentissant | sur le pavé des cou.rs [.]   2:4|4:2

This is how Baudelaire actually wrote the opening stanza of the *Chant d'automne*—in alexandrines.

The standard alexandrine has a *binary* form: i.e. it is in two equal parts. When it first appeared in French, in the Middle Ages, it actually consisted of two six-syllable lines yoked together, with a stress and a pause in the middle. The term used for this pause was *caesura*, a Latin word meaning 'a cut'. For reasons that we have just demonstrated, the line evolved into a unified whole and the medial pause disappeared, but the stress at the point – the sixth syllable – remained, and is still called the *caesura*. It is the *major stress* of the line, second only to that on the line-ending which carries the rime. When the alexandrine is written, it carries no indication for the eye as to where the caesura falls. On occasions, there may be punctuation at this point, as in

50   Qu'il soit dans ton repos, qu'il soit dans tes ora.ges [,]

or

51   Le dése.rt est muet, la ten.te est solitai.re [.]

But very often there is no punctuation, and we must interpret the stresses for ourselves.

52   Le Mon.de est rétréci | par notre expéri:en.ce [.]

And even where there is punctuation, it may not occur exactly at the caesura:

53   O que ma quille écla | te! ô que j'ai.lle à la me.r [!]

Therefore, in reading, we place the caesura by 'feeling' the number of syllables. It is absolutely essential that it occur at the mid-point (except in special cases where the rhythm deviates from the norm, which we will discuss in due course), and there can be no question of reading an alexandrine without knowing, and showing, where the caesura falls. It is the keystone of the line's structure. The image of an arch, with a keystone at its central point, is indeed borne out by the characteristic melodic curve of the 'convex' alexandrine, which may be considered to be its basic form. Here are two examples;

54   Mais la natu,re est là, qui t'invite et qui t'ai˙me [;]

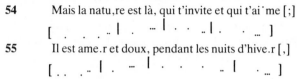

55   Il est ame.r et doux, pendant les nuits d'hive.r [,]

To describe the form of these lines, we need a certain terminology. We define the alexandrine as a line of twelve syllables, divided by the caesura into two equal parts of six syllables each. Each half of the line is called a *hemistich*. This is a word of Greek origin, and in English it is pronounced *hemistik*, and not *hemistitch* as is sometimes heard; and its plural is *hemistichs*, pronounced *hemistiks*, In this book, we indicate the first hemistich by the letter [A] and the second by [B]: thus [1A] refers to the first hemistich of the first line, [2B] to the second hemistich of the second line. Each hemistich will normally contain one subsidiary stress, dividing it into two stress-groups, each of which is called a *segment*. Thus typical lines such as **54** or **55** above consist of four segments. Unlike the hemistich, which is of fixed length, the length of the segment varies, and this produces a *metrical pattern* which is expressed in terms of syllables. The pattern of **54** is 4:2|3:3 and that of **55** is 4:2|4:2. This pattern decides the rhythm of the line. In writing it, the caesura is represented by an upright stress-bar, and the segments are separated by colons. In any regular alexandrine the figures on either side of the stress-bar must total six.

In both **54** and **55**, [A] has an upward slope and [B] a downward one. The two segments which make up [A] are both unstable, since the first segment requires the second to complete it, and when we reach the caesura we anticipate another hemistich to complete the line. This instability produces a rising tone which normally reaches its peak at the caesura, from which point it descends, probably to middle pitch at the end of the first segment [B] and to neutral or low pitch at the end of the line. This gives the characteristic 'convex' melodic line which is associated with the alexandrine. However, this is no more than a basic pattern, and if all lines followed it, even allowing for variation in position of the minor stresses, the result would be monotonous. In fact there will be many variations resulting not only from the varying lengths and disposition of the segments but also from the meaning of the words and from the type of punctuation used. Unless the poet deliberately decides otherwise, the caesura will be the fulcrum around which the melodic line of the alexandrine turns; but he may if he wishes use it as the low-point, rather than the high-point, of the line. For instance, in **56** it seems to me very likely that we would give a downward slope to the word *plongerons* on the caesura, in order to reinforce its sense. The semicolon on the line-ending suggests that the line ends at neutral: if a fullstop had occurred here, it would have gone down to low pitch. The line which follows it, closed by an exclamation mark, is certainly unstable. So one may arrive at a rendering such as:

56   Bientôt nous plongĕrons | dans les froi˙dĕs ténè˙bres;

     [.   ˙˙   ·   ·   · ... | .   .   ˙˙   ·   · ...

     Adieu, vi˙vĕ clarté | de nos étés trop cou.rts [!]

     [. ˙˙   ·   ·   ·   ˙˙˙ | ·   ·   ·   ˙˙   .   ˙˙˙

In all the cases we have so far considered, the stress-bar indicating the caesura is placed between two words. This happens if the word on the caesura ends in a stressed vowel or a sounded terminal consonant (e.g. *tombeau* or *bloc*). The stress-bar is then written after the terminal vowel or consonant. If [B] begins with a vowel, a terminal consonant in [A] will in fact attach itself to the syllable following, so that we ought in fact to write

57   Je vais m'exercer seu|l à ma fantasque escri˙me [,]

But this practice may be felt to be a little pedantic, and one may prefer to place the stress-bar between the words; though in a phonetic transcript one would show the transference of the consonant.

     Je vais m'exercer seul | à ma fantasque escri˙me [,]
     [jĕ vè mèg sèr sé sœ | lá má fà tá skè skri˙m]

The advantage of writing the stress-bar between words is apparent in cases such as

58   Je te do˙nnĕ ces vers | afin que si mon nom [ ]

and

59   Contrĕ quelque univers | immobile en sa fo˙rce [ ]

in which it is not the terminal [s] which is carried over when the line is spoken, but the [r] ·which precedes it; so that the division 've|rs afin que' or 'unive|rs immobile' may seem rather awkward. This, however, is left to the reader's discretion. But in phonetic transcript no problem arises, and one writes [vè|rá fë] and [ü ní vè|rí mò bí *là* sá fò˙rs].

But in many cases it is obligatory to write the stress-bar through the word rather than after it. This is always so when the word on the caesura ends in a mute [e]. This situation, which occurs frequently in verse, is illustrated by the following examples:

60 Un souvĕni.r, un son. | ge, une invisible ima.ge [.]

61 Pascal avait son gou | ffre avec lui se mouvant [.]

To understand this practice, it is necessary to consider the problems raised by the presence of neutral [ĕ] in such a position. The neutral [ĕ] can never occur on the sixth syllable, since this syllable bears stress: and as we have seen, [ĕ] cannot be stressed. Therefore, if the word on the caesura ends in [e], it is the preceding stressed vowel which falls on the sixth syllable, and the final [ĕ] must be muted by absorption into the word following. For this to happen, the grammatical phrase which composes [B] *must* begin with a vowel. This is the case in **60** and **61**, and indeed in every alexandrine in which the word on the caesura ends in an unstressed [e].

Why should this be so? Why cannot the neutral [ĕ] simply be taken over into [B] as an unstressed syllable? Let us consider as an example Baudelaire's

·**62** Le Printemps adora|ble a perdu son odeu.r [.]
    · · ·· · · ···   · · ·· · · ···

Here the final [e] of *adorable* has simply disappeared, just as it would do if the word occurred on the line-ending. Hence, in metrical terms, the hemistich and the syntactical phrase coincide exactly, and the line has a strong caesura. But supposing Baudelaire had written

    Le Printemps adora|blĕ ne reviendra pas [.]
    · · ·· · · ··· · · · · · ···

this would no longer be the case. For although [A] still has six syllables, the syntactical phrase which composes it is heard as having seven. The caesura is therefore weakened and the line metrically ambiguous. It lacks a clear fulcrum on which to turn. This situation is entirely unacceptable to the French ear, and is never allowed to occur.

To the English-speaking reader brought up on different rhythms the point may seem unimportant. That it is not so to the French poet is shown by the fact that, in order to conform to it, he accepts the most remarkable limitations on his freedom to use words in the alexandrine. In the first place, he can never use a plural verb on the caesura, since the final *-ĕnt* cannot be elided. Even if [B] begins with a vowel it cannot absorb this syllable, owing to its final [t]. (It is in fact possible to use *-aient* on the caesura, since, as we saw on page 38, in this combination the *-ent* is absorbed into the preceding vowel and is metrically non-existent, so that Hugo can write

63   Les cho.sĕs qui sortaient | de son nocturne esprit [ ]
        .   ¨ .   . .   ···   . .   . . ¨ . ···

But otherwise, plural verbs with a terminal *-ent* cannot occur in this position.) This restriction is obviously a considerable handicap to the poet.

Even more regrettable is that, although words ending in [e] occur commonly on the caesura, they can never do so in the plural form. For the addition of an *-s* would make it impossible to elide the final [e], and the syntactical phrase in [A] would have seven syllables, not six. So **60** could not have been written in the form

Des souveni.rs, des son.|gĕs ...

nor could Baudelaire have given us **61** as

Pascal avait ses gou.|ffrĕs ...

From these examples it will be apparent why, when the word on the caesura ends in an unstressed [e], it must be cut off with its preceding consonant and absorbed into [B]. For this reason, the stress-bar is always written through the word, and immediately after its stressed syllable.

It will also be apparent from what has been said that a phrase cannot normally end on the fifth or seventh syllable of an alexandrine, since this would confuse the stress of the caesura. But otherwise the poet enjoys complete freedom in the placing of his minor stresses. They will result from his sense-groups or syntactical phrases. The reader is likewise free to make what use of them he chooses. More often than not there will be no doubt as to where they occur, since in this respect the rhythms of verse conform generally to those of prose; but verse does permit greater freedom than normal language, since rhythm is an essential and not a merely incidental quality. In general usage, for instance, an adjective preceding a noun does not bear stress. But in verse it can do, particularly if its positioning is unusual. Baudelaire, for instance, places the adjective before the noun in

64   Bientôt nous plongĕrons | dans les froi˙dĕs ténè˙bres [;]
          · ·· ·   ·   · ··· | ·   ·   ·   ·· · · ···

and it is the obvious position in which the minor stress of [B] will fall. This may also be true of *noirs* in

65   Sous les noi.rs acajous, | les lia˙nĕs en fleu.r [,]
          ·   ·   ··   · · ··· | · · ·· ·· ·   ···

In some cases the subsidiary stress may be merely technical, as for instance in [B] in

66   Je te do˙nnĕ ces vers | afin que si mon nom [ ]
          · · ··   ·   · ···   · ·   ·· · ·   ···

Here there is a clear syntactical break after *que*, as the reader will see if he refers to page 6, and the sentence is not resumed until the beginning of the following stanza, and this is likely to produce at least nominal stress. In such cases, minor stress may fall on words which are syntactically quite unimportant. This would not be possible with a major stress, which in any case cannot fall on a neutral [e]. In practice, we may if we wish dispense with at least one of the minor stresses in the alexandrine, if the sense justifies this. In

67   Li˙brĕs commĕ la me.r | autour des som.brĕs î˙les [.]

the subsidiary stress in [A] necessarily falls on the first syllable. In [B] we may choose to place it on *sombres*, though the last syllable of *autour* is also a possibility. Or we may choose to ignore it entirely and stress only the rime-word. This is entirely at the reader's discretion. In a line such as

68   Ca˙lmĕ commĕ la me.r | en sa sérénité [,]
          ··   ·   ·   · · ··· | ·   ·   · · ···

there can really be no very convincing reason for introducing a subsidiary stress into [B], since a smooth unbroken flow entirely fits the sense.

On the other hand, it is possible to have more than one subsidiary stress in a hemistich if the sense requires it. Punctuation usually makes it clear when this is called for. Hugo showed a particular fondness for enumerative effects which multiply stress:

69　　　Eh bien! oubli:ez-nous, | maison, jardin, ombra.ges [!]
　　　　　.　..　.　.　...　　|　.　..　.　.　...

or the much more aggressive

70　　　Cheval, foule aux pieds l'ho|mme, et l'homme et l'homme et
　　　　　.　..　.　.　...　|　.　.　..　.　..　.
　　　　　　l'homme!
　　　　　　...

in which the poet attains a deliberately agitated rhythm intended to suggest the large scale of the slaughter. We would represent the rhythm of this line as 2:4|2:2:2.

We have quoted a number of lines in which subsidiary stress falls on the first syllable of [A], as it does in **67** and **68**. When this happens we have a 1:5 rhythm. If this rhythm occurs in [B], an odd situation arises, since it means that the subsidiary stress falls on the syllable immediately following the caesura. Poets generally avoid this, since a stress is most effective when contrasted with unstressed syllables, and a subsidiary stress adjacent to a major one is likely to be completely overshadowed. And yet the effect can be handled successfully. Here are two lines, one by Racine and one by Vigny:

71　　　L'assassiner, le per|dre? Ah! devant qu'il expi.re [,]
　　　　　.　.　.　..　.　...　|　..　.　.　.　.　...

72　　　Refermant ses grands yeux, | meu.rt sans jeter un cri [.]
　　　　　.　.　..　.　.　...　|　..　.　.　.　.　...

The first of these has the rhythm 4:2|1:5, and the second 3:3|1:5. Racine's line is highly dramatic, and it is clear that the syllable *Ah!* represents a sigh, or a cry, of appreciable length. It is not, as it may sometimes be at the beginning of a line, an ejaculation to be passed over quickly. But it cannot overshadow *perdre* on the caesura, which is crucial to the sense of the line. Similar considerations apply to **72**, Vigny's description of the dying wolf which was once known to every schoolboy who knew anything at all about French verse. *Meurt* is very important, but so too is *yeux* on the caesura: for those dying eyes have moved the hearts of countless readers. In reading these lines, two things are clear. First, there must be a difference of pitch between the two words around the caesura. If one is at high pitch, the other is at middle. And no less important, in both cases the syllable on the subsidiary stress is very considerably lengthened. It has to be. Otherwise its effect will be lost.

The rhythm 5:1 occurring in either hemistich will likewise result in two stresses falling on consecutive syllables. Although this will be generally avoided, it can on occasions be used to good effect, as Hugo demonstrates when he writes

73   Il faut que l'he ˙ rbĕ pou|sse, et que les enfants meu.rent [,]

In reading, the antithesis between *pousse* and *meurent* will be brought out by the fact that the former, on the caesura, is at high pitch, while the latter is at neutral, since the line clearly ends with a falling cadence. And here too we will make the most of the contrast in vowel-length on the line-ending. In such cases the short segment will be prolonged in order to prevent it being overshadowed by the subsidiary stress. A similar lengthening of a single syllable occurs at the beginning of **67** and **68**, where the stress on the first word produces the rhythm 1:5 in [A]. The voice will naturally dwell on 'libres' and 'calme', even though there is no adjacent stress to compete with them. And if the short segment is stretched, then, relatively, the long segment is shortened: i.e. read more quickly.

Grammont has argued convincingly that what is involved here is a principle of general application, and a feature which probably does more than any other to account for the importance of the subsidiary stress within a line. He suggests that in a four-segment line, each segment tends to occupy a quarter of the time spent in speaking that line. What is involved is only a tendency, not a verifiable fact. A single syllable cannot be stretched to the same length as the five other syllables which make up the hemistich. But it will be read more slowly, whereas the longer segment will be read more quickly. This seems to be the case. It applies not only to hemistichs with a 1:5 rhythm, but also to 2:4 or 4:2. Only a line which has the rhythm 3:3|3:3 will be read at an unvarying speed. In the case for instance of **64**, which has a rhythm of 2:4|3:3, we shall read *Bientôt* slowly, and the second segment of four syllables, *nous plongerons*, a good deal more quickly. We have already suggested that this second segment will have a falling slope; so in all respects our rendering will reinforce meaning. In the second hemistich the speed of reading will even out.

The same principle applies to

74   J'entends le vent dans l'ai.r, | la me.r sur le récif [,]

which has the rhythm 2:4|2:4. *le vent dans l'air* and *sur le récif* are
read more quickly than *J'entends* or *la mer*, and this movement of
the voice gives movement to the line.

But in **75** a problem arises. [A] has the rhythm 1:5, but it is
obvious that this cannot be stretched, since this opening syllable is
merely the conjunction *Et*.

75   Et, comme un long linceul | traînant à l'Orient [,]
          ··   ·   ·   ·   · ··· | · ·· ·   · · ···

This kind of hemistich is not uncommon, and it goes without saying
that one would not attempt to treat a conjunction in the same way as
one would an evocative word such as *meurt* or *ah*! What happens in
this case, I think, is that the first segment is followed by a slight
pause. Since the conjunction cannot be significantly stretched, this
is a case in which punctuation really does result in a pause. In [B] of
this line, the word *traînant* will be read more slowly than the final
segment, so here again we obtain an appropriate reading.

A conjunction such as *et* or *mais*, occurring at the beginning of a
line, will only produce a 1:5 pattern when it is isolated by punctuation. And in that case the punctuation is also indicated by pitch: for
when the first syllable of a line bears stress, it begins not at neutral as
would normally be the case but at middle or high pitch. This applies
to all lines with initial stress. But when an initial conjunction is not
separated from the subsequent sentence by punctuation, it has no
particular stress and the line begins at neutral. This we hear in

76   Et les soi.rs au balcon, voilés de vapeurs ro.ses [.]
          · ·   ··   · · · ···   · ·· · · ·   ···

The rhythm is 3:3|2:4, and the initial conjunction does not modify
the speed of reading.

If the alexandrine begins with a word charged with considerable
emotional force, its effect on the melodic line will depend on how
closely it is integrated into the syntax of the sentence. Ejaculations,
not uncommonly found in this position in the verse of classical
tragedy, are syntactically separate from the main sentence which
follows, and equally isolated from the melodic pattern. In the
following example of 1:5|1:5 rhythm, the opening segment is raised
by strong stress, and the main melodic line is likely to begin from
neutral with the second segment:

77   Dieux! quels ruisseaux de sang | cou˙lĕnt autour de moi [!]
          [·· | ·   ·   ·   · ··· | ·· |.   ·   ·   · ···]

In [B], of course, the stressed syllable of *coulĕnt* is much prolonged. The opening syllable of

78   Va: je te désavoue, | et tu me fais horreu.r [.]

[¨ | . . . · ˜ | · · · ‥ | . ‥]

may be regarded as similarly isolated. However, we may also regard it as belonging to the main sentence, and in that case it will introduce a downward slope running through the line:

Va: je te désavoue, | et tu me fais horreu.r [.]

[¨ | · · · · ‥ | . · · ‥ | . ‥]

In either case *Va* and *horreur* will be prolonged, the former probably by an initial pause. Most often there is no ambiguity, and a stressed opening syllable which is closely linked in terms of syntax with the segment following will produce a downward melodic slope running through the hemistich and perhaps through the line.

79   J'ai ˙mĕ le son du Co.r | le soi.r, au fond des bois [;]

[¨ | · · · · ‥ | . ¨ | · · · ‥]

80   Pen.chĕ sa tê ˙tĕ pâ.|le et pleu.rĕ sur la me.r [,]

[¨ | · · · · ‥ | . ¨ | · · · ‥]

81   Triste, et le jour pour moi | sera commĕ la nuit [.]

[¨ | · · · · ‥ | . ¨ | . · · ‥]

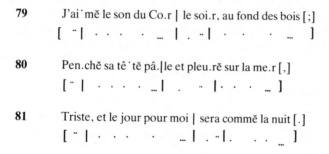

In any alexandrine, the melodic form of [B] is determined above all by whether the line is stable or unstable. The classical alexandrine, as used in the seventeenth and eighteenth centuries, was generally end-stopped: i.e. ended in punctuation. But this does not imply that it was necessarily or even predominantly stable. A question mark, exclamation mark or colon produces instability, causing the line to end at middle or high pitch; and a glance at any of Racine's plays demonstrates that he makes abundant use of this effect. A long sequence of alexandrines would be monotonous if all ended on the same pitch. Even a sequence of stable lines offers the variation between the ending at neutral (the comma) or low pitch (the full stop).

82   Tout ce qui de mon cœu.r fut l'uni˙quĕ dési.r,

[. . ⊣ · · ⸱⸱ ‖ · ·⸌ · ·⸱⸱]

Tout ce que j'aimerai jusqu'au dernier soupi.r [.]

[⸱⸱ | . . . . ⸱⸱‖· · · ·⸳⸳ | . ⸱⸱]

Here, in contrast, is a sequence of end-stopped unstable lines:

83   Ce changĕment est grand, ma surpri.se est extrê˙me:
         Titus entre mes mains remet tout ce qu'il ai˙me!
         Dois-je croi.rĕ, grands dieux! ce que je viens d'ou:i.r?
         Et, quand je le croirais, dois-je m'en réjou:i.r [?]

And even in classical times the open-ended or run-on line, which is necessarily unstable, was by no means exceptional.

84   Pour fruit de tant d'amou.r, j'aurai le triste emploi
         De recueilli.r des pleu.rs qui ne sont pas pour moi [.]

The run-on line is often confused with enjambement, a quite different feature of French verse to which we must now turn our attention. Enjambement may occur either on the caesura or on the line-ending. In either case, it involves a change in the balance of the alexandrine. Equilibrium around the caesura is, as we have seen, the fundamental principal of the binary alexandrine: nevertheless, on occasions the poet may deliberately upset this equilibrium, and in so doing produce striking rhythmic effects. He does so only exceptionally, and it is by contrast with the pattern of the more frequent regular lines that his variation forces itself on our attention. Enjambement does not involve neglect of the regular stresses of the line but rather a deliberate displacement which sets up a counter-rhythm.

Enjambement occurs within a line when a segment overruns the caesura in such a way as to set up a rhythm which runs contrary to normal metrical stress. It displaces the major internal stress of the line from the caesura to some other syllable—not the fifth or the seventh, for that is so close to the normal position that it would give an impression of bungled rhythm, but to a position which clearly is not that of the regular caesura. The line then has no centre and no symmetry; but it is not disorganized. For enjambement to be effective, we must feel that the lack of balance is purposeful.

Vigny opens his poem *Le Cor* with a perfectly regular line:

85   J'ai˙mĕ le son du Co.r, | le soi.r, au fond des bois [;]

         ⸱⸱ · · · · ⸱⸱ | · ⸱⸱ · · · · ⸱⸱

which has the rhythm 1:5|2:4. The short segments will be lengthened in reading: *Cor* is stressed on the caesura because it is central to the theme of the line and the poem. And he closes the poem with an isolated line which strongly recalls the one with which he began—and yet at the same time differs from it. It differs because the poet has been speaking of the death of Roland, the sound of whose horn echoed, from a pass in the Pyrenees, through medieval literature. The memory of that horn evokes sadness. And the poem concludes with the words:

86   Dieu! que le son du Cor est tri/ste, au fond des bois [!]

The word *Cor* is still on the caesura, but this no longer bears a major stress: for this has been transferred to *triste* on the eighth syllable. The rhythm of the line is 1:5:2/4. A sloping stress-bar is here used to indicate that the major stress no longer coincides with the caesura, but is displaced.

What is the effect of this? The line begins with an isolated exclamation, stressed, lengthened and raised to middle pitch. And the remaining five syllables of [A] do not complete a meaningful phrase. There is still stress on the sixth syllable, but it is not major and the segment is quite unstable, since *que le son du Cor*—leaves the mind in suspense. For the sense to be complete, we need two more syllables: *est triste*. It is on the eighth syllable that the major stress falls, and as a consequence the melodic slope runs straight through the caesura to reach high (or possibly low) pitch on the word *triste*. One might suggest the following reading:

[dy̆œ̆ ... | kĕ le sò dü kò rè ᵗʳⁱ | stó fò dè ᵇʷá]

A line of this kind may be said to have a *delayed stress*, and the effect is termed *enjambement on the caesura*. The term *enjambement* is known to every student, but its significance is less generally understood. It means literally *striding over*, and in this case it is the caesura that is crossed. The effect is both to move the main stress and to intensify it when it occurs in its unexpected position. It is as if the mental energy which is normally dissipated at the caesura is bottled up and explodes a few syllables later. Thus enjambement is not a failure to use the caesura. It is a quite deliberate effacement of the stress on the caesura in order to place it, with additional force, at a later point. If Vigny had written:

Le son du Co.r est tri|ste, au fond des som.brĕs bois [!]

the word *triste* would have made much less impact on the imagination
than it does in the line which he in fact wrote.

In **86** the presence of enjambement is clearly shown by punctuation. But this is not always the case. There is no punctuation in
Baudelaire's line

87   Derrièrĕ la mura.ille immen./sĕ du brouilla.rd [;]

.   .. .

but there is none the less enjambement on the caesura. Certainly
the first six syllables—*Derrièrĕ la muraille*—seem to form a complete hemistich, but they do not because of the presence of the
adjective *immense* which cannot stand on its own and must be
attached to *muraille*. Although metrically situated in [B], in terms
of sense the adjective belongs to [A] and not to the words that
follow it—*du brouillard*. As a result the caesura is eroded, and the
pitch slope runs straight through it to reach its high point on the last
syllable of *immense*. The rhythm of this line will be expressed as
2:4:2/4. It will be noted that it is the syntactical form of the sentence
that imposes enjambement. If the poet had written

Derrièrĕ la mura.|ille immen.se et menaçan.te [;]

there would have been no enjambement since *immense et mena-
çante*, being two adjectives both describing *muraille*, belong together
naturally and form a perfectly satisfactory hemistich. The same may
be said of

88   Trouveront dans ce sol lavé comme unĕ grè.ve [,]

. . ..

where there is no displacement of stress and no enjambement, even
though *lavé* is an adjective describing *sol* in the previous hemistich.
The point is that the whole of [B] is an adjectival phrase describing
sol, and so forms a perfectly satisfactory unit. No single part of it
needs to be attached to [A]. Enjambement on the caesura always
has the effect of *dislocating* [B] as a sense-unit and therefore as a
stress-unit, as is clearly seen from such patterns as 2:4:2/4 or 1:5:2/4.
A word or small group of words at the beginning of [B] is attached
inseparably to [A] by its syntax, while having no such close relationship with the remainder of its own hemistich. So in **86** [B] consists of
two unrelated phrases—*est triste au fond des bois*, as it does also
in **87**, where we have *immense : du brouillard*. The fragment which

crosses over the caesura is called the *rejet*, and in a rhythmic formula such as 2:4:2/4 it is represented by the figure which appears immediately before the sloping stress-bar. If it is to intensify stress, the *rejet* must consist of one, two or three syllables, not more. A *rejet* of four syllables is perfectly possible, but is too far from the caesura to make a dramatic contrast of stress. When we read

89   En passant sur le pont de la Tourne/lle, un soi.r,

·   ·   ··   ·   ·   ··   ·   ·   ·   ···   ·   ···

we recognize that there is enjambement, since *le pont de la Tournelle* is a name which cannot possibly be divided between two sense-groups. The rhythm of the line is 3:3:4/2. So the symmetry of the line has been upset, but we do not get the feeling that the poet is anxious to impress upon us that he was on the pont de la Tournelle and not on the pont Neuf. Whereas we realize beyond doubt that in **86** the key to the whole line is *triste*. Out of such subtleties of rhythm is poetry made.

Where there is enjambement on the caesura, the sixth syllable almost always retains some stress: but it is a subsidiary, not a major stress. In the examples we have quoted, [A] remains a perfectly coherent stress-unit, and is not dislocated, even though it is not complete. *En passant sur le pont* makes perfectly good sense, but to understand the line as a whole we need to add something to it. In such cases the caesura may be said to be *eroded*. This is the effect which Hugo obtains in

90   Ellĕ tient à la main unĕ ro./se, et regarde [.]

·   ·   ··   ·   ·   ··   ·   ·   ···   ·   ·   ···

in which the rhythm is 3:3:3/3. But enjambement on the caesura does happen quite frequently as a result of [A] being dislocated. If, for instance, the first two or three syllables of [A] form a phrase which is not linked by syntax with the rest of the line, then the remaining syllables may well be insufficient to form a complete sense-group, and so will overrun the caesura. This is liable to happen as a result of enjambement on the ending of the previous line. And it is in this form that students most readily recognize—or think they recognize—enjambement, because if the sense overruns the line-ending it usually means that the line ends without punctuation. As a result, it is usual to associate enjambement with an open-ended line. But this is not a reliable guide. The essential feature of enjambement is displacement of stress, which results in dislocation of the hemistich. In the case of enjambement on the caesura it is [B] that is dislocated: but enjambement on the line-ending means that the *rejet* goes into the line following, and as a result it is [A] of the second line which is dislocated.

Here are three examples:

91   Tout en parlant ainsi, le saty.rĕ devint
           Démesuré; plus grand d'abo.rd que Polyphè˙me [,]

92   Une ondulation majestueu.se et lente
           S'éve.ille, et va mouri.r à l'horizon poudreux [.]

93   Mais les vrais voyageu.rs sont ceux-là seuls qui pa˙rtent
           Pour parti.r; cœurs légers, sembla˙blĕs aux ballons [;]

In each case the sense of [1B] is completed by a short *rejet* in [2A]: *le satyre devint* [] démesuré [;]; *Une ondulation majestueuse et lente* [] s'éveille [;], *ceux-là seuls qui partent* [] pour partir, and this *rejet* has no syntactical connection with its own line. As a result, [2A] is in every case dislocated. In our first example, *Démesuré; plus grand* is incoherent; in the second, *S'éveille, et va mourir* makes sense but is divided between two clauses; and this is also true of the third, *Pour partir; cœurs légers*. The rhythm of the second line of **91** would be represented as 4/4:4 ; that of **92** as 2/4:4:2, and of **93** as 3/3:3:3.

This effect cannot occur by chance in good verse. The alexandrine is built from grammatical clauses, and meaning and metre either run together or offset each other. The vast majority of grammatical clauses and sentences will be coterminous with line or hemistich. When the poet departs from this practice, he produces a substantial rhythmic jolt, and this jolt must have a purpose. The *rejet* always bears strong stress on its last syllable: it represents a climax, and dominates the line in which it occurs. In **91**, Hugo is giving *démesuré* a force appropriate to its meaning, greater than it could have in any other position. In **92** Leconte de Lisle is emphasizing the contrast between the strongly-stressed *s'éveille* and the more weakly stressed *mourir*; and in **93** Baudelaire is changing an apparently commonplace truism—

    Mais les vrais voyageurs sont ceux-là seuls qui partent [ ]

into an observation of startling originality by adding the unexpected words *pour partir*. So in each case the enjambement is functional. This must be reflected in our reading. If the first line is unstable as in our examples (and it usually will be) then our intonation must clearly show that the sense is incomplete, and the melodic pattern of [1B] will leap over the line-ending and be continued into, or answered by, the *rejet*. If we accept that *démesuré* suggests an upward slope, we could read

Le satyrĕ devint [] démesuré [;]

[lĕ sá ᵗⁱ | rĕ dĕ vë [] dé mĕ zü ʳᵉ]

In **92** *s'éveille* is likely to have a similar slope. But in **93** the first line is likely to end at high pitch, since we have to counteract, by tone of voice, the impression of completeness which the words would otherwise give. In this case the *rejet* will have a falling slope.

... ceux-là seuls qui par.tent [] pour parti.r [;]

[sœ̀ là sœ̀ kí ᵖá.ʳᵗ [] púr pár ᵗí.ʳ]

It will be noted that the use of enjambement does not lead to the sacrifice of the pause on the line-ending. To omit or skimp the pause would merely lead to a muddling of metre, whereas what is wanted is a strong awareness that meaning is running counter to metre. This may in fact lead us to lengthen the pause which separates the *rejet* from the previous line. This could well be the case in **93**. Having completed the line which, as we said, expresses a platitude, we would by a marked pause increase the sense of expectancy with which we await the *rejet* which is to change its meaning. This pause increases stress, as it would do in normal speech: for *je te – hais*, with a slight postponement of the verb, is a good deal more forceful than *je te hais*.

The alexandrine in which the *rejet* occurs is necessarily irregular, since stress falls on its first segment and the caesura is eroded. We would say of such a line that it has a *premature stress*. As is the case with enjambement on the caesura, if the *rejet* is to be rhythmically forceful it must be short. If the phrase carried over extends the whole length of the hemistich, there is no enjambement, since its final stress falls on the caesura and stress is not displaced. But with enjambement on the line-ending it is possible to have a *rejet* of one syllable only, since the pause between the lines keeps the rhythm firm. Hugo demonstrates this:

94   Là, l'om.brĕ fait l'amou.r; l'Idy˙llĕ nature˙lle
         Rit; / le bouvreu.il avec le verdier s'y quere˙lle [,]
         ··· · · ·· · · · · ·· · ···

Here the second line has the rhythm 1/3:5:3, and the main stress falls strongly on the first syllable. But, as **91** illustrates, a four-syllable *rejet* can be effective provided that the sense reinforces it.

The *rejet* is most effective when, as in the examples we have quoted, it is isolated by punctuation from the rest of the line. But the same principles apply even if it is not so isolated, if [A] is dislocated so as to form two syntactical phrases. An example of this is Vigny's

95   Mais il renon.ce et dit: 'Que votrĕ volonté
        Soit faite et non la mienne et pour l'éternité [!]

Here *Soit faite et non la mienne* is a dislocated hemistich and the rhythm of the line is 2/4:6. We may say much the same of *A grands flots le parfum* in

96   Un po.rt retentissant où mon â.mĕ peut boi.re
        A grands flots le parfum, le son et la couleu.r [;]
        .   .   ..

and so stress falls on *flots*, since the *rejet* is closely attached in terms of meaning to the verb *boire* in the previous line. The rhythm is 3/3:2:4.

A run-on line does not necessarily, or even generally, produce enjambement, but it is certainly true that when enjambement occurs the line which leads up to the *rejet* will more often than not end without punctuation. The essential feature of the *rejet* is that we must feel it to be closely attached to the previous line, and punctuation would discourage this. However, there are occasions when the previous line is merely an interpolation, and the *rejet* in fact continues the sense of a still earlier line, or of an earlier part of the line, and in such a case there will be punctuation. In the following example, the main sense-sequence is the sentence *Ses agneaux* [...] *bondissent*, but a short clause has been interposed, and as a result we have enjambement even though the first line is end-stopped:

97   Ses agneaux,/dans le pré plein de fleu.rs qui l'encen.se,
        Bondi/ssĕnt, et chacun, au sole.il s'empourprant [,]
        .   ...

In this case as in all others we identify enjambement by the dislocated hemistich: *Bondissĕnt : et chacun.* Another rather unusual example of enjambement is heard in the following lines (taken, like the quotation above, from Hugo's *Pasteurs et troupeaux*):

98   Et, là-bas, devant moi, le vieux gardien pensif
        De l'écu˙/mĕ, du flot, de l'a˙lguĕ, du récif,
        Et des va˙/guĕs, sans trêve et sans fin remué˙es [,]
        .   ...

The enjambement between the first two lines is clear enough: the phrase *le vieux gardien pensif de l'écume* overruns the line-ending. But there is also enjambement between [2] and [3], despite the comma at the end of [2]. This is because *Et des vaguěs* completes the list which runs through the previous line. In terms of meaning, [3] is divided into three phrases: *Et des vagues : sans trêve et sans fin : remuées*, the second of these phrases being an interpolation between the noun and the adjective. [A] is therefore dislocated and the caesura eroded. So, although cases of enjambement with end-stopped lines are not common, the reader should bear in mind the fact they do occur. And it is even more important to remember that an open and run-on line does not necessarily imply enjambement.

There is no point in merely recognizing enjambement: to read intelligently one must understand what is its function in any particular case. In this last example it has a dual purpose. The stressed *rejet* in the first segment of [3] brings to a strong climax the list of natural features in the previous line which are being watched over by the *vieux gardien pensif*. And, by disturbing the rhythm of the remainder of the line, Hugo reinforces the idea of the restless movement of the sea, the vast expanse of which is suggested by the long phrase *sans trêve et sans fin* which spreads across the caesura, breaking the natural bounds of the line.

There is another type of enjambement which is in some respects the mirror-image of that which we have discussed. It uses not a *rejet* but a *contre-rejet*, a short phrase at the end of a line which attaches itself syntactically to the line following. When Vigny's she-wolf makes off with her cubs, leaving her spouse to his fate at the hands of the hunters, the poet justifies her with the words:

99   Mais son devoi.r était de les sauver, afin
            De pouvoi.r leur appren.dre à bien souffri.r la faim [,]

Here *afin* is a *contre-rejet*, detached by punctuation from [1] and leading on naturally to [2]. Unlike the *rejet*, the *contre-rejet* is only lightly stressed: indeed, it tends to take stress off the line-ending. The rhythm of **99** is 4:6/2, with the major stress falling on *sauver*. Thus there is enjambement on the caesura as well as on the line-ending. This is indeed very commonly the case. When a phrase overruns the caesura, it often leaves only a short segment on the line-ending which the poet runs on to the next line. The *contre-rejet*, of course, must not be physically joined to the line following: the pause must be maintained in all cases of enjambement. The tone of voice is sufficient to show the link, for a *contre-rejet* is always unstable, raising the voice to middle or high pitch, and this makes it clear that the phrase is unfinished. Since it is itself unstressed, it tends to throw stress on the word or phrase at the beginning of the line which follows it. This is apparent in Verlaine's

100   Et pour sa voix, lointaine, et calme, et grave, elle a
         L'inflexi:on des voix chè.rĕs qui se sont tu˙es [.]

in which both *grave* and *l'inflexion* are stressed, but not *a* on the line-ending. Similarly, when Leconte de Lisle writes

101   Un vent léger s'éve.ille à l'horizon, et ri˙de
         Les flots de la poussiè.re, ainsi qu'un lac limpide [.]

he throws stress on to the word *flots* and so reinforces his image of the dust as a shining lake. However, the effect of the *contre-rejet* is essentially on rhythm rather than stress. It does not bring a line or sentence to a climax as does the *rejet*: rather, it tends to soften the contours of the line and to introduce unexpected rhythms, particularly when associated with enjambement on the caesura. Thus Gautier uses it to create a feeling of vagueness in his evocation of Notre Dame by moonlight:

102   ... L'Archĕvêché
         Se dessinait au pied de l'église, dont l'om.bre
         S'allongeait ...

Baudelaire uses it to great effect to suggest despair and the total derangement of his life:

103   – Et de longs corbilla.rds, | sans tambou.rs ni musi˙que,
         Défi˙lĕnt len˙tĕment dans mon â./me; l'Espoir,
         Vaincu, pleu./re, et l'Angoisse atro˙cĕ, despoti˙que,
         Sur mon crâ.ne incliné | plan.tĕ son drapeau noi.r [.]

The use of *l'Espoir* in [2] above may serve to remind us that the *contre-rejet* is not invariably to be recognized by absence of punctuation on the line-ending, although this is normal: its essential feature is its dislocation from its own line and its close link with a line following. In this present case, the use of punctuation is due to the interpolation of the word *vaincu* into the phrase *L'Espoir pleure*; and it is the word *pleure* which benefits from the stress thrown by the *contre-rejet*, and not *vaincu*.

Mallarmé uses more or less continuous enjambement to quite different effect when he evokes the dream-like atmosphere of his *Après-midi d'un faune*:

104   Ces nym.phĕs, je les veux perpétuer./
                                             Si clai.r,
         Leur incarnat léger, | qu'il volti.gĕ dans l'ai.r
         Assoupi / de somme.ils touffus. /
                                             Aimé-je un rê.ve?
         Mon doute, amas de nuit anci:e˙/nnĕ, s'achè.ve
         En maint rameau subtil, | qui, demeurés les vrais
         Bois mê˙/mĕs, prouve, hélas! que bien seul je m'offrais
         Pour triom./phĕ, la faute idéa˙lĕ des ro.ses [.]

Lines such as these take enjambement as far as it can be taken.
They are highly exceptional. Whatever liberties poets may take in
particular circumstances, the basic feature of the alexandrine is its
binary form fixed by the caesura. Mallarmé's experiments seem
ultimately to lead in the direction of free verse: but what he himself
was doing was an acrobatic balance on the caesura. This would have
been quite unthinkable to the classical theorists of the seventeenth
and eighteenth centuries, who did their best to outlaw enjambement
of any kind. Their successors rebelled against this prohibition: Hugo
in particular boasted of his success in 'dislocating' the alexandrine,
but in practice his revolution stopped far short of complete liberation
from traditional form. For the restrictions of the alexandrine are the
basis of its strength. The fact that Mallarmé did not want the strong
cadences of rhetoric led him to lighten its form but not to destroy it:
and the lines quoted above represent calculated variations which are
effective precisely because we feel them to be exceptional. No one
could respond to their rhythms if he was unaware of the basic rhythm
of the alexandrine. The evolution of enjambement greatly increased
the fluidity of the line, but was no less dependent on the feeling for
the hemistich than was the classical alexandrine. When we read

         Mon doute, amas de nuit [...]

we expect a stress on the sixth syllable, but are not given it. [A] is in
fact highly unstable, and requires the addition of stressed *ancienne*
to resolve the tension. This variation of rhythm depends on
an underlying awareness of expected rhythm. In the same way
Baudelaire's

         Défi˙lĕnt len˙tĕment dans mon â./me [...]

has a kind of emotional length which cannot be measured simply in
syllables. We are rhythmically disposed to expect the phrase to end
with the caesura, on *lentĕment*, and it does not. We are conscious of
dans mon âme as an extension. In the line which follows, the stress

thrown on *pleure* by the *contre-rejet*, and that on *atroce* by enjambe-ment on the caesura, both result from our awareness that the poet is deviating from his regular beat. The liberation of the alexandrine thus led not to a slackening of its metrical form but to a more subtle use of the possibilities that this form offered. The alexandrine is a structure of words in equilibrium around its caesura. To vary the balance by moving its main stress is simply to exploit its possibilities, but to abandon the concept of a fulcrum would be to condemn it to immobility.

It is as a variant of the binary form that we must consider the ternary alexandrine, in which the medial caesura is replaced by two caesuras occurring at four-syllable intervals and so dividing the line not into hemistichs but into three segments. This pattern, abundantly used by Hugo, is sometimes described as the *Romantic* alexandrine to distinguish it from the other, which has been given the name *classical*. These terms are best avoided. They had some justification in the nineteenth century, since the development of the modified form was part of the Romantic revolt against classical tradition. However, the vast majority of alexandrines written by Romantic poets were binary, and there is no such thing as a poem written entirely in ternary alexandrines; therefore, the binary form belongs to classical and Romantic poets alike. The term *classical alexandrine* should be reserved for the binary metre as used by the seventeenth and eighteenth centuries, subject to the conventions of classical theory. The term *Romantic alexandrine* is superfluous. The distinc-tion to be made is not between two periods of literary history but between two metrical arrangements of the alexandrine, one of them standard—the binary—and the other—the ternary—an interesting variation.

The alexandrine does not necessarily become ternary by reason of being divided into three parts, or having two strong interior stresses. It can only be so when neither of these stresses falls on the sixth syllable. Hugo's line

105   Je suis veuf, je suis seul, et sur moi le soir tom.be [,]

is binary, and has a rhythm of 3:3 | 3:3, or possibly 3:3 | 5:1. *Seul* on the caesura is stressed. The line is therefore perfectly regular. When there is enjambement on the caesura, an alexandrine may develop ternary characteristics. Thus:

106   Pauvre ê/tre! ellĕ se sent très gran./dĕ vaguĕment [;]

We may read this line so that the stress on the caesura is purely vestigial, and the two effective stresses of more or less equal value. But whether we regard the rhythm as 2:4:2/4 or as 2:6/4, this is essentially a case of enjambement on the caesura. Enjambement quite often produces a ternary form, as in

107   Tout en parlant ainsi, le saty.rĕ devint
              Démesuré; | plus grand d'abo.rd | que Polyphè˙me [,]

which represents the ideal form of the ternary alexandrine, with the rhythm 4|4|4. It is this which is the true ternary alexandrine, since it can be felt to have a firm metrical form comparable to that of the binary alexandrine, whereas the irregular lines are merely examples of the many possible variations of the binary form. When we read lines such as

108   Je marcherai | les yeux fixés | sur mes pensé˙es [,]

109   Et je voguais, | lorsqu'à travers | mes liens frê.les [,]

110   Elle est l'Infan.|te, elle a cinq ans, | ellĕ dédai˙gne [,]

we have no doubt that we are listening to a clearly identifiable rhythm which does not depend on a central caesura, even by implication. But the ternary alexandrine does not hold together so firmly as does the binary, and so the two forms, when used, are always interwoven, generally with the binary form predominating. This is why the ternary form should perhaps be regarded as a variant of the binary rather than as a metre in its own right. Its effect is to change rhythm, but it is difficult to generalize on what the effect of this change is. It is certainly true that it gives a sense of movement—or can do, when the meaning of the words suggests this—since it substitutes two main stresses for the expected one, and it may well produce a variation in the speed of reading. Grammont has suggested that it produces an effect of speeding up. But he himself quotes, under the heading *Expression d'un mouvement rapide*, an example in which the words *à pas lents* effectively rule out such a possibility, and appears unaware of the inconsistency.

111   Leur bou˙chĕ, d'un seul cri, dit: Vivĕ l'empereu.r!
            Puis, à pas lents, | musique en tê˙|tĕ, sans fureu.r [,]

That this implies movement is beyond doubt: but it is slow movement.

    The reader may care to judge for himself the effect in the following stanza:

112   Qui trouble ainsi les flots | près du sérai.l des fe˙mmes?
           Ni le noi.r cormoran, | sur la va˙guĕ bercé,
           Ni les pie.rrĕs du mur, | ni le bruit caden.cé
           D'un lou.rd vaisseau rampant sur l'on˙de avec des ra˙mes [,]
                .   .   .   . .. | .   .   . .. | . . . ...

I would suggest that the change in rhythm causes us to think in terms
of movement, and that, in this particular context, it is likely to
suggest the beat of oars. Since the boat is *lourd*, this beat will be
slow, as is further implied by the use of the word *rampant*. On the
other hand, speed is certainly suggested in

113   On se rencon.tre, ô choc hideux! les deux armé˙es
            .   .   . .. | .   .   . .. | .   .   .   ...
           Se heu.rtĕnt, de la même épouvan.te enflammé˙es [,]
            . ... ‖   .   .   .   . | .   .   ...

Here the clauses 'les deux armées [] se heurtent' is a straightforward
example of enjambement on the line-ending, resulting in an eroded
caesura; an effect which not uncommonly occurs after a *rejet*.
     Although the ternary alexandrine offers an effective variant on
the binary form, it lacks the tonal range produced by the contrasted
major and subsidiary stresses in the latter line. Nor can the placing
of the caesuras be significantly varied without producing an amor-
phous and arhythmic effect. But it does enlarge the potential of the
alexandrine form, and offers a further demonstration that this is
very far from being the monotonous and limited form which is
sometimes thought to be by those unfamiliar with it.
     We may conclude our remarks on the alexandrine with some
considerations directly relevant to the needs of the non-French
speaking student. Why does this line, full of variety as it is, often
strike him as prosaic and uninteresting? The first and most obvious
reason is that to the eye a sequence of alexandrines, more than any
other metre, resembles a passage of run-on prose, and will be read
as such. This is further encouraged by the fact that its rhythms are
not normally obtrusive, and in general result from word-groupings
not dissimilar to those of prose. The factors which give it metrical
variety—the caesura, sub-stresses, and melodic line—are in no way
indicated on the printed page, and unless he has been trained in the
skill of verse-reading, the student is likely to be but dimly aware of
them. Even if he is aware of them, their application (at least until
through experience it becomes spontaneous) is likely to be half-
hearted unless accompanied by a genuine desire to make the lines
yield of their best. Further, these features are not only absent from

the printed page, but are impossible to reproduce fully except with the use of the vocal organs; and verse today is almost always read mentally. When we so read, we do reproduce in the mind the effects of the vocal organs, but only to a restricted degree. Whereas sense and syntax can be fully assimilated, stress and pitch (not to mention phonetic harmonies) scarcely impose themselves on our awareness.

These are real difficulties of which the teacher must take account. His answer to them is to ensure that, whenever possible, the verse is read aloud. He will insist that the reading be a good one, and that the student understands the difference between good and bad reading: that he is aware of what is implied by the poet's choice and arrangement of words in any line. He will make it clear that a poem is not written to be read once only, and indeed cannot be so read with any profit. He will also at every opportunity encourage the student to enjoy the sound of words and cadences, and stress (however difficult this may be when poetry is incorporated into an educational curriculum) that the prime function of poetry is to give enjoyment. While a poem is by no means all emotion, it cannot be created without a certain intensity of emotion on the part of the poet: and it can speak only to a mind which is susceptible to this feeling and capable of transforming it into personal experience. To do this, the student must understand not only the poet's words, but also the implications of their sound and metre.

The student to whom the material discussed in this chapter represents unfamiliar ground would be wise, I think, to apply it first to poems which already have some appeal for him. Routine exercises of scansion applied to some lines can open up new possibilities in reading them. Lines, stanzas, and some whole poems should be learnt by heart with their most effective melodic patterns, which need to be thought about and should in some cases be committed to paper. The experience so gained will pass inevitably to the reading of other poems. No one is expected to like all poetry, but most of the poetry to which the student is introduced will have some merit: and if a poem seems dull, this may well be because it is not being read properly. The object of education, in this field, at least, should in the long run be the development of personal taste, but for taste to have any value it must be properly informed. The student will therefore make it his business to know some poems very well indeed, which means having at his disposal their full potential. When he has done this, he will never again read any alexandrine as if it was merely a line of words on a page.

Chapter Four
PHONETIC PATTERNING

RHYTHM, as we have so far considered it, results from the recurrent beat which is the product of metre and of syntax, sometimes working together but sometimes diverging so as to introduce subtle modifications. The sense of a line can modify its stresses and consequently its melody. But we have not so far given attention to the texture of the line itself, to the sounds of which it is composed. Clearly these too form part of its rhythm, even though they are not governed by the laws of prosody; nor are they necessarily related to its meaning. The pleasure which we derive from reading a line of verse comes partly from the sound of the words themselves, and partly from the way in which these sounds are arranged to give form and coherence to the line. The reader of French verse will probably be most readily aware of such patterning when it is related to the cadences of rhetoric, which involves the repetition of words and the balancing of one phrase against another. In our own time, the art of rhetoric is generally held in disrepute, being at best identified with verbosity and pretentiousness, and at worst with the deliberate attempt to mislead the hearer. But in fact rhetoric is simply the art of using cadenced language to persuade the hearer to share the speaker's emotions or convictions, and is not in itself either morally or aesthetically suspect, though it is certainly open to abuse. It is closely akin to verse, and in France, from the seventeenth to the nineteenth century at least, it was considered one of the natural resources of poetry. It is no longer in fashion, partly because the qualities we value in poetry are no longer those of the public speaker, but also because it is essentially a spoken art, whereas we tend more and more to read verse silently to ourselves. Any consideration of the potential and dangers of rhetoric would take us far beyond the scope of this book. We must, however, be conscious of it as a source of rhythm.

Hugo opens his poem *A Villequier* with the word 'Maintenant', which he repeats six times introducing new clauses until at the end of stanza V he comes to his main sentence: 'Je reprends ma raison devant l'immensité'. If read merely with the eye, the sequence of clauses which leads up to this line gives an impression of superfluity and of verbosity, but if read aloud the rhythmic beat which it produces powerfully affects the imagination. Similarly, in a typical line from the same poem, Hugo balances one phrase and one hemistich against another:

114   L'â.mĕ de deuils en deuils, l'ho˙mmĕ de rive en ri.ve,
       Roule à l'éternité [.]

Again, the effect of the repetition is clearly to set up a rhythm. Indeed, it represents the simplest form of rhythm: a single repetition, but with sufficient variation to make it interesting. We have phrase balanced against phrase, and image against image.

In this case the cadenced language reflects the binary nature of the alexandrine. But a threefold rhythm is equally possible, as Lamartine demonstrates:

115   Elle a passé sans bruit, sans nom, et sans retou.r [:]

116   J'ai trop vu, trop senti, trop aimé dans ma vi˙e [;]

These two lines do not have the same metrical rhythm. The first is divided 4:2|2:4 and the second 3:3|3:3. But the repetition of *sans* and of *trop* gives to each a characteristic rhetorical cadence which modifies the rhythm of metre.

In the examples we have quoted rhythm is established by the repetition of words and phrases and the contrast of images. But if we consider the following:

117   Tes jou.rs, som.brĕs et cou.rts commĕ les jou.rs
       d'auto.mne [,]

we notice an additional feature. Not only is *jours* repeated, but advantage is also taken of the rime which it makes with *courts* on the caesura. Without this, the line would lose its imposing rhythm. But this is not all. When we hear *tes jours, et courts, les jours* we respond also to the repeated [é] which introduces the rimes, as we do indeed to the [k] of *courts|comme* around the caesura, and the sequence in [o] which we hear in *sombres, comme* and *automne* [ó tòn]. These effects blend together to give the line a distinct tonality which is pleasing to the ear. In the following line there is no repetition of words:

118   Et, seu˙lĕ, tu descends le sentier des tombeaux [.]

but we nevertheless hear a phonetic rhythm. There is the threefold repetition of [s] which is heard in *seule, descends, sentier*, reinforced in the last two cases by the vowel [à]. And there is another triple effect, that of [t] in *tu, sentier, tombeau*, as well as the repeated [o] of [tò bó] which rounds off the line so strongly. We feel that the sounds of which the line is composed are woven into a satisfying pattern which enriches the rhythm of the line.

An effect of this kind is not simply rhetorical, though it may be associated with rhetoric. It is phonetic; that is to say, it depends on the repetition and balance of phonemes. We shall have more to say about phonemes as we proceed, but for the moment we may define them as the individual sounds out of which language is made. (A more exact definition will be found in the Index.) What we are concerned with is not the sounds themselves, but the rhythmic effect which may be produced by their repetition. Let us consider the following stanza by Lamartine:

119   Commĕ lui, de nos pieds secouons la poussiè.re;
         L'ho˙mmĕ par ce chemin ne repa˙ssĕ jamais:
         Commĕ lui, respirons au bout de la carriè.re
         Ce calme avant-coureu.r de l'éterne˙llĕ paix [.]

Here we have, with varying degrees of identity, a correspondence of sound at the beginning of each of the four lines: *comme* in [1], *l'homme* in [2], *comme* again in [3] and *calme* in [4]. In [1], the [p] of *pieds* is answered by that of *poussière*. The consonantal structure of this last word is [p s r], and we hear it again, in a slightly different order, in the [r p s] of *repasse* in [2], and as [r sp r] in *respirons* in [3]. These words are linked together by their sound. At the end of [3] the word *carrière* [k r r] anticipates *coureur* [k r r] in [4], and its initial [k] is also echoed in *calme*. Now let us go back to [2]. If we pronounce first *par ce chem-* and then *repassĕ jam-* we will be conscious of a remarkable similarity of sound. The consonants of the first we represent as [p r s dh m] and of the second as [r p s j m]. They are identical, except that in the first case we have [dh] and in the second [j]. The reader familiar with phonetic terminology will recognize that [dh] is the voiceless form of [j]: they are the same phoneme, but the first is produced without the use of the vocal cords. (We shall consider relationships of this kind more fully in Chapter Seven.) However, similarity is not limited to the consonants. In the first phrase we have the vowels [á ĕ ĕ] and in the second [ĕ á á]. So we may say that the stanza as a whole is characterized by an abundance of phonetic correspondences of considerable subtlety. Clearly this is in some way associated with the fact that Lamartine's language is usually heard as 'musical' by those whose ear is attuned to the sound of French verse.

It will be apparent that phonetic patterning may not only re-inforce or modify rhythm: it may also enrich the texture of the line as a whole. It will do so only provided we are trained to hear it. If we skim through the lines, absorbing only their meaning, it will be wasted on us. In that case we shall not really be reading the verse at all, since verse is made up not only of meanings and images but also of sounds skilfully distributed. The reader familiar with English verse will recognize that phonetic patterning is a feature by no means confined to French. Any poet writing in any language will in some way take advantage of resemblance of sound in composing his lines. Before we go on to examine this feature as it affects French verse, it may be helpful to the student who is comparatively un-familiar with that field if we consider briefly how it is used in English. A well-known example occurs in the opening lines of Coleridge's *Kubla Khan*, in which the words which I have italicized are linked by a common initial consonant:

> In Xanadu did *Kubla Khan*
> A stately pleasure -*dome decree*
> Where Alph the sacred *river ran*
> Through caverns *measureless* to *man*
> Down to a *sunless sea*.

The effect is very striking both because the words involved are placed on the line-ending, and also because initial consonants are involved. But the matter may be more complex than this. When, later in the same poem, we come across 'a damsel with a dulcimer' we immediately recognize the same repetition of initials: but here the full corre-spondence is between the [d m z l] of *damsel* and the [d l s m] of *dulcimer*, the [s] in the second group being the voiceless form of the [z] in the first. Indeed, we may well suppose that the image of a maiden playing this particular instrument presented itself to Cole-ridge's mind largely as a result of the phonetic association of the two words. Phonetic association can be a great deal more complex than this. Here are some fairly typical lines from Goldsmith's *The Deserted Village*, in which the poet describes how the schoolmaster

> With words of learned length and thundering sound
> Amazed the gazing rustics ranged around [.]

We tend to dismiss such effects as 'alliteration' or 'assonance' without realizing their complexity. Our phonetic symbols are not adapted to represent the sounds of English: but the reader will note the correspondence in [w] with which the couplet opens—*With words*; the repeated vowel followed by [d] in *words* and *learned*; the

[1] of *learned length*; the [th] of *length* and *thundering*; and the four-times repeated [nd] which we hear in *learned, and, thundering, sound*. In the second line, *Amazed* and *gazing* repeat two phonemes, and share the same vowel as *ranged*; and there is a triple sequence of [r] in *rustics ranged around*. These effects are in addition to the rime between *round* and *sound* which is required by metre. We find even more complex effects in Tennyson's *Choric Song of the Lotos-Eaters*:

> ... and the clouds are lightly curled
> Round their golden houses, girdled with the gleaming
> world [.]

This description of the gods who 'lie beside their nectar' clearly springs from a mind which is no less aware of sound than of meaning. *Clouds* and *curled* share the same consonantal structure [k l d], which in the second line changes to [g l d] in *golden, girdled*, and at the beginning and end of *gleaming world*. The vowel of *clouds* recurs in *round* and *houses*, and that of *curled* in both *girdled* and *world*. These examples in English may help to clear up a difficulty which students sometimes find in approaching the subject of phonetic patterns. It may be felt that because a sound is dispersed throughout a line it cannot really be heard as a pattern. But this is not so. In rime, sounds must be identical in their arrangement, but not so in a free pattern. We do not hear *girdled* as a bad rime for *world*, but as a free correspondence of sound. And the same is true of the other relationships. Both the examples we have quoted here are self-conscious, in that the poet clearly intends that we shall hear an association of sounds, but they are not artificial. They are as natural to his way of thinking as are rhythm, metre, and rime: but all these features, while deriving from an instinctive awareness of the potential of language, must be disciplined and enhanced by imagination and intellect if they are to play their part in poetry. The effects obtained in French tend often to be less obtrusive than in these English examples, but are no less important.

In order to appreciate fully the phonetic content of a line, it may be useful to make a *phonetic abstract*. This is how we would represent the line by Lamartine which we have already analysed:

120	L'ho˙mmĕ par ce chemin	ne repa˙ssĕ jamais [.]
	m m	m
	á	á á
	p r s ʧ	r p s j

The object of such an abstract is to represent whatever phonetic features may be felt to contribute to the rhythm and texture of the line. Since it is useful to have a term to describe these effects, I call each of the patterns set out here a *phonetic cluster*, a term which will be defined more precisely in due course. The first cluster noted involves a triple repetition of [m], and the second a similar repetition of [á]. This effect, which I call a *triplet*, is one of the commonest rhythmic patterns into which phonemes fall within a line. These particular triplets I describe as *simple* because only one phoneme is repeated in each. The last pattern is a *doublet* because it involves one repetition (i.e. two occurrences) but in this case it is *compound*, since a number of phonemes are involved in the group which is repeated. In a compound doublet or triplet, it is not necessary that the phonemes recur in the same order, provided we hear them together. In the examples we quoted from Coleridge's *Kubla Khan*, the patterns on the line-endings are simple doublets, while that which links 'damsel' to 'dulcimer' is a compound doublet. An effect such as that of the [r] of 'rustics ranged around' is of course a simple triplet, and it has a very pronounced rhythmic effect. An arrangement such as this I describe as a *symmetrical triplet* because the elements of which it is composed are spaced at more or less equal distance from each other. We have an example of a simple triplet so arranged in

121 Tu te tairas, ô voix sini˙strĕ des vivants [!]
  t   t   t

and a compound symmetrical triplet in

122 Magnifi˙quĕ, total et solitai.rĕ, tel [ ]
    t l   l t   t l

But the triplet is more often arranged *asymmetrically*, in which case it consists of a doublet with either an *echo* (giving the rhythm [..|.]) or a *pre-echo* (which gives [.|..]). The elements of a doublet are placed close together, while the echo or the pre-echo is at a greater distance: usually in the other hemistich, if the line is an alexandrine. An example of a simple triplet so arranged is

123 La fleur se fâne et l'oiseau fuit [.]
    f   f   f

and of a compound triplet:

124 Et de ses pieds palmés frottant le pavé sec [ ]
     p é   pa é   pa é

The rhythm of **123** would be represented as [f f: -f], and of **124** as [p é pa é| pa é], with the upright stress-bar representing the caesura.

Most effective phonetic clusters are either doublets or triplets or combinations of them. But there may be cases where a cluster is heard simply by reason of the frequency of repetition of its elements. Regardless of its rhythmic arrangement, it may then be described as *prevailing cluster*. Here are examples:

125   Derriè.rĕ la mura.ille immen./sĕ du brouilla.rd [;]
      r   r   r   r   r

126   Ils mê˙lĕnt un moment | leur on.de et leur murmu.re [,]
        m   m m | m   m
      l   l |l   r   l   r   r   r

This is the effect which is commonly known as *alliteration* (or, if vowels are used, as *assonance*).

The recognition of phonetic effects is a matter for the reader's discernment, but his response to them will be facilitated if he recognizes the form which they are likely to take. In Baudelaire's line

127   Ta main se glisse en vain sur mon sein qui se pâ˙me [;]

the thrice-repeated nasal vowel of *main, vain,* and *sein* is heard as a symmetrical triplet, and this effect is associated with a prevailing cluster in [s]. A sound-picture of the line may look something like this:

        Ta main se glisse en vain | sur mon sein qui se pâ˙me [;]
           ë   ë | ë
              s   is |s   s   is
         m | m   m

There is no great difficulty in recognizing that [ë] is the dominant effect, since it is associated with the metrical stresses of the alexandrine. The importance of [s] derives from the frequency of its occurrence. The [m] triplet is much less obtrusive, but nevertheless helps to give form to the line. Likewise, when we read Leconte de Lisle's

128   Baigné d'unĕ lueu.r qui sai˙gnĕ sur la nei˙ge [,]

the asymmetric triplet [è-|è è] is clearly heard, both as a result of stress and also because it is combined with a repeated [n]. But we also note the effect on the tonality of the line resulting from the occurrence of [ü], [l], and [r] in *une lueur* and *sur la*. This constitutes a compound doublet.

```
Baigné d'unĕ lueu.r | qui sai˙gnĕ sur la nei˙ge [,]
    ènў           |        è˙nў         nè.
   ü   lü   r |               ür l
             |       s        s
```

But some strong effects are not so immediately obvious. We are aware on first reading that there is some kind of sound association in Hugo's

129   La fenêtre enfin libre est ouvert à la bri˙se [,]

and we realize that this is in part dependent on the echo of *fenêtre* [ètr] heard in *ouverte* [èrt]. But what is involved is actually a triplet, since [t] is sounded in *libre est*, and this gives us [rèt]. And there is also a compound doublet heard in *libre* [líbr] and *la brise* [l brí]. We set this out as follows:

```
La fenêtre enfin li | bre est ouverte à la bri.se [,]
    f         f     |
      ètr           |   rèt        èrt
                 lí | br             l  brí
```

It is very difficult to give clear predominance to any effect in this line. The [f] doublet is strongly heard at the beginning of the line; the second cluster is associated with the important words *fenêtre* and *ouverte*, and the third with the no less important, and stressed, *libre* and *brise*. The line is an interesting example of the way in which phonetic effects blend.

The examples that we have so far considered are for the most part *linear*: i.e. they are internal effects within the line. However, phonetic clusters may also be *run on*, in which case they pass from one line to the next, or *interlinear*, i.e. a feature of a sequence of lines. In the following example, Baudelaire rimes on successive caesuras:

130   Mon chat sur le carreau | cherchant unĕ litiè.re,
            Agi˙tĕ sans repos | son co.rps maigre et galeux [;]

It is also possible to rime on a subsidiary stress. When we read

131   Les plus ra.rĕs fleu.rs
            Mêlant leurs odeu.rs
            Aux va˙guĕs senteu.rs de l'a.mbre [.]

it is impossible not to hear *senteurs* as part of the rime-sequence. This is not necessarily true of *leurs* in [2] since this word lacks all stress. But it may still make some contribution to the sound, not only through its vowel but through its consonants:

Les plus ra.rĕs fleu.rs
l   l r r l   r
Mêlant leurs odeu.rs [ ]
　 l　 l r　　 r

In the following lines by Lamartine, I have indicated two run-on clusters (one in [èў], the other in [à] in which all save the first occurrence are based on the caesuras:

132   La nuit tom.be, ô mon â | me! un peu de *ve.ille* enco.re!
Ce coucher d'un *sole.il* | est d'un au᾿trĕ l'auro.re.
Vois comme avec tes *sens* | s'écrou᾿lĕ ta prison!
Vois comme aux premier *vents* | de la précoce auto᾿mne,
Sur les bo.rds de l'*étang* | où le ruisseau frisso᾿nne [,]

But run-on clusters, like others, may be based on consonants. This we hear in Hugo's

133   Je dis que le tombeau qui sur les mo.rts se fe᾿rme
　　　　　　　　　　　　　　　　　m r　　 f rm
Ou.vrĕ le firmament [,]
f rm m

in which *morts*, *ferme*, and *firmament* are phonetically linked. A similar effect is heard in

134   Mes yeux verraient partout le vide et les dése.rts;
　　　　　　　　　　　　　　　　　　　　déz r
Je ne dési.rĕ rien de tout ce qu'il éclai.re [ ]
déz r

and is enriched by the fact that *désire* and *éclaire* together suggest the sound of *déserts*. Run-on clusters such as these, in which a group of phonemes in one line are echoed in the next, may call for a certain degree of extra stress in reading if they are to be effectively heard. This is apparent if we compare the restrained effect of Lamartine's

135   Que me font ces vallons, ces palais, ces chaumiè.res,
　　　　　　　　　　　　　　　　　　 ch m r
Vains objets dont pour moi le charme est envolé [?]
ch rm

with Gautier's strong linear doublet:

136   Les chimè.rĕs du cauchĕma.r [ ]
        ch m r   ch m r

In this latter case we may say that the effect is obviously self-conscious: indeed, it may be thought to be the *raison d'être* of the line. In the case of Lamartine, we may be less sure. But in his lines we may note other effects. In [1] we have *font* followed by *vallons* [ò ò], and *vallons* followed by *palais* [á á]. In [2] we have *dont*, and then *moi* [wá] and *charme* [á]. This similarity may be pure chance: but a more likely explanation is that there is present in the poet's mind a certain phonetic rhythm, and just as one alexandrine suggests another, so one sequence of sound predisposes the poet to think of another sequence in which the same sounds are present. This, I would suggest, is in general the explanation of the existence of the phonetic cluster. Certainly the poet may often use it quite consciously: but it derives from an unconscious tendency which is as natural to him as the faculty to think in rhythm. We know very little of the way in which we choose our words when we speak, but we normally assume that they are selected by a process of rational association. In the case of the poet, no such clear priority is given to reason. Words and phrases suggest themselves to him not merely by reason of their meaning, but equally because of their rhythm and phonetic composition. If this were not so, riming verse, which requires him to give a particular sound to the final word of each line, would be an absurdity, totally alien to the proper function of language. But in fact it is nothing of the kind. The poet is not only a man of vision, but a man whose vision necessarily expresses itself in language: and language to him is a tangible, physical thing, and not, as it so often is to us, a series of conventional sounds and symbols. The phonetic cluster is not merely an ornament. It is a rhythmic distribution of phonemes; and it is this arrangement which our phonetic abstract seeks to demonstrate.

Before we proceed, one point must be made very clear to the reader to whom this field of study may be a new one. The phonetic cluster is not a visual effect. It can only be heard. When we read

137   Amante ou sœu.r, soyez la douceu.r éphémè.re [ ]

the eye may draw our attention to the [s] which links *sœur* with *soyez*. But this is merely part of a rich compound doublet—the riming of *-te ou sœur* [tú sœ̀.r] with [dú sœ̀.r] which cannot be seen, but must be heard. Repetition of sound does not necessarily involve the repetition of printed letters. And the converse is perhaps even more important. For in French the letters of the alphabet are not used consistently in such a way that each represents one sound and one sound only; and therefore the recurrence of a letter in a printed line is no indication of the presence of a phonetic cluster. This is well illustrated in Hugo's lines

138   Et les peu ˈplĕs [...]
Tremblaient, sentant sur eux ces deux yeux fixĕs lui.re [.]

In this last line the letter *x* occurs four times, and yet does not form a cluster. In two cases—*eux* and *yeux*—it is silent; in another—*deux* —it has the sound of *z*; while in *fixĕs* it is pronounced as [ks]. There is in fact a phonetic cluster in [s], but the occurrence of this letter at the end of *ces* and *fixĕs* plays no part in it, since in these words it is silent. Only in *sentant* and *sur* is [s] written as *s*: in *ces* it appears as *c*, and in *fixĕs* it occurs as part of the sound represented by *x*. Letters such as *c* or *x* should never be used in phonetic transcript, but only those which represent one single and unambiguous sound. For this reason, it is advisable to use phonetic symbols.

Our object so far has been to establish the existence of the phonetic cluster as a recognizable phenomenon. We must now consider its significance. And before we do so, it may be well to define the phenomenon we have observed. We may say that a phonetic cluster is a recognizable correspondence of sounds, usually within a line or a stanza, which cannot be explained by the requirements of metre. The qualification is added so as to exclude metrical rhythm and rime, not because they are essentially different but because they are governed by rules, whereas the phonetic cluster is free: it does not have to be there to make the line good, nor does it necessarily have any single, specific function. It is simply a feature of the line. In some respects we may compare it with meaning. An alexandrine does not have to mean anything in order to be good, but in fact it generally will mean something because the writing of poetry normally implies the representation of a meaningful vision, and its meaning will modify the form of the line and contribute to our aesthetic pleasure in reading it. Since it is in the poet's nature to think in terms of sound, then it is also likely that a line will contain some degree of phonetic patterning, and we cannot be said to appreciate the line fully unless we have some awareness of it. When we say that a cluster must be 'recognizable', we do not mean that the untrained ear will recognize it, any more than it will recognize, for instance, that a line contains twelve syllables, or that the medial stress has been displaced. One learns to recognize such things only by acquiring good reading habits.

Most books on French versification have been concerned with reducing it to rules, and since phonetic patterning is not governed by rules it has tended to be overlooked. So much so that no adequate terminology exists to describe it, and we have to make our own. The tendency to ignore it has also been encouraged, one may think, by the habit of reading with the eye rather than with the voice; and it is likely to result from excessive concentration on meaning. Massive effects of alliteration or assonance may often be recognized if they can in some clear way be related to the meaning of the line. But phonetic clusters result from the sound of words, and do not necessarily reflect their meaning. And so the critic often does not hear them: or if he does hear them, is liable to dismiss them as the result of pure chance. Indeed, the meaningless question is sometimes posed: 'Did the poet actually *intend* this effect?' and if it cannot be demonstrated that he did, the effect is ignored. The question is meaningless because we are bound to assume that the poet intends what he writes, but whether he does so consciously or by instinct is impossible to decide, and usually irrelevant to the appreciation of the verse. A poet does not plan a line as a mathematician does an equation. Certainly his intelligence is very much at work in giving it its final form, but the material out of which it is built is partly the result of happy accidents, or, if one prefers a more grandiose term, of inspiration. The poet himself cannot necessarily 'explain' what he has created: all that he knows is that in its finished form it satisfies him, at least to a sufficient extent to justify its publication. He will leave to others the task of analysing its qualities.

Even so, if we are to use a phonetic cluster we need to know why we are doing so. To *use* a cluster means in the first place to recognize it: i.e. to read a line with a certain awareness that it exists. It may also mean that in reading aloud we give it a certain degree of emphasis. And since a line may contain several interlocking clusters, we will choose to emphasize, or to be most aware of, those which seem to us to have some kind of significance. The purpose of a phonetic abstract is to enable us to recognize what resources of this kind a line contains, and then to decide which of them (if any) make a significant contribution to the effectiveness of the line. Many such effects may well be beyond analysis, and this is no cause for regret, for in all great poetry there must be some element of the mysterious. However, if we were conducting an orchestra, respect for the 'mystery' of a symphony would not lead us to be careless about the details of its form, which are the vehicles by which that mystery is conveyed. In the same way, if we understand what can be understood about the phonetic form of a line, this does not lessen its power. On the contrary, it enables us to re-create it from the printed page with much greater imaginative force than would otherwise be the case. In order to do this, we must have some criterion of its significance. The student will also know that, in writing a commentary on a poem, it is a good principle that if one mentions any point one should be in a position to furnish some reason for thinking that point interesting. It is therefore not enough merely to identify a phonetic pattern and call attention to it. One needs to be able to say something about it.

Possibly the first reaction, on hearing an effect which might be classed as alliteration or assonance, is to assume that there must be some direct relationship between the repeated sounds and the meaning of the line. This possibility certainly exists, but comparatively rarely, since phonetic clusters result from the poet's natural tendency to create harmonies of sound, which does not necessarily imply that the sound suggests meaning. This possibility is a very delicate question indeed, and one which we cannot examine without some consideration of the nature of linguistic sound. For this reason, consideration of this question will be postponed until later in this book. For the moment we are concerned simply with patterns, regardless of the quality of the individual phonemes which compose them. A cluster is a repetition of any identical (or in some cases similar) sound, regardless of what that sound may be. The question we have to examine now is: what effect does such repetition have on the line, regardless of the individual qualities of the repeated phoneme?

There are, I think, three possible effects. The first is concerned with musicality, or its opposite, which is cacophony. Repetition of a phoneme, or a complex of phonemes, will affect the musicality of a line. In order to appreciate this, it is necessary to distinguish between the concepts of *noise* and *sound*. Noise is disorganized and formless. It can produce no satisfying aesthetic response. We either ignore it or it jars the nerves. Sound on the other hand possesses recognizable characteristics which can be comprehended by the mind. It possesses a certain interest. It is in this category that ordinary language falls, at least if we understand the language. Each language makes use of a small selection from the wide range of phonemes which can be produced by the human voice, and each has its characteristic intonations. The poet gives further identifiable form to language by his use of metre and also by his rimes. Thus, in general, we find verse more pleasing to listen to than ordinary speech, assuming of course that its content is such as to merit our attention. The reason for this is that the texture of verse (its sound and its rhythms) has recognizable form. The use of verse moves language further away from noise and closer to musical sound. Language cannot attain to the purity of musical sound, and indeed would not wish to, since an excess of musicality can distract from our response to sense; but by producing identifiable patterns of sound it achieves an effect in some ways comparable to music. A line which is rich in phonetic effects posses-ses audible form while one that is devoid of them is more random and hence closer to noise. This does not mean that the more phonetic clusters a line contains the better it is, since effects which are inappropriate or ostentatious are unlikely to be pleasing. Like rime or rhythm, phonetic patterning is a resource which must be used with taste. When we hear a line such as

139   Votrĕ co.rps modelé par le doigt de Dieu mê˙me [ ]
                  m d l   l d   d   d   m   m
           ò r   ò r   ò

we hear the effect as musical: but in a serious poem we should not wish to be encountering lines of this kind too often.

Therefore, our first conclusion is that when we are particularly struck by phonetic patterning in a line or lines, we should consider the possibility that the effect obtained is simply one of musicality.

But the matter goes further than this. Phonetic patterns are *persuasive*. When Pope writes

The sound must seem an echo of the sense [.]

he is making a statement about verse which may or may not be true. However, his sequence of initial [s] heard in *sound, seem, sense* makes his statement seem as if it were self-evidently true. What has happened is that a phonetic resemblance between words has been interpreted by us as in some way reinforcing their rational link. We are all of us familiar with the use of simple (and indeed sometimes quite complex) phonetic patterns in advertising slogans—'Guinness is good for you' [g g + vowel sequence], 'Jeyes's hygienic toilet tissue' [j j t t + other subsidiary effects] or 'Drinka pinta milka day'—and it is true to say that almost all the catch-phrases of commercial television (or American politics, as 'I like Ike' or 'Tricky Dick' illustrate) can be broken down into phonetic clusters. Adver-tisers and propagandists are aware of the powers of suggestion carried by words which have been integrated into a phonetic pattern. It may seem frivolous to compare great poetry with commercial jingles, but our comparison concerns not quality or seriousness but elementary method, and it is not surprising that those who seek to persuade us to part with our money or trust should have studied the secrets of rhetoric and verse. When wedded to a phonetic pattern—even one of which we are not consciously aware—words take on the sound of truth, and what is in fact merely an assertion becomes an aphorism. Good verse possesses a quality of inevitability which makes us feel that the words and their meaning are inseparable, and that to rephrase them would be absurd.

Phonetic patterning may not only suggest truth: it may also make apprehension of that truth pleasurable. It can totally change one's response to a meaningful statement. When Hugo tells us

140   Que l'oiseau perd sa plume et la fleu.r son parfum [,]

he expresses images of death (in themselves far from pleasant) with a sumptuous quality of sound redolent of romantic beauty; and in so doing he not only reinforces truth but also gives pleasure. This effect is obtained largely by interweaving sound-patterns. The rhythm of the line is enhanced by the strong triplet [p p| –p] which is heard in *perd*, *plume*, and *parfum*, being reinforced in the first and last of these words by the presence of [r]. In [B], the words *fleur* and *parfum* are linked by the doublet in [f], producing a terminal cluster. These rhythmic effects are backed up by clusters in [l] and [sá], and the phonetic relationship as a whole may be set out as follows:

[kĕ lW̌á zó pèr sá plü | mé lá flœ̀.r sò pár fœ̀ [,]
      p r   p | p r
                | f œ̀.r   r fœ̀
l   l | l l
   á z   sá | á   s   á

In cases such as this, where a number of clusters are interwoven, the strongest patterns may be described as *dominant* and the others as *subsidiary*. To some extent such a distinction may be subjective and will represent a personal interpretation, but often it will be clear and unambiguous. There can be little doubt that in this line the asymmetric triplet is dominant in the line as a whole, and the terminal doublet [f œ̀.r| r fœ̀] is dominant in [B]. The other effects are subsidiary. In Baudelaire's

141   Commĕ de longs échos | qui de loin se confon.dent,
       Dans unĕ ténébreu. | se et profon.de unité [,]

the first line offers a prevailing cluster in [o], but we may feel that the truly dominant effect is the nasal triplet [ò] which forms part of this, and which is further echoed by *profonde* in [2]. The sense of inevitability or truth of the line is reinforced by the terminal doublet [kò fò.d] where the repeated [ò] itself suggests an echo (to be followed by the further echo of [prò fò.d]). But apart from this, the metrical coherence of [1] is reinforced by a compound doublet which repeats five consonants in each hemistich in the same order. This is a subsidiary effect, but nevertheless very elegant. We may represent the total pattern as follows

```
Commĕ de longs échos | qui de loin se confon.dent [,]
          ò           |               ò ò
    kò            kò  | k          kò
        d  l   z      |     d  l   s
```

This line serves well to illustrate the third function of phonetic patterning, which is to reinforce metrical or syntactical rhythms. This function is closely linked to the concept of musicality, and also to that of meaning. It is only to be expected that the poet, who is thinking in a particular rhythm, will summon up not only recurring stresses but also recurring phonemes. The [ò|òò] illustrates one of the forms most frequently taken by the asymmetric triplet—a pre-echo in [A] followed by a doublet in [B]. The other common form is the reverse of this: a doublet in [A] followed by an echo in [B]. The rhythmic effect of both is similar. The second cluster noted above shows [k] occurring in the beginning and end of each hemistich. And in the third cluster, the compound doublet [d l z| d l s] is neatly balanced around the caesura. All these effects serve to strengthen the form of the alexandrine.

Clusters will not normally occur with this preciseness, since the poet does not calculate the exact number of phonemes and their placing in his line. Nevertheless, their distribution is normally related to metrical rhythm. They may be characteristic of the line as a whole, as in the following examples:

```
142     Toi, forme immorte˙llĕ, remon.te [ ]
        t              t              t
           òrm     mòr      r mò

143     Pour soulever un poids si lou.rd [ ]
        p   s  l       p   s  l
           ur   u                  u.r

144     Et de ses pieds palmés | frottant le pavé sec [,]
                   p    pa     |           pá
              é  é       é     |                é  è
```

Effects of this kind are most common in shorter lines. In the alexandrine, a dominant cluster characteristic of the line will be accompanied by other effects which distinguish the hemistichs. In

the following, there are strong dominant clusters running through
the line: [m] in **145**, [d] in **146**, but they are closely linked with more
localized patterns:

145   Mais la tristesse en moi | mon.tĕ commĕ la me.r [;]
    m   m | m   m   m
          t st s | ò   ò

146   Une oasis d'horreu.r | dans un dése.rt d'ennui [!]
                 d | d   d   d
              r   r | r
     n   s s | z   z   n

Alternatively, the dominant clusters may be characteristic of the
hemistich rather than the line. This also has the effect of reinforcing
metre, as we hear in the following examples:

147   Ca˙lmĕ commĕ la me.r | en sa sérénité [,]
    k lm k   m l m | s s

148   Nos cœu.rs que tu connais | sont remplis de rayons [!]
      k   k   k | r   r

149   L'Irrépara˙blĕ ron. | ge avec sa dent maudi˙te [ ]
      r   r   r | d   d

150   O Toison, moutonnant | jusquĕ sur l'encolu.re [!]
     t   t | üsk sür   k ü.r

151   Vous n'avez pas voulu | qu'il eût la certitu˙de [,]
    v   v   v |
                 lü | lü   l   ü

But, as the last example illustrates, such patterns are always free:
here the cluster which dominates in [B] actually begins in [A]. What
is involved is simply a rhythmic tendency: the phrasing of the line,
whether metrical or syntactical, is likely to be reflected in its clusters.
Thus a ternary rhythm is stressed in

152   Je marcherai | les yeux fixés | sur mes pensées [,]
        é | sé | sé

and in

153   Tu te tairas, | ô voix sini˙ | strĕ des vivants [!]
    t t t r | | tr
                     si i˙ | s   i
             | v | v v

though in the latter case the association is less rigidly metrical. Clusters often follow sense-groups, as in

154   Et rongé d'un dési.r sans trê./ve; et puis à vous [,]
            r   r   r /

where the triplet in [r] supported by [e] overruns the caesura as a result of enjambement; and in

155   Voyez-vous, nos enfants | nous sont bien nécessai.res [,]
        v   v
                 n z | n   s   n s s

even without enjambement, the opening phrase has its [v] doublet and the remainder of the line is characterized by the [ns] triplet.

Clearly, clusters are as flexible as the line itself. If we are to appreciate their effect on the line, it is very useful to have terms by which we can describe their positioning and indeed their function relative to the arrangement of the line as a whole. With this purpose in mind, I propose the following terms which I find useful in analysing phonetic abstracts:

1. THE DEFINING CLUSTER

This marks the beginning and end of a metrical unit (hemistich or line) by a repetition of a phoneme or phonemes. It is therefore usually a doublet, such as we hear in

156   Vient de la vi˙lle [;]
        v   v

157   Jeter l'an.cre un seul jou.r [?]
        j   j

In general, a doublet is only effective when the two elements are in fairly close proximity: but in the case of the defining cluster it is the positioning of the phonemes which gives them metrical importance and makes them significant. They may therefore be effective even when quite widely spaced.

158   Va˙lsĕ mélancolique et langoureux verti˙ge [.]
        v   v

159   Vo˙lĕ contrĕ l'assaut des rafa˙lĕs sauva.ges [,]
        v   v

160   Vains objets dont pour moi le charme est envolé [?]
        v   v

161   Commĕ je traversais le nouveau Carrousel [.]
      k   k

These are all simple doublets. But compound effects are not uncommonly heard:

162   Li˙brĕs commĕ la me.r autour des som.brĕs î˙les [.]
      l i   i l
         brĕ   brĕ

163   Ce qu'ellĕ cherche, amie, est un lieu saccagé [ ]
      s   k   dʒ   s k j
             l   l

164   Les souveni.rs lointains lentĕment s'élever [ ]
      l è s   v   sé l v

165   Ainsi, parfois, quand l'â.me est tristĕ, nos pensé˙es [ ]
            s p   p s

166   Un soi.r, t'en souvient-il? nous voguions en silen:ce [;]
         s   s   s   s

The extreme elements of a triplet may equally well serve as a
defining cluster:

167   Fai˙tĕs des fo.rmĕs que Dieu fond [.]
      f   f   f

168   Le vent du soi.r s'élè|ve et l'arrache aux vallons [,]
      l   v   l v   v l

169   S'envo˙lĕnt un moment | sur leurs ai˙lĕs blessé˙es [ ]
      s   l   s   l   l s

For an example of the defining cluster applied to the hemistich,
note the [tèr tèr] doublet in *155* in the Index.

2. THE PIVOTAL CLUSTER

This is the mid-line cluster which, in the case of the alexandrine,
usually spans the caesura. It combines well with the defining cluster,
and it will be noted that in some of the examples given above the
middle element of a triplet has this function. Often, however, an
independent cluster occurs:

170 Les souveni.rs lointains | lentĕment s'élever [ ]
       l ë t ë | là tà
  l ès v   s'é l vé

171 Cettĕ chanson d'amou.r | qui toujou.rs recommen.ce [?...]
         u r | u u r
  s   s   s

172 Va ˙lsĕ mélancoli | que et langoureux verti.ge [.]
      élà kó | é là gu
  v | v
       i | i.

But the pivotal cluster is often found without the defining cluster:

173 Et le mê ˙mĕ sole.il | se lè.vĕ sur tes jou ˙rs [.]
         s lè | s lè

174 J'entends le vent dans l'ai.r, | la me.r sur le récif [;]
          l è .r | l è.r

175 Je pen'se à la nègre | sse, amaigrie et phtisi ˙que [,]
         ègr | ègr
      s | s   s

3. LIMINAL AND TERMINAL CLUSTERS

The term *liminal* is used to describe a cluster which is characteristic of the beginning of a line or phrase, and *terminal* to describe one characteristic of its end. Liminal clusters give a strong phonetic colouring to the opening words of phrases such as *Demain, dès l'aube* [d d], *Moi, mon âme est fêlée* [m m m], *Calmĕ commĕ la mer* [k-lm k m l m]. *Ma maison me regarde* [m m m]. We have already drawn attention to some terminal patterns on p. 73, and the reader will have noted many others. It is possible to have a terminal doublet to round off both [A] and [B], as in

176 C'est un pays plus nu | que la te.rrĕ polai.re [;]
     [p p ü ü]| [è.r   è.r]

or

177 Toutĕ sono.re enco.r | de vos derniers baisers [;]
      [o.r ò.r]| [è é è é]

but the effect is normally reserved for the line-ending, as in

178   Ce coucher d'un sole.il | est d'un au˙trĕ l'auro.re [.]
                           ó r   óró r

or

179   Ont, dans les plis de cettĕ peau [,]
                           p   p

A simple doublet is quite enough to give a strong phonetic ending to a line, but richer effects are common. Here are a few line-endings culled at random: *ellĕ dêdaigne* [è dé dè], *ainsi qu'un lac limpide* [k l kl], *d'unĕ brusquĕ secousse* [ü üskĕ sĕk s], *ramiers amoureux* [rám ám r], *mon cadavrĕ verdi* [d vr v rd], *qu'ellĕ t'ouvre toujours* [tú r tú úr], *par tous étaient cités* [t sétè s té], *que Madeleinĕ baigne* [èn èn], *étrange et pénétrant* [etrà:étrà]. In the following stanza by Baudelaire, the vowel of each rime-word is repeated in such a way as to form a terminal cluster:

180   Quand, les deux yeux fermés, en un soir chaud d'auto˙mne,
                                                     ó   ó ò

Je respi.rĕ l'odeu.r de ton sein chaleureux,
                   ǿ   ǿ

Je vois se dérouler des riva.gĕs heureux
                        ǿ   ǿ

Qu'ébloui˙ssĕnt les feux d'un sole.il monoto˙ne [;]
        [ǿ]   ò   ò ò ò

4. LIMINAL AND TERMINAL ECHOES

An *echo* involves the repetition of identical phonemes at the beginning or end of consecutive segments, hemistichs, lines etc. If a vowel is involved, this produces free rime or assonance. The liminal effect is not common except in rhetorical repetition, though we have quoted an example on p. 72 where the lines of a quatrain open with the matching sounds *comme, homme, comme,* and *calme.* We hear liminal echoes in [ás] in the last three lines of the stanza

181   Pour n'ê˙trĕ pas changés en bê˙tĕs, ils s'eni.vrent
           D'espace et de lumiè.re et de cieux embrasés;
           La gla˙cĕ qui les mo.rd, les sole.ils qui les cui.vrent,
           Effa˙cĕnt lentĕment la ma˙rquĕ des baisers [.]

Since the beginning of a line does not normally bear stress, liminal effects will be heard only if we choose to give them some slight emphasis in our reading. Terminal effects, on the other hand, are naturally stressed. A common form of the terminal echo is the rime on the caesura, which we heard above in

182   Je vois se dérouler les riva.gĕs heureux
                                    œ́   œ́
           Qu'éblouissĕnt les feux [...]
                          œ́

and a triple sequence of terminal echoes is heard in

183   Et qu'un peu ́ plĕ muet | d'infâ ́ mĕs araigné ́ es
           Vient ten.drĕ ses filets [...]

The difference between the terminal cluster and the terminal echo may be demonstrated in the following examples. The line

184   Et, nous montrant l'épi | dans son germe enfermé [,]

ends in a terminal doublet, since the repeated [èrm] occurs in the same segment: whereas in

185   Je dis que le tombeau qui sur les mo.rts se ferme
           Ou ́ vrĕ le firmament [,]

we have a terminal echo, since *ferme* and *firmament* are in consecutive lines. This last example demonstrates that it is possible to have a terminal echo based on consonants alone. It has already been pointed out (on page 78) that the effect here is really a triplet based on *morts* [m r], *ferme* [rm] and *firmament* [rm m]. The terminal echo is also heard in Verlaine's

186   Toutĕ sono.re enco.r | de vos derniers baisers,
                                       è zé
           Laissez-la s'apaiser [...]
                è zé

in addition to the terminal cluster which rounds off both [A] and [B] in the first line. The interesting pattern *laissez-la sa-* [lè sé : lá sá] may also be noted.

5. CONTRAPUNTAL ECHO

I use this term to describe an echo which runs counter to normal metrical stress. To be effective one of its elements must be stressed, usually the second, which falls on the line ending; the first, which in the case of the alexandrine occurs in [A], may bear no stress at all and yet be effectively heard when read aloud. Examples are the [às] and the [ès] doublet in the following lines respectively:

187   Cettĕ chanson d'amou.r | qui toujou.rs recommen.ce [?...]
          à s | *à* s
                   u.r | u.r

188   Et mon esprit subtil, | que le roulis care˙sse [,]
          ès | è˙s
                   il | li

In both these lines there is a supporting contrapuntal echo which links the stress on the caesura to the minor stress of [B]. In this case it is 'contrapuntal' only in the sense that, contrary to normal metrical practice, the strongest stress falls on the first element.

A common form of contrapuntal echo matches the minor stress of [A] with the major stress on the line ending:

189   Dans l'astre au front d'argent | qui blanchit sa surfa˙ce [,]
          ás | á˙s

190   Le dése.rt est muet, | la ten.te est solitai.re [.]
          è r | è. r

191   Il est ame.r et doux, | pendant les nuits d'hive.r [,]
          è r | è r

192   Entends, ma chè.re, entends | la dou˙cĕ nuit qui ma˙rche [!]
          má dh   r | ma˙rdh

Conversely, the stressed word on the caesura may be echoed by a minor stress in the second hemistich:

193   Un bouquet de houx ve.rt et de bruyè.re en fleu.r [.]
                           è r   è r

194   Allumaient dans nos cœu.rs une ardeu.r inquiè˙te [ ]
                           œ r   œ r

195   Ce Simoïs menteu.r qui par vos pleu.rs grandit [,]
                     œ r   œ r

More free-ranging effects than these are possible, such as the following in which the caesura is not used:

196   Je passe; enfant, troupeau, s'effa ˙cĕnt dans la bru ˙me [.]
            ás   á s

197   A n'aimer, en ce monde ame.r où la chai.r rè ˙gne [ ]
                                         è r   èr

198   J'ai rêvé dans la grotte où na.gĕ la sirè ˙ne
            rè   rè

The contrapuntal echo normally requires a certain amount of stress
in reading to make it effective; and one of its interesting characteristics is that it makes possible some modification of metrical
stress. It is always possible to put the main stress on the second part
of the cluster, thus using it as a true rime or assonance. If this is not
done, what we hear is a sort of *diminuendo* rime, producing a falling
away or muted effect.

6. RUN-ON AND INTERLINEAR CLUSTERS

A *run-on cluster* is one which extends from one line to the next;
while the term *interlinear* may be used to describe a pattern which
characterizes a whole series of lines.

One of the most familiar of run-on clusters takes the form of an
echo of the rime-word on the caesura following, or from one caesura
to the next. We have already quoted examples of the former (**182,
183, 186**) and of the latter (**130**). And other examples (page 78)
demonstrate that this kind of echo can be effective between the
line-ending and subsidiary stresses in the next line. But this last kind
of echo will normally only be effective if it occurs on a word which is
important in terms of sense. When we read

199   Elle a pour nourrisson l'universe ˙llĕ faim;
          C'est vers son sein qu'en bas les raci ˙nĕs s'allon.gent [.]

we hear the correspondence between [fë] and [së] because there is a
break in the syntax after the word *sein*. And for the same reason we
hear the echo between *ménagerie* and *vis*:

200   Là s'étalait jadis unĕ ménageri ˙e;
          Là je vis, un matin, à l'heu.re où sous les cieux [ ]

The *phonetic copula*, in which a compound doublet is divided
between the end of one line and the beginning of the next, is
generally associated with enjambement, when its effect is to establish phonetic continuity between the line and the *rejet* which follows:

201   Mais les vrais voyageu.rs sont ceux-là seuls qui pa˙rtent
                                                    pa˙rt
         Pour parti.r; [...]
         p   r párt r

202   Contrĕ quelque unive.rs immobile en sa fo˙rce
                                               sá fò rs
         Défoncera [...]
            fò s rá

203   Se dessinait au pied de l'égli˙sĕ, dont l'om.bre
                                             ò   lò
         S'allon.geait [...]
             lò

It may however be effective on occasions even without enjambement:

204   Ce matelot ivrogne, inventeu.r d'Améri˙ques,
                                       d   m r
         Dont le mira.gĕ [...]
         d   m r

205   La mer, la me.r, toujours recommen.cé.e!
                                     rĕko   à sé
         O récompen.se après unĕ pensé˙e [ ]
         rékò   à s

Interlinear clusters, on the other hand, do not normally have this
close association with metre or syntax: they are freely scattered
from line to line and their effect is cumulative. In order to be heard,
they must normally be dominant in some of the lines within which
they occur.

206   Ho˙mmĕ, si, le cœur plein de joie ou d'amertu˙me,
              si
         Tu passais vers midi dans les champs radi:eux,
                  s   i i   i
         Fuis! la natu˙re est vide et le sole.il consu˙me;
           i   i   s   s
         Rien n'est vivant ici, rien n'est triste ou joyeux [.]
               i   isi   is

Effects of this kind will often not show up in a linear analysis. But in
the work of a poet such as Gautier they may be extremely complex
and self-conscious:

207   Ce fe.r que le mineu.r cherche au fond de la te.rre,
         Aux brumeu.sĕs clartés de son pâ.lĕ fanal,
         Hélas! le forgĕron quelquĕ jour en doit fai.re
         Le clou qui fermera le couve˙rclĕ fatal [.]

Among the sounds of which there is significant repetition in these
lines are the following:

[èr]	fer, cherche, terre, faire, fermera, couvercle.
[f]	fer, fond, fanal, forgeron, faire, fermera, fatal, fanal.
[k-l]	que le, clarté, quelque, clou, couvercle.
[l-t-r]	la terre, clarté.
[a]	clarté, pâle, fanal, fatal.
[ò]	fond, son, forgeron.
[f-r-j]	forgeron, jour en .. faire.
[u]	jour, clou, couvercle.

The reader may find some comfort in the knowledge that virtuoso
effects of this kind are rare. Normally, interlinear patterning depends
upon the persistent repetition of comparatively few sounds. In his
sonnet *Correspondances* Baudelaire uses combinations of [fr] and
[è]—*parfums, frais, chairs, verts, prairies*—and it is as a result of
following this phonetic pattern that his perfumes become green:

208   Il est des parfums frais commĕ des chai.rs d'enfants,
                    rf   fr | f
             è   rè | è.r
         Doux commĕ les haubois, ve.rts commĕ les prairi˙es [,]
                                  | è.r   rèr

and then blends *comme* with the [p r] of *parfums* to produce *corrompus*. The nasal [ò] is echoed in *triomphants* which introduces
[à]; and this latter nasal, strongly supported by sibilants, persists
through the remaining lines of the poem.

209   – Et d'autrĕs, corrompus, ri˙chĕs et tri:omphants,
                                                          à
         Ayant l'expansi:on des cho.sĕs infini˙es,
             à   à
                  s   s   dh   z
         Commĕ l'am.brĕ, le musc, le benjoin et l'encens,
                  à   à   à à
                       s   j   s s
         Qui chan.tĕnt les transpo.rts de l'esprit et des sens [.]
               à   à   à
               dh   s   s   s s

In making a phonetic abstract, it is always necessary to indicate clearly if the patterns to which one is drawing attention are inter-linear. In the first line of **209**, [à] would not appear as part of any linear pattern, the line being dominated by [ò] and [r], and has no significance other than as introducing the sequence which follows. In general, it is more difficult to represent interlinear clusters in abstract form than linear ones; and as the effect is cumulative rather than rhythmic, the best way of indicating its presence will often be simply to list the words concerned.

The terms and method of analysis that we have described help us to understand how a line or verse 'works' phonetically. To say of a line such as Nerval's

210   Un pur esprit s'accroît sous l'éco˙rcĕ des pie.rres [!]

that 'it sounds very musical' is not really helpful. We hear it as having phonetic form because *un pur esprit* offers a liminal doublet in [p r] which is echoed on the line-ending in *pierres*, and *s'accroît* and *sous l'écorce*, arranged around the caesura, produce a compound pivotal doublet [s kr | s k rs]. The combination of these gives a balanced and pleasing quality to the line. Further, [A] ends in the terminal doublet in [á] which is heard in *s'accroît*, and [r] forms a prevailing cluster throughout the line. We may show these effects as follows, and so represent in abstract form the phonetic qualities of the line:

```
Un pur esprit s'accroît |  sous l'éco˙rcĕ des pie.rres [!]
   p  r  pr             |                        p    r
      s    s   kr        | s        k   rs
              á    wá     |
      r    r      r       |       r              r
```

The general effect is one of equilibrium, with variety introduced by the asymmetric triplet [pr pr|-pr], and in terms of sense the phonetic linking of *pur esprit* and *pierres* greatly strengthens the line.

If we examine in a similar manner Leconte de Lisle's

211   Sur les cô.tĕs du ciel son pha.rĕ constellé [.]

we note that the hemistichs are linked by both liminal and terminal echoes: the [s] of *sur* and *son* and the [èl] of *ciel* and *constellé*. And indeed [s] is present in all these words, reinforcing the metrical form of the line. No less striking is the compound doublet [kò.t|kò t] heard in *côtes* and *constellés*. These patterns are linked and all come together in the final word *constellés*, thus producing a very elegant line.

Sur les cô.tĕs du ciel | son pha.rĕ constellé [.]
```
s              s  | s              s
              èl |               èl
    kò.t          |       kò   t
```

To these firm effects we may add the more subdued contrapuntal
echoes which are heard in each hemistich: in [A], the [lè] of *les*
echoed inversely in *ciel*, and in [B] the echo of *son* [sò] as [òs] in
constellé. It is interesting that the word *phare* plays no part at all in
this rich phonetic patterning. One may suppose that *Sur les côtĕs du
ciel* and *constellés* came into the poet's mind by phonetic association
in exactly the same way as the proposal of a rime suggests its answer,
and it then remained for him to find exactly the right word, in terms
of its imaginative impact, with which to complete his line.

For our final example, we take the closing line of Vigny's *La
Maison du berger*:

212   Ton amou.r tacitur|ne et toujou.rs menacé [.]

The two effects which strike us most forcefully are the combination
of [t] and [ás] heard in *Ton amour taciturne* in [A] and *toujours
menacé* in [B], and the triplet in [u+r] heard in *amour* and *toujours*.
A more subdued but very pleasing effect is heard in the chiastic
doublet [n m|m n] heard at the beginning and end of the line in *Ton
amour* and *menacé*, and supported by the [n] of *taciturne* on the
caesura. We set these patterns out as follows:

```
Ton amou.r tacitur | ne et toujou.rs menacé [.]
 t    á     tás     |    t              ás
   n m              |  n          m n
       u.r     r    |      u   u.r
```

What does this tell us about the quality of the line? I think it would
be agreed that the second two clusters, with their nasal consonants,
vibrant, and long rounded vowel, give an effect of great musicality.
They interlock and suggest equilibrium. The quality of individual
sounds will be discussed in our final chapter, but here I will suggest
simply that the [u] is a constricted sound which serves well to give
sonorous expression to a feeling of melancholy. The effect of these
two clusters is subdued. But this is not the case with the first, which
is strongly heard: and here there is no equilibrium. The echo in [ás]
is contrapuntal; and [t] heard three times in [A] occurs only once in
[B], and not at all in the final segment of the line—*menacé*. Thus the
phonetic quality of the line changes, and becomes softer, towards
the end. It produces a diminuendo effect. This weakening of
phonetic force which leads to the word *menacé*, this co-existence of

balance with unbalance, together with the association of *amour* and *toujours* through their vowel sounds, goes far, I think, to explain the haunting and memorable quality of the line.

But before we leave this example, it may serve to draw our attention to another point of some interest. The force of the [t] cluster seems to depend not only on the fact that it is a voiceless stop (and the significance of this will be discussed in our closing chapter) but on its being situated, in three out of its four occurrences, at the beginning of a word. If our investigations had been into alliteration, the point would certainly have come up earlier, for it is usually assumed that in alliterative patterns the initial consonant does have some special importance. In our discussion of phonetic clusters we have treated all phonemes as being of equal importance, except for possible association with rhythms and with words which play a crucial part in the meaning or imaginative impact of a line. Yet if we look back over our examples I think we shall find many cases in which the fact of a consonant being in an initial position does seem to add to its force. Certainly it is better to underestimate this than to overestimate it, since lines tend to be a complex of patterns which we simply will not hear if we pay undue attention to initials. But the matter does call for some comment. Initial consonants are not different in function from others, but they tend to be associated with dominant patterns. One wonders why this should be so. In French, stress falls not on consonants but on vowels, and then only when they occur in a final position. Further, it is in the nature of the language that an initial consonant is rarely heard as an initial, since important words are almost always preceded by a particle with which they merge: generally a definite or indefinite article or a pronoun which phonetically is indistinguishable from the word itself. The initial phoneme heard in *la maison* or *nous voyons* is [l] and [n], not [m] and [v], and stress in both cases falls on [ò]. One possible explanation is our habit of reading verse with our eyes rather than our voice, for on the printed page the space between the words draws attention to the initial, whereas in speech there is no pause to correspond to that space. This point may explain why some critics more readily notice initial effects than others, but hardly why poets use them. My own suggestion, for what it is worth, is that the word is a mental concept. When we wish to give particular emphasis to the meaning of a word, we do stress its initial consonant, which suggests that it is present in our mind as a meaningful unit. If taken by surprise, we may sometimes bring out words in incoherent relationships, and it may require a conscious effort of re-phrasing to give them syntactical form. We may suppose then that words are the prime units out of which the poet assembles his metrical patterns;

and if this is so they may tend to be associated in his mind by reason of their initial consonant just as they are by their capacity to rime. It is a matter of common experience that we all respond to initial alliteration: even in ordinary speech it can produce comic effects at times, just as can unintentional rime. But the poet's feeling for language is a good deal more sophisticated than that which we bring to ordinary speech, and it would be a mistake to suppose that his faculty for sound association is limited to, or even strongly dominated by, initials. This is abundantly demonstrated by the line we have just discussed by Vigny, in which no less than twenty-one out of its total of twenty-seven phonemes are effectively integrated into patterns.

In our study of phonetic patterns, we have made little use of the traditionally accepted terms *alliteration* and *assonance*. These terms may be appropriate in certain cases when phonetic clusters are deliberately made obtrusive. But it seems to me that the distinction they make between consonants and vowels is irrelevant. And in any case they refer only to the cumulative effect of sound-patterning. A doublet would not traditionally be held to fall into either category (three occurrences of a consonant being the minimum usually qualified as alliteration), and yet, as we have seen, the doublet is fundamental to the concept of the phonetic cluster. So I would suggest that while it is perfectly correct to speak of alliteration in the case of a line such as

213   Et tout le reste est littératu.re [.]
         t   l r t   l t r t r

the point is made much more clearly if we say that it has a prevailing cluster in [t l r]. If he does choose to use the words *alliteration* and *assonance* in writing a commentary on a poem, the student should always indicate quite clearly the sounds to which he is referring. To say of a line merely that it 'contains alliteration' gives absolutely no indication of what he actually hears when he reads it.

Chapter Five
STANZA FORM

RHYTHM is possibly the only feature which is absolutely essential to all verse and to all poetry. And in regular verse, rime is one of the most potent sources of rhythm: indeed, the fact that the word is commonly spelt 'rhyme' in English draws attention to the fact that both concepts derive their name from the same Greek term which means 'rhythm'. Rime is a form of phonetic patterning, but differs from phonetic clusters in that it is a regular metrical feature. It must occur in a position of metrical stress (almost always on the line-ending), and so it reinforces the regular rhythm imposed by the metre. But the poet may vary its effect in two ways. He will propose and answer his rimes in a certain order: and the order may vary from poem to poem, and occasionally within the poem. Also the distance between each rime-word (in terms of syllable-count) may vary. A long line means that the rimes are widely spaced, and the rhythm is slow. A short line means that rimes recur rapidly: we are therefore more conscious of them, and the rhythm is fast. In this context, expressions such as 'slow' and 'fast' do not refer to the speed at which we actually read the words, but rather to the sense of movement and progress that we have when the rimes recur frequently. Moreover, every so often and almost always at regular intervals, the poet may introduce a pause in his rime-sequence. This is represented on the printed page by the blank line which separates one stanza from the next. Its metrical function is to make us aware of the stanza as a rhythmical unit, and to give us a brief moment in which to assimilate the rime-pattern which it concludes. More often than not such breaks would be inappropriate in narrative verse, which tends to be written in long blocks of lines; but in lyrical verse, which gives pleasure through its rhythms and combinations of sound, they have an important function. So lyrical verse is written in stanzas—i.e. a group of lines held together by a rime-pattern—and may often use shorter lines, and even lines of varying length, in order to enhance our awareness of the rhythms formed by rime and metre.

The poet's choice in this matter is not necessarily conscious. His poem may originate from a small number of lines which suggest themselves to his imagination either complete or in fragments which invite the use of one metre rather than another. A poet does not merely decide to write on a particular subject. With the subject, he is likely to conceive the manner in which it will be treated, and this is likely to lead him to his metre.

However, rime does not function merely by reinforcing metrical stress. It creates its own particular kind of rhythm, coinciding with that of metre, but based on the anticipation of *words* associated with recurring sound. It is therefore linked with meaning, and is apprehended by the intelligence. The most obvious link is a purely negative one: a word cannot rime with itself, and even excessive similarity of meaning or form can weaken it and leave us with a sense of dissatisfaction. This would not be so if all we were looking for was identical sound occurring with an expected stress. But the expectation aroused by rime is not merely negative. Some years ago the Lancashire comedian George Formby used to sing a song about a Chinese laundryman called Mr Wu. It was in riming couplets, one of which took the surprising form of

> He's got a naughty eye that flickers
> When he's ironing ladies' – blouses [,].

Everyone who heard the song knew perfectly well that the second line should not end in 'blouses', and had already prepared himself to hear something quite different. Here the rime was so outrageously false that the listener didn't even feel let down: indeed, he got more satisfaction from the slight imaginative effort needed to correct the rime than if it had been given to him in the correct form in the first place. So we must recognize that in certain cases at least we may anticipate not merely a sound but a word. In fact, this must always be to some extent the case when we know a poem well. We are only fully sensitive to rime, as to all other features of verse, when we have read the poem more than once, in which case the arrival of each new rime-word creates the expectation of another which we already vaguely anticipate. The importance of this lies in the fact that in good riming, the rime should always fall on words which are important to the sense or feeling of the poem. When Vigny writes of his wolf:

214   Il nous regarde enco.re, ensuite il se recou˙che [,]

he creates in our our mind a certain subdued expectancy which is resolved by the line following:

215   Tout en léchant le sang répandu sur sa bou˙che [,].

This resolution of tension is effected specifically by the word 'bouche', and consequently the image is reinforced: moreover, an effective link is established not merely between words and lines but also between images. If we feel that a word occurs on the line-ending merely to make the rime, we feel a sense of inadequacy. This is only too often the case when attempts are made to translate riming verse from one language to another. In the original, the rimes are integrated meaningfully into the fabric of the poem, whereas in the translation new words must be found, often having no function other than to complete the rime.

Riming involves two distinct and even contradictory processes. A rime-word leads us to expect something which is both similar and different: or, as Baudelaire put it in one of his projected Prefaces for *Les Fleurs du mal*, it achieves its effect by a combination of mono-tony and surprise. All forms of rhythm involve a balancing of the similar with the dissimilar. Thus we reject not only rimes which are excessively similar in form or meaning, but also those that are so obvious or hackneyed as to involve no element of surprise at all. There was a time when sentimental ballads were prone to rely heavily on such matches as 'June' and 'moon' or 'love' and 'above', with the result that one led so inevitably to the other that all sense of contrast or of the unexpected was lost. Cliché riming of this kind would be intolerable in serious verse, simply because of its obvious-ness and its facility. As Pope, following Boileau, puts it,

> If crystal streams with pleasing murmurs 'creep',
> The reader's threatened (not in vain) with 'sleep' ...

In fact, good poets do have recourse to cliché rimes—*ombre* and *sombre, amer* and *la mer, automne* and *monotone* occur in some of the finest of nineteenth-century poems—but their richness is such that they give sensuous satisfaction when they come even though we know very well that they are on their way. They contribute to the emotional quality of the poem, and would do so even if the poet was not riming on them. Rime, then, subjects us to various kinds of stimuli. In narrative verse, we may require little more of it than a phonetic reinforcement of metrical stress with words not too facilely chosen: while in lyrical verse it is likely to be a much more active feature. In general, as is the case with all features of rhythm, we should not expect it to be too obtrusive, but even this principle is extremely flexible: what would be obtrusive in one type of verse may be most pleasurable in another.

Skill in riming involves matching significant rime-words and also integrating them into the lines to which they belong. In the lines we quoted from Vigny's *La Mort du loup*, we have the impression that both terms of the rime must have come into the poet's mind almost simultaneously, since 'recouche' and 'bouche' belong so naturally to the scene they describe. But in fact this effect of simultaneity derives from the poet's natural skill in the handling of words. If a line, complete with rime-word, has suggested itself to his imagination, then that rime-word attracts other potential rimes to it as a flower will attract bees. Each rime-word circulating in the poet's mind gives rise to new possible lines, and the final choice of an answer to the rime will depend not merely on the qualities of the word itself but on the appropriateness of the new line which grows out of it. Thus the rime may itself play an active part in composition. Baudelaire describes the process admirably in *Le Soleil* when he speaks of himself walking through Paris.

> **216** Je vais m'exercer seul à ma fantasque escri`me,
> Flairant dans tous les coins les hasa.rds de la ri`me,
> Trébuchant sur les mots commĕ sur les pavés,
> Heurtant parfois des ve.rs depuis longtemps rêvés [.]

In this description, several activities operate more or less simultaneously. The scene which he has before his eyes suggest words: these words jolt his imagination and suggest rimes which in turn attach themselves to new lines, which may sometimes be already half-formed in his mind. The process thus described is largely intuitive and difficult to break down into a strict chronological sequence: one thing leads to another, but image, rime, and metre interact and modify each other. Certainly, the final verse may require a good deal of conscious pruning and polishing, for the poet is not only an artist but also a craftsman. Valéry has laid great stress on the interdependence of these qualities. For him, a poem may first take shape simply as a rhythmic sequence, a metrical pattern which subsequently attracts to itself, as it were, thought and imagery. He describes the poet at work

> **217** Je cherche un mot (dit le poète), un mot qui soit:
> féminin,
> de deux syllabes,
> contenant P ou F,
> terminé par une muette,
> et synonyme de brisure, désagrégation;
> et pas savant, pas rare.
> Six conditions – au moins!

Obviously, this may not represent the conscious working method of other poets, but each in his own way must face similar problems. Baudelaire, laying less stress on the rôle of intelligence, speaks of poetry as *sorcellerie évocatoire*. But whatever the approach, language itself plays an active part in the creation of a poem, and it is for this reason that rime is not a mere technical restriction but a thought-process which follows its own logic, independent to no small extent of the poet's rational faculties.

The rime-unit or stanza is therefore more than a metrical feature of verse: it is an imaginative structure which grows out of the association of certain rime-words. This is one of the distinguishing features between good and mediocre verse. Rime may be perfectly good so far as conformity to rules is concerned, but if it gives us the sense of being merely 'added on' to a thought-sequence which has really no need for it, then the verse does not justify its existence. It must be noted that such a structure does not necessarily grow, as logical thought does, from a beginning, through a middle, to an appropriate end. Rime may influence not only the lines which follow it but also those which precede. In the terminology adopted in this book I speak of a rime being *proposed* and *answered*. When a poet proposes a rime he places a word in such a position in his line that we expect it to conjure up a word of corresponding sound in a subsequent line. To say this is to look at the proposal and answer of a rime from the reader's point of view, which will often also be that of the poet. But it is not invariably so. The poet does not necessarily compose his lines in the order in which we read them: there are many cases in which it is the second rime-word which comes first into his mind, and the first one evolves subsequently as an answer to it. This does not matter to us unless we are particularly interested in the way in which the poet's mind works, and in a good poem the elements will usually be so carefully balanced that it is difficult for us to know which came first. But Hugo gives us at least one example of inverted structure of which we may be certain. This occurs in the two closing stanzas of *Booz endormi*.

218   Tout reposait dans U.r et dans Jérimadeth;
       Les a˙strĕs émaillaient le ciel profond et som.bre;
       Le Croissant fin et clai.r parmi ces fleu.rs de l'om.bre
[4]   Brillait à l'occident, et Ruth se demandait,

       Immobile, ouvrant l'œil à moitié sous ses voi˙les,
       Quel dieu, quel moissonneu.r de l'éternel été
       Avait, en s'en allant, négligemment jeté
[8]   Cettĕ fauci.llĕ d'o.r dans le champ des étoi˙les [.]

Here we are given the clue not by any weakness in the verse itself but by the fact that no such place is known as *Jérimadeth*. This is a name which Hugo invented in order to make the rime. (Indeed, the story goes that, rather in the manner of Valéry on the previous page, Hugo was muttering to himself: 'Je rime à *-dait* ... Je rime à *-dait* ...' and that he finally resolved his problem by turning the phrase into a place-name.) Normally, a made-up word will not provide a satisfactory rime, since much more is required than similarity of sound; but in this case the name contributes so richly to the atmosphere (particularly when associated with Ur, which was a real place) that we feel it to be a genuine and satisfying poetic creation. But what concerns us here is that, in creating it, Hugo already knew that he was riming with *et Ruth se demandait* at the end of the stanza. Thus for him it was the last line which proposed the rime, not the first. Indeed, we can go further. These two stanzas exist in order to lead up to the image contained in the final line—that of the moon seen as golden sickle lying in a field of stars. They are independent of the remainder of the poem, and are linked to it simply by the words *Ruth se demandait*. Therefore the image of the last line must have been present in the poet's mind before he began to construct the stanzas. The poet's thought worked inversely to the manner in which he finally presents his image to the reader.

We cannot conclude from this that [8] as it now stands existed before [4], or even that [4] existed before [1]. There is a high degree of simultaneity in the composition of a stanza, and rime association plays an important part in it. Nevertheless, it is tempting to speculate. Hugo begins from a visual association of the moon and a golden sickle. This he sees through Ruth's eyes, and it leads her to think of God as a harvester, for she is a simple girl who has been gleaning in the fields after the harvest. She knows nothing of Jehovah or of His purpose for her (hence *quel dieu...* with a small letter, which is one of the most potent touches of the image, since it implies the linking of her mortal destiny with something beyond her comprehension). So the source of the image is three phrases:

> Le croissant ...
> Quel dieu, quel moissonneur ...
> Cettĕ faucille d'or dans le champ des étoiles.

and the lead-in phrase

> Ruth se demandait...

The image is then filled out, perhaps by

> Avait, en s'en allant, négligemment jeté

for this springs straight from the peasant girl's imagination. *S'en allant* is appropriate for she has just seen the other workers leaving the field in which she herself has lain down to sleep, and *négligem-ment jeté* hints at the immeasurable majesty of a God (suggested to her by the vastness of the sky) who could afford to leave behind him, quite casually, in a field, a sickle of pure gold. Having thus proposed a new rime with *jeté*, Hugo answers it with the obvious choice—*été*. We may be reasonably sure that the words occurred to him in this order, and not the other way round, since *été* is not essential to the theme and is there to make the rime. In terms of meaning it is in fact slightly inappropriate, since autumn and not summer is the season of harvest. However, there is nothing clumsy about the matching, and *l'éternel été* is a much more satisfactory phrase to describe eternity than would be *l'éternel automne*. The fact that [6] and [7] are open-ended encourages one to think that the last three lines developed in close association in the poet's mind, but as we have seen not necessarily in the order in which they finally occur.

So Hugo now has for his last stanza:

> Quel dieu, quel moissonneur de l'éternel été
> Avait, en s'en allant, négligemment jeté
> Cettĕ fauci.llĕ d'o.r dans le champ des étoi˙les [.]

He now needs only his first line, which we may assume was com-posed last since it is only a 'fill in', the substance of the stanza lying in the lines which he has completed. The content of the line is governed by the word *voiles*, which is one of the few rimes available to match *étoiles*. It only remains for Hugo to derive from this his image of the sleeping Ruth, and his stanza is finished.

But the concluding image is not yet linked to the poem as a whole. For this purpose a penultimate stanza is needed. Hugo needs it because he has not yet been able to bring in the words *Ruth se demandait* (or their equivalent) which are necessary to introduce the final image, and also in order to build up to his climax, for which purpose a single isolated stanza would be inadequate. He also needs to introduce the crescent moon to prepare us for the final line. So he begins with *Ruth se demandait* in a key position at the end of the stanza and leading on to the next, and in the line before it we have *le croissant*. This Hugo amplifies with the adjectives *fin et clair*. These words may perhaps have suggested *fleurs* by the phonetic associa-tion of [f l r], and by completing his line with the poetic flourish *ces fleurs de l'ombre*, the poet prepares us for the association of the sky with the field with which he is to round off the poem. We now have

> Le croissant fin et clair parmi ces fleurs de l'om.bre
> Brillait ... et Ruth se demandait [,]

and the words *à l'occident* are added to fill out the last line. Both these lines must propose new rimes, and in the case of *ombre* there is very little choice. It must be answered by *sombre*, from which we conclude that the image

Les astres émaillaient le ciel profond et sombre [;]

derives from its final rime-word.

Can we be sure that *ombre* came first? I think so. After all, Hugo had to complete his sentence of which *le croissant* is the subject before finishing [2]. If he had worked the other way round, he might have found it quite impossible to match the rime of [2] at the end of [3] without remodelling his sentence. We may therefore assume that he finished this sentence first and then developed [2] from the rime-word *sombre* which it gave him.

Once again, then, he has produced the three last lines, first, and requires an opening sentence to complete the stanza. And we know that this was so since he invented the place-name *Jérimadeth* to answer *se demandait*. Doubtless he had already thought of *Tout reposait* [...], for the quietness of the fields pervades the stanzas. The introduction of the place-name *Ur* is exactly right, for it was the birth-place of Abraham and so the starting-point of the great religious saga of which the story of Boas and Ruth is but an episode. And since there was no other biblical place-name which would suit his purpose, Hugo made one up. And his stanzas were complete.

If, in the libraries of Heaven, Hugo has access to a copy of the present book (and I do not know whether the publishers intend to send one to that destination) I have a feeling that he may read the above paragraphs with a good deal of merriment and some deprecatory comments on the futility of academic speculation. Of course, things may not have happened that way at all: the process of composition does not follow a clear time-sequence. The final assembly of a stanza does indeed require careful and conscious thought: yet before that final stage the poet must anticipate and discard numerous possibilities, and might often be hard put to say in what order the component parts of his verse had presented themselves and been accepted as 'just right'. My conjectures are, I think, if not historically correct, at least typical of the process by which rime and image, fertilized by imagination, grow into a stanza.

The construction of stanzas such as these requires not only that rimes shall be answered, but that they shall be proposed and answered in a fixed order. The pattern so formed is called a *rime-scheme*, and as we have seen it exercises a considerable influence on the manner in which the poet expresses himself. A rime-scheme is expressed symbolically by the use of lower-case italic letters, the same letter being used for both the proposal and the answer of a rime. The rime-scheme of Hugo's verse would be indicated by the formula *abba*, which means that in each stanza a rime is proposed in the first line and another in the second: this second rime is then immediately answered in the third line, while the answer to the first is postponed until the line following which ends the stanza. Normally a poet will stay with the same rime-scheme throughout his poem, since this makes of each stanza a clearly-felt metrical unit in a chain. He may, however, very occasionally modify his sequence of rimes: in *Booz endormi*, for instance, Hugo introduces some stanzas in which the rimes are answered in a different order. We shall consider the possible effect of this later. Any rime-scheme may, at the poet's discretion, be combined with lines of different length, though any such variation of length will normally occur at regular intervals and so itself form part of the pattern.

The simplest of all rime-schemes is the *couplet*, in which every two consecutive lines propose and answer a new rime. This arrangement, in French, is very often used with the alexandrine, with two significant results, one negative and the other positive. The negative result is that the rimes are often unobtrusive. They are distant from each other, owing to the length of the lines; they occur with a complete regularity which we tend easily to take for granted; and since each is answered in the line following its proposal, the rhythm of anticipation and satisfaction is quite invariable. The couplet is particularly suited in this respect for long sequences of lines, unbroken into stanzas, such as one may have in narrative verse or in drama, in which the overall function of the writing is not too dissimilar from prose, and it would be inappropriate to be too conscious of the verse-form. However, the couplet does also have a positive feature which gives it its own characteristic rhythm, and enables it, when appropriately used, to express poetry of the highest order. We have spoken of the alexandrine as a binary form in which the second hemistich is felt to answer the first. The couplet is an extension of this principle, and involves a conscious balance not only between two hemistichs but between two lines. It is felt as a unit in which the second line answers or amplifies the first. In this way, rime is rhythmically linked with meaning.

French classical tragedy (and some comedy) is written in flowing sequences of alexandrines arranged in couplets, with no metrical pauses (through of course there may be actual pauses between lines and even within a line when speech passes from one character to another). In general, though not invariably, the sentence-arrangement follows the rhythm of the couplet:

219   Tu ne t'attendais pas, sans doute, à ce discou.rs;
           Mais ce n'est point, Arbate, un secret de deux jou.rs.
           Cet amou.r s'est longtemps accru dans le silen.ce.
           Que n'en puis-je à tes yeux marquer la violen.ce,
           Et mes premiers soupi.rs, et mes derniers ennuis!
           Mais, en l'état funeste où nous sommĕs réduits,
           Ce n'est guè.rĕ le temps d'occuper ma mémoi.re
           A rappeler le cou.rs d'une amoureu˙se histoi.re.
           Qu'il te suffi.sĕ donc, pour me justifier,
           Que je vis, que j'aimai la rei˙nĕ le premier [;]

Since sense and metre run closely together, the majority of classical
alexandrines are end-stopped (i.e. have terminal punctuation); but sentences may sometimes end in mid-line, setting up dramatic counter-
rhythms:

220   Non, je n'écoutĕ rien. Me voilà résolu˙e;
           Je veux parti.r. Pourquoi vous montrer à ma vu˙e?
           Pourquoi venir enco.re aigri.r mon désespoi.r?
           N'êtĕs-vous pas content? Je ne veux plus vous voi.r [.]

Since rime by definition consists of a proposal and at least one
answer, normally situated on the line-ending, the couplet may be
considered its embryo form from which all other rime-schemes are
derived. It functions as part of a larger structure. Sequences of riming
couplets—known *as rimes suivies* or *rimes plates*—were a feature not
only of the classical verse of the seventeenth and eighteenth centuries
but also of the work of the Romantics in the nineteenth century. But
just as awareness of the alexandrine itself as a binary form was to some
degree modified and rendered more flexible in this later period, so the
unity of the couplet tended to be sacrificed to freer concepts which
suited, for instance, Hugo's flowing narrative style, in which the sense
would frequently overrun the couplet. Here is an extract from *La
Légende des siècles* in which the couplet has ceased to be a metrical unit,
and the rime has no function other than to reinforce the line-ending.

221   Je songeais, méditant tout bas cettĕ consi˙gne.
           Des jets d'éclai.r mêlés à des plu˙mĕs de cy˙gne,
           Des flammè˙chĕs rayant dans l'om.bre les flocons,
           C'est tout ce que nos yeux pouvaient voi.r. – Attaquons!
           Me dit le sergent. – Qui? dis-je, on ne voit perso˙nne.
           – Mais on entend. Les voix pa˙rlĕnt; le clairon so˙nne,
           Partons, sortons; la mort cra˙chĕ sur nous ici;
           Nous sommĕs sous la bombe et l'obus. – Restons-y.
           J'ajoutai: – C'est sur nous que tom.bĕ la bata.ille.
           Nous sommĕs le pivot de l'action. – Je bâ.ille,
           Dit le sergent. [...]

On the other hand, later poets have explored contrary possib-ilities of development by using the couplet as a self-contained unit. We have already noticed a striking example of this, Verlaine's *Colloque sentimental* (p. 18), in which each couplet encapsulates a fragment of dramatic dialogue. The twentieth-century poet Jean Cocteau demonstrates a very forceful use of the couplet:

222   Sole.il, tu vernis tes chromos,
      tes paniers de fruit, tes animaux.

      Fais-moi le corps tanné, salé;
      fais ma grandĕ douleu.r s'en aller.

      Le nè:grĕ, dont brillĕnt les dents,
      est noi.r deho.rs, ro.sĕ dedans.

      Moi, je suis noir dedans et ro.se
      deho ̇rs, fais la métamorpho.se [.]

The lines are comparatively short—eight syllables—which means that the rimes are quickly answered and therefore prominent. Each gives its character to its own stanza: the effect is light, rather like a dance-movement. Some of the rimes are self-conscious, almost humoristic—*chromos*|*animaux, rose*|*métamorphose*—and the latter is associated with an unexpected enjambement which is a sort of pirouette. The brevity of the stanzas gives great tautness, which Cocteau nurtures by suppressing the expected initial capital of the second line. This does not mean that the pause on the line-ending disappears, but that the mind leaps over it more rapidly. Each couplet has the quality of an aphorism. There is a vivacity about these verses which prevents them from being monotonous. The poet may be sunbathing but the mood is anything but languid. The flexibility of the metre is increased by the variation from line to line of the position in which the internal stress occurs.

We would represent this metre as an *aa bb cc* etc, as distinct from the more usual form of *rimes suivies,* which is *aabbcc* etc. It serves very well to indicate the function of the stanza-pause, which isolates and makes us conscious of the rime-unit. In *Pasteurs et troupeaux* Hugo uses a continuous sequence of *rimes suivies* without metrical break. Let us consider the effect if he had isolated his couplets:

223   Le vallon où je vais tous les jou.rs est charmant,
      Serein, abandonné, seul sous le firmament.

      Plein de ron.cĕs en fleurs, c'est un souri.rĕ tri ̇ste.
      Il vous fait oublier que quelquĕ cho.se exi ̇ste,

Et, sans le bruit des champs remplis de travailleu.rs,
On ne saurait plus là si quelqu'un vit ailleu.rs.

Là, l'ombrĕ fait l'amou.r; l'idy˙llĕ nature˙lle
Rit; le bouvreu.il avec le verdier s'y quere˙lle.

Et la fauvette y met de trave.rs son bonnet;
C'est tantôt l'aubépine et tantôt le genêt;

De noirs granits bourrus, puis des moussĕs rian.tes,
Car Dieu fait un poè.me avec des varian.tes.

It is clear why Hugo did not choose to write his poem in this manner.
The pauses between the couplets fulfil no purpose. They simply
impede progress, and we feel that Hugo is slow in getting to the
point. But when we read the lines as he wrote them (see **265**), the
verse carries the ideas forwards and the mind registers not individual statements but a cumulative development of impressions.

The poet will only use the couplet as an isolated stanza when he
has some specific reason for doing so. In general, the rimes are so
closely placed and so obvious in their effect that they need no
reinforcement, and the rime-unit is too short to enclose anything
other than brief and comparatively simple statements. But for the
lyric poet the unbroken sequence of lines is equally limiting. In this
form his rimes get lost in the onward movement of his material: we
do not pause to savour them and so are largely unaware of their
sensuous appeal. Therefore he will generally prefer longer stanzas,
which give him freedom to develop his thought and imagery and at
the same time set up a rhythmic pattern in which the rime is of
considerable importance. The use of the stanza in lyric verse derives
in the first place from its early association with music. Both songs
and folk-dancing are built out of repeated sequences of movement.
In the song, each stanza is different in content from others, but
follows the same melodic pattern. In dance, of course, the movement is also physical. The earliest lyric verse was by definition
written to be sung to accompaniment if not necessarily by the lyre at
least by some musical instrument. But the division into verses has
long survived the partial divorce between poetry and music. This is
partly because the words themselves have come to be heard more
and more as a form of music in their own right, and also because
whereas narrative may be sustained for an indefinite period, emotion
cannot. Each stanza offers the possibility of developing its own
emotional force and the poem becomes a sequence of imaginative
experiences. In practice, the poet may not avail himself of all the
potential of the stanza-form, and it may sometimes be no more than
a riming-unit; but when he composes he thinks in the rhythm which

his stanza-form imposes, and if his work is good its resources will enhance his expression.

The most common and generally useful of all lyric stanzas is the *quatrain*, which contains four lines and two rimes. It may be (though rarely is) formed by linking together two consecutive couplets, giving the pattern *aabb ccdd* etc, as Vigny does in *Le Cor* or Baudelaire in *Ciel brouillé*. But in this form the rime-scheme and the stanza-form cannot be said to add much to each other. This type of stanza is in fact only a slight rhythmic variation on the sequence of couplets, with the disadvantage that if the couplet is self-contained and strong the stanza is weakened and, in effect, broken into two. As a result the poet usually prefers one or other of two remaining possibilities for the arrangement of his rimes, both of which involve interleaving his couplets. In the one, he alternates his rimes, giving the pattern *abab*. In the other, he encloses one couplet within the other, giving *abba*.

The first of these possibilities—*abab*—is called *rimes croisées* since the rimes cross over each other. The second—*abba*—is called *rimes embrassées* since the outer rime embraces the inner. Both these forms have the advantage that the couplet, being divided, no longer pulls against the stanza form. They produce different mental rhythms. When *rimes croisées* is used the rime is always answered after an interval of one line, and this continues throughout the poem, giving an unchanging rime-scheme interrupted at four-line intervals by a pause. Apart from this pause, the stanza is not self-contained in form, though so far as its content is concerned, it may be as self-contained as the poet chooses. This arrangement is very suitable when the poet wishes to establish a high degree of continuity in this poem while exploiting the advantages of stanza-division. On the other hand, *rimes embrassées* gives each stanza its self-contained mental rhythm. The rime proposed in [1] is not answered until the end of the stanza, and after the intervention of a couplet in [2-3] in which, naturally, the rime is answered more rapidly. The features of *rimes embrassées* are therefore (*a*) rhythmic variation within the stanza, and (*b*) a sense of completeness, since each stanza rounds off a pattern. Owing to its position, the central couplet is rarely self-contained in terms of sense, and so it strengthens rather than weakens the form of the stanza. If the poet chooses to write in *rimes embrassées*, we are likely to be rather more conscious of the sensuous force of his rimes and rhythms than if he uses *rimes croisées*. With the latter, the rime-scheme moves constantly forward as the sense of his words unfolds, whereas the latter offers a movement partly independent of sense, since the last line recalls the first. Whichever form is used, it will be noted that the first two lines of the quatrain follow the same pattern: the first rime is proposed in [1] and the second in [2]. The difference is to be found only in the second half of the stanza. In *rimes croisées* the rimes are answered in the same order and in *rimes embrassées* in inverse order. This has the effect that, owing to the required alternation of rimes, if *rimes croisées* are used each stanza must begin with a rime of the same gender, whereas in *rimes embrassées* the gender of the first rime constantly changes. (This distinction will be discussed in the next chapter.) If we use capital letters to indicate a feminine rime, the possibilities open to the poet in *rimes croisées* are either *aBaB cDcD eFeF* or *AbAb* etc, while *rimes embrassées* gives either *aBBa CddC eFFe* etc or *AbbA cDDc*.

While the theoretical distinction between these two types of quatrain may be perfectly clear, its practical effect is less so, and the student called on to assess the significance of one rime-scheme rather than another in a particular poem will be compelled to use his own judgement to decide whether the poet has made any real use of their potential. What is certain is that the poet will generally continue the same rime-scheme throughout this poem. This is because his mind is working in that rhythm, and also because each stanza is given unity by its rime-scheme just as is a verse of a song by its melody. However, on rare occasions, he may wander from one rime-scheme to another, and the question arises as to whether such a variation has any significance. A case in point is Musset's *Souvenir* in which the first stanza has *rimes embrassées* and the remainder *rimes croisées*, except for the two closing stanzas which revert to the original form. The poem begins:

224	J'espérais bien pleurer, mais je croyais souffri.r	*a*
	En osant te revoi.r, place à jamais sacré ́e,	*b*
	O la plus chè.rĕ tom.be et la plus ignoré ́e	*b*
	Où dorme un souveni.r!	*a*
	Que redoutiez-vous donc de cettĕ solitu ́de,	*c*
	Et pourquoi, mes amis, me preniez-vous la main,	*d*
	Alors qu'unĕ si douce et si vie.ille habitu ́de	*c*
	Me montrait ce chemin [?]	*d*

But does it really matter that the first stanza has the rime-scheme *abba*, and the second *abab*? The fact of a changed rime-scheme does not necessarily oblige us to attribute aesthetic significance to it. It is possible that the poet composed his opening and closing stanzas first and that, for the body of the work, he either found the more complicated rime-scheme difficult to sustain or for some other reason he found himself thinking in an *abab* pattern, which is in fact that of his model, Lamartine's *Le Crucifix*. Hugo's choice of *rimes embrassées* in *Booz endormi* is highly appropriate to the sumptuous quality of Lis lines; but the fact that in two of his stanzas—the tenth and the fifteenth—he changes to *rimes croisées* is less easy to explain. He was a master of rime and metre, and would have had no difficulty in fitting all his twenty-two stanzas into the same rime-scheme, had he thought this necessary. We may say the same of Leconte de Lisle, who in *Le Sommeil du condor* (written without stanza divisions) uses mainly *rimes embrassées*, but twice in the course of this short poem changes to *rimes croisées*. Critics sometimes associate such changes with the meaning of the lines concerned, but personally I rarely find such explanations convincing. In a quatrain, a change in rime-scheme becomes apparent only at the end of the third line, since the order of [1-2] remains the same, and this is therefore not an effective way of enhancing a change of meaning which has occurred two lines previously at the beginning of the stanza or rime-group. For such a change to strike us forcibly it seems to me that the poet would have to modulate from, for instance, quatrains to couplets, which he rarely does. The more probable explanation is that, on rare occasions, lines may present themselves in the poet's mind in such a way as to suggest an irregular rime-scheme, and that he may find such an irregularity perfectly acceptable if it does not too strongly disturb his over-all effect. Few good poets, however, would go as far as Musset, who in his *Nuits* uses *rimes mêlées*, in which rime-schemes are freely intermingled, for this weakens the link between rime and metrical form. However, it can be perfectly effective in free verse, which may use rime and assonance in any combination, or not at all.

It is tempting to seek to demonstrate the different effects of *rimes croisées* and *rimes mêlées* by transposing lines written in one pattern into the other; but the difficulty is that the transposition is likely to read like a distortion of the original and so real comparison is impossible. However, I will make such an attempt. Here are the opening stanzas of Leconte de Lisle's *Épiphanie*:

225   Ellĕ pa˙ssĕ, tranquille, en un rê.vĕ divin,
        Sur le bo.rd du plus frais de tes lacs, ô Norvè.ge!
        Le sang ro.se et subtil qui do.rĕ son col fin
        Est doux comme un rayon de l'au˙bĕ sur la nei.ge.

        Au murmu.re indécis du frêne et du bouleau,
        Dans l'étincellĕment et le cha˙rmĕ de l'heu.re,
        Ellĕ va, reflétée au pâle azu.r de l'eau,
        Qu'un vol silenci:eux de papillons effleu.re.

Quand un sou˙fflĕ furtif glisse en ses cheveux blonds,
Unĕ cen.dre ineffable inon.dĕ son épau˙le;
Et, de leur transparen.ce argentant leurs cils longs,
Ses yeux ont la couleu.r des bellĕs nuits du Pô.le.

Here is a transposition into *rimes embrassées*:

Sur le bo.rd du plus frais de tes lacs, ô Norvè.ge,
Ellĕ pa˙ssĕ, tranquille, en un rê.vĕ divin;
Le sang ro.se et subtil qui do.rĕ son col fin
Est doux comme un rayon de l'au˙bĕ sur la nei.ge.

Dans l'étincellĕment et le cha˙rmĕ de l'heu.re,
Au murmu.re indécis du frêne et du bouleau,
Ellĕ va, reflétée au pâle azu.r de l'eau
Qu'un vol silenci:eux de papillons effleu.re.

Quand un sou˙fflĕ furtif glisse en ses cheveux blonds,
Unĕ cen.dre ineffable inon.dĕ son épau˙le;
Ses yeux ont la couleu.r des bellĕs nuits du Pô.le,
Et, de leur transparen.ce, argen.tĕnt leurs cils longs.

The reader must decide for himself whether I have done any greater violence to the original than the failure to change the gender of the rime in passing from the first to the second stanza. My own conclusion is that in the second the rime-scheme is more striking, but that the difference is hardly such as to give significance to an occasional change from the one rime-scheme to the other.

If the line is shorter, then any variation in the rime-scheme will be more apparent, since proposal and answer recur more rapidly. Here is Gautier using octosyllabics with *rimes croisées*:

226   Carmen est maigre–un trait de bi˙stre
        Ce˙rnĕ son œil de gitana.
        Ses cheveux sont d'un noi.r sini˙stre,
        Sa peau, le dia˙blĕ la tanna.

        Les fe˙mmĕs di.sĕnt qu'elle est lai˙de,
        Mais tous les ho˙mmĕs en sont fous:
        Et l'archĕvè˙quĕ de Tolè˙de
        Chan˙tĕ la messe à ses genoux [;]

Baudelaire uses the same metre in *Le Chat*, with a delicate rhythm and *rimes embrassées*:

227   Dans ma cerve˙llĕ se promè˙ne,
        Ainsi qu'en son appartĕment,
        Un beau chat, fort, doux et charmant.
        Quand il miaule, on l'entend à pei˙ne,

> Tant son tim.bre est ten.dre et discret;
> Mais que sa voix s'apai.se ou gron.de
> Elle est toujours riche et profon.de.
> C'est là son charme et son secret [.]

The pre-eminence of the quatrain among stanzas derives from the fact that it is the simplest and strongest form of interwoven couplets, as forceful as the simple couplet and at the same time ampler and more adaptable. Just as the couplet is the basis of the quatrain, so the quatrain may be the basis of longer stanzas, which involve one at least of the rimes being answered more than once. Baudelaire in *La Chevelure* uses a five-line stanza which is in fact a quatrain of *rimes embrassées* with an extra line added at the beginning, giving the pattern *abaab*. In *Moesta et Errabunda* he uses a quatrain of *rimes croisées* with a fifth line added which echoes the first:

228　　　Commĕ vous êtĕs loin, paradis parfumé,
　　　　　Où sous un clair azu.r tout n'est qu'amou.r et joi˙e,
　　　　　Où tout se que l'on ai.me est di˙gnĕ d'ĕtre aimé,
　　　　　Où dans la volupté pu.rĕ le cœur se noi˙e!
　　　　　Commĕ vous êtĕs loin, paradis parfumé!

The use of a refrain is a familiar feature of lyric poetry. Since in this stanza the final word of [5] is identical with that of [1], it appears to offer an exception to the general rule that a word cannot rime with itself. However, this is not strictly speaking a rime. A refrain may repeat a rime-word already used, but this is not obligatory, and it may not rime at all, at least in the case of songs and ballads. What is essential is that it shall repeat a phrase in such a way as to constitute a rhythmic feature of the stanza. Where whole phrases and lines are repeated in a poem (as in the *pantoum*) the normal representation of the rime-scheme by letters proves inadequate.

The unity of the stanza normally derives from the intermingling of two rimes; but in a long stanza more may be used. Vigny created an interesting seven-lined verse which links together a quatrain of *rimes croisées* and a quatrain of *rimes embrassées*, overlapping in such a way that the fourth line is common to both. This uses three rimes in the pattern *ababccb*, and despite its length possesses a strong sense of unity.

229　　　Nous marcherons ainsi, ne laissant que notre om.bre
　　　　　Sur cettĕ te.rre ingrate où les mo.rts ont passé;
　　　　　Nous nous parlerons d'eux à l'heu.re où tout est som.bre,
　　　　　Où tu te plais à sui.vre un chemin effacé,
　　　　　A rêver, appuyée aux bran.chĕs incertai˙nes,
　　　　　Pleurant, commĕ Diane au bo.rd de ses fontai˙nes,
　　　　　Ton amou.r taciturne et toujou.rs menacé [.]

This stanza is particularly interesting in that it uses an odd number of lines which may be divided in a number of different ways. Here we have a two-line sentence followed by one of five lines, but the arrangement 3:4 or 4:3 is equally possible. In it, one may feel, Vigny has developed the most fluid of the French stanzas.

There is no theoretical limit to the length of a stanza, but in practice it must not be too long or too complex for us to be conscious of it as a rime-pattern repeated throughout the poem. For this pattern to be felt, the rimes must change with each stanza. But to this general principle there are some striking exceptions, in which a rime is carried from one stanza to the next in such a way as to produce a complex counter-rhythm. Such effects demand a high degree of virtuosity on the part of the poet—for the result would otherwise be confusion—and the pleasure of reading verses of this kind is heightened by our awareness of the skill with which the poet manipulates his rimes. He must make us respond to two patterns, one set up by his stanza form and the other by his rime-scheme, which are related but do not coincide.

This is the case with the *terza rima*, an Italian verse-form immortalized by Dante in his *Divine Comedy*. It consists of three-line stanzas in which the middle line rimes with the first and third of the stanza following. Thus each rime is answered twice and re-inforces the stanza form while at the same time overrunning it and so establishing strong continuity. The scheme may be represented as *aba bcb cdc ded* etc. Here is how Gautier uses the form to satirize the gloomy austerity of Spanish monks in a painting by Zurbarán:

230   Deux tein˙tĕs seulĕment, clair livide, ombrĕ noi.re;
       Deux po.sĕs, l'unĕ droite et l'autre à deux genoux,
       A l'artiste ont suffi pour pein.drĕ votre histoi.re.

       Fo˙rmĕ, rayon, couleu.r, rien n'exi˙stĕ pour vous,
       A tout objet réel vous êtĕs insensi˙bles,
       Car le ciel vous eni.vre et la croix vous rend fous,

       Et vous vivez muets, inclinés sur vos bi˙bles,
       Croyant toujou.rs enten.dre aŭx plafonds entr'ouve.rts
       Éclater brusquĕment les trompe˙ttĕs terri˙bles [!]

A poem in this form always ends in a quatrain, which requires an additional isolated line to round off the whole with the pattern *aba b*:

231   Quels rê.vĕs faitĕs-vous? quellĕs sont vos pensé˙es?
       Ne regrettez-vous pas d'avoir usé vos jou.rs
       Entrĕ ces murs étroits, sous ces voû˙tĕs glacés?

       Ce que vous avez fait, le feriez-vous toujou.rs?

But the most familiar verse-form which uses an overrunning rime is the *sonnet*, which also came to France from Italy at the time of the Renaissance. It was used with great skill by French poets of the sixteenth century and, after a period of eclipse, came into favour again in the nineteenth century. Despite its apparently slight form— for it consists of only fourteen lines—it has been the vehicle of some of the finest of verse. Being of fixed length, the poem as a whole forms a single complex rime-pattern composed of stanzas linked by overrunning rimes. The first eight lines, called the *octet*, consist of two quatrains, and the remaining six, the *sestet*, of two tercets: and they may, if the poet so wishes, be written without a break between them, in which case only the rime-scheme establishes their form. A certain amount of freedom is allowed in the arrangement of the rimes. In this respect, it is traditional in books on versification to distinguish between *regular* and *irregular* sonnets, but the distinction has no real significance. What is important in the sonnet is that sense and form should be felt to reinforce each other.

This effect is most strongly felt if the same two rimes run through the quatrains of the octet, and particularly if *rimes embrassées* are used, since this form delineates the quatrains most strongly. Thus the octet will often take the form *abba abba*, though *abab abab* is permissible. Indeed, the poet may change his rime, and use for instance *abba cddc*, though the introduction of the superfluous rime may be felt to weaken the unity of the octet. Other things being equal, we prefer the poet to turn the limitations of the sonnet to advantage, rather than relax them, and a unified rime-scheme in the octet contrasts effectively with the more complex riming of the sestet.

The sestet uses three rimes, spread over two tercets or three-lined stanzas. The first tercet proposes and answers one rime, and also proposes a second which is to be answered in the final tercet, which also introduces and answers a final rime of its own. One of the most frequently used patterns is rather similar to the *terza rima*. The first tercet opens with a couplet, after which comes a line which forms a quatrain when taken with the final tercet. This can give a combination such as *aa/b ccb*, effectively ending in a quatrain of *rimes embrassées*, or *aa/b cbc*, which has the effect of *rimes croisées*. But other arrangements are possible, such as that in which the sonnet ends with a riming couplet. This form, popularized in England on the model of the Shakespearean sonnet, is less often found in French. It is also true to say that the French sonnet tends to respect the relationship between the stanzas and the development of the theme more scrupulously than is the case in English. Traditionally the first stanza states the theme and the second develops it, and each may well be a complete sentence. In the sestet, the poet modifies his approach to the theme, possibly emphasizing a particular aspect of it; and at least in the sixteenth century the closing line was likely to have the quality of an aphorism summing up the whole.

In the sixteenth century, Ronsard and Du Bellay are the two masters of the form whose work the student is most likely to read, and in the nineteenth century Baudelaire, and to a lesser extent Verlaine, who produced a small number of excellent examples. The line most commonly used is the alexandrine, but Baudelaire quite often uses shorter lines. We have already quoted a Baudelairean sonnet (on page 6) and at the end of this book will be found a detailed commentary on another by Ronsard. It is comparatively rare to find a sonnet with lines of varying length, but Baudelaire's *La Musique* demonstrates the possibility of alternating long and short lines:

232   La musi˙quĕ souvent me prend comme unĕ me.r!
            Vers ma pâle étoi.le,
        Sous un plafond de brume ou dans un vaste éthe.r,
            Je mets à la voi.le;

        La poitrine en avant et les poumons gonflés
            Commĕ de la toi.le,
        J'escala˙dĕ le dos des flots amoncelés
            Que la nuit me voi.le;

        Je sens vibrer en moi tou˙tĕs les passions
            D'un vaisseau qui sou˙ffre;
        Le bon vent, la tempête et ses convulsions

            Sur l'imme.sĕ gou˙ffre
        Me be.rcĕnt. D'autrĕs fois, ca˙lmĕ plat, grand miroi.r
            De mon désespoi.r!

The sonnet is the only fixed verse-sequence which has survived into modern French, but there was in the nineteenth century a renewed interest in certain medieval verse-forms such as the *rondeau*, the *virelai* and the *ballade*, which required the poet to make rhythm not merely by combinations of rimes but also by the repetition of whole phrases. This type of composition had been natural in an age which was still strongly aware of the link between poetry and song and dance, for the returning phrase is very much like the culmination of a series of movements which brings the dancers back into the position from which they began, or like the returning theme of a fugue. One of the most pleasing of these effects, to the modern ear, is that of the *rondeau*, a short poem of three stanzas in which the opening line also figures as the final line of the poem, and often as the last line of the middle stanza too. Charles d'Orléans's *Le Temps a laissié son manteau* is one of the best-known examples in the French language. Here is another from the work of the same poet:

233   En regardant ces be˙llĕs fleu.rs
      Que le temps nouveau d'Amours pri˙e,
      Chascunĕ d'ellĕs s'ajoli˙e
      Et fa.rdĕ de plaisans couleu.rs.

      Tant enbasméĕs sont d'odeu.rs
      Qu'il n'est cueu.r qui ne rajeuni˙e
      En regardant ces be˙llĕs fleu.rs

      Les oyseaux deviennĕnt danseu.rs
      Dessuz maintĕ bran.chĕ fleuri˙e
      Et font joyeu.sĕ chanteri˙e
      De contrĕs, deschans et teneu.rs
      En regardant ces be˙llĕs fleu.rs [.]

It will be noted that the same two rimes are used throughout the poem. If we indicate identical lines by adding an apostrophe, the rime-scheme may be shown as *a'bba aba' abbaa'*.

Another verse-form in which the same two rimes run throughout the poem, from stanza to stanza, and effective patterning is introduced by the recurrence of whole lines, changing their position from stanza to stanza in a regular but complex sequence, is the *pantoum*, a form apparently of Malayan origin and introduced into French by Gautier. The example which every student will encounter at some stage of any serious study of French verse is Baudelaire's *Harmonie du soir*:

234   Voici venir les temps où vibrant sur sa ti.ge
      Chaquĕ fleu.r s'évapo.re ainsi qu'un encensoi.r;
      Les sons et les parfums tou˙rnĕnt dans l'air du soi.r;
      Va˙lsĕ mélancolique et langoureux verti.ge!

      Chaquĕ fleu.r s'évapo.re ainsi qu'un encensoi.r;
      Le violon frémit comme un cœu.r qu'on affli.ge;
      Va˙lsĕ mélancolique et langoureux verti.ge!
      Le ciel est triste et beau comme un grand reposoi.r.

      Le violon frémit comme un cœur qu'on affli.ge,
      Un cœur ten.drĕ, qui hait le néant vaste et noi.r!
      Le ciel est triste et beau comme un grand reposoi.r;
      Le soleil s'est noyé dans son sang qui se fi.ge.

      Un cœur ten.drĕ, qui hait le néant vaste et noi.r,
      Du passé lumineux recue˙illĕ tout vesti.ge!
      Le soleil s'est noyé dans son sang qui se fi.ge.
      Ton souveni.r en moi luit comme un ostensoi.r!

Each stanza apart from the first repeats two lines from the stanza immediately preceding it, but changes their position: the second line becomes the first and the last becomes the third. The intention is to create an almost hypnotic and musical effect by sheer repetition with rhythmic variation. The result is powerful, but obviously limited, since the rational content of the poem is overwhelmed by its sound. This is quite different from the normal function of rime and stanza-arrangement, which is to enhance and enrich meaning. What is evoked here is the suggestive quality of sound and rhythm: and we may say the same, for instance, of Mallarmé's *sonnet du Cygne* which rimes throughout on the same vowel-sound and so deliberately sacrifices the delicate contrast of the traditional sonnet form.

In reading Baudelaire's sonnet *La Musique*, we are forcibly reminded that the shape of a stanza or poem is fixed not only by its rime-scheme but also by line-length. More often than not the poet will use the same number of syllables in each line throughout his poem, since this gives the steady and unobtrusive rhythm which generally suits his purpose. If he chooses to vary his line-length, he will always do so in such a way as to form a recognizable pattern (unless, like La Fontaine, he wishes to produce an effect of whimsicality); and the effect of variation will be to make us more conscious of metrical rhythm. In *La Musique*, the poet's unexpected alternation of twelve- and five-syllable lines (unexpected, since when lines are so alternated an easily recognizable relationship such as 12:6 or 12:8 is almost invariably adopted) has obviously been suggested to him by his theme, since both music and the sea suggest mobility. Only the last line is static: we feel the rest to be in constant motion. In *L'Invitation au voyage* Baudelaire uses five-syllable couplets each separated from the next by a seven-syllable line, thus obtaining the extreme lightness of the short line without monotony. Verlaine uses four- and three-syllable lines to similar effect in *Chanson d'automne*. In all such cases, the lyrical quality is paramount: and even when longer lines are used, the poem approximates more closely to a song if, by varying his line-length, the poet makes us more than usually conscious of his metre and hence of his rimes. He may, as Lamartine does in *Le Lac* or Hugo in *Tristesse d'Olympio*, introduce variation of line-length only in certain stanzas, or to a greater extent in certain stanzas: and this will clearly correspond to some change in the emotional tone of the sections concerned.

But if the intermingling of short lines with longer ones produces a light and lyrical effect and avoids monotony, what is the effect of introducing the occasional shorter line into a series of alexandrines? The question needs to be asked because we find from experience that poets are particularly prone to do this when they wish to suggest a certain quality of poignancy. Indeed, if there is such a thing as an elegiac stanza in French, then it is a quatrain consisting of three alexandrines rounded off with a shorter fourth line of six or eight syllables. This is the form which Lamartine uses in *Le Lac*:

> **235** Ainsi, toujours poussés vers de nouveaux riva.ges,
> Dans la nuit éternelle emportés sans retou.r,
> Ne pourrons-nous jamais sur l'océan des â.ges
> Jeter l'an.cre un seul jou.r?
>
> O lac! l'année à peine a fini sa carriè.re
> Et près des flots chéris qu'ellĕ devait revoi.r,
> Regardĕ! je viens seul m'asseoi.r sur cettĕ pie.rre
> Où tu la vis s'asseoi.r [!]

If it be agreed that the final short line not only enhances the lyrical quality of the stanza but also introduces a certain note of sadness (admittedly, only if the meaning of the words justifies this interpretation), can we suggest why this should be so? There are two possible reasons. The first is that the short line suggests incompleteness. It leaves us not dissatisfied but, so far as our metrical expectation is in the question, unsatisfied. There is a clash between the finality of the sense and the apparent lack of finality of the metre, and we are left as it were in mid-air: a situation which has the effect of heightening the emotions. To this we may add a further possible explanation. In our discussion of scansion, we endorsed the view that a short segment of an alexandrine, in reading, tends to be lengthened and a long segment to be correspondingly shortened: that is, stress-units of different length tend towards equalization. Is this not also true of lines? Do we not in fact tend to read a short line more slowly than a long one? The reader will judge for himself (Baudelaire's *L'Invitation au voyage* makes an interesting test case, when read aloud) but my own answer would be in the affirmative. The elegiac stanza, in that case, ends with a *rallentando*, which in itself suggests solemnity. It goes without saying that this tendency— for it is no more than that—should not be exaggerated into a mannerism: but if intelligently used, it can make a significant contribution to the emotional force of the verse. If it be objected that these two explanations are self-contradictory—the first being based on its shortness and the second suggesting that it is not short after all—we must answer that we are dealing with two different concepts of length. Nothing can alter the fact that in terms of syllable-count the last line is short; but speed of reading is a matter of time, not of syllable-count. A line may be read quickly or slowly without this in any way affecting our feeling of its metrical length.

I would suggest that variation in the speed of reading tends to introduce a disturbed quality, and to heighten emotion, in any verse where long lines alternate with shorter ones: always with the proviso, of course, that effects of this kind can only be significant if the sense of the words permits. Verlaine offers a particularly dramatic demonstration of this in his poem which begins:

236   Je ne sais pourquoi
         Mon esprit ame.r
    D'une aile inquiète et fo ˙llĕ vo ˙lĕ sur la me.r.
         Tout ce qui m'est che.r
         D'unĕ ai ˙lĕ d'effroi
    Mon amou.r le couve au ras des flots. Pourquoi, pourquoi [?]

I should personally find it quite impossible to resist the temptation to increase the speed of reading when speaking the long lines. And it is, I think, with this effect in mind that Lamartine changes his metre in *Le Lac* when his elegiac tone gives place to disturbed passion:

237   O temps, suspends ton vol! et vous, heu.rĕs propi ˙ces,
             Suspendez votre cou.rs!
         Laissez-nous savourer les rapi ˙dĕs déli ˙ces
             Des plus beaux de nos jou.rs!

         Assez de malheureux ici-bas vous implo.rent:
             Coulez, coulez pour eux;
         Prenez avec leurs jou.rs les soins qui les dévo.rent,
             Oubli:ez les heureux [.]

What is involved in such cases is clearly not just an intensification of lyrical power. The interleaving of long and short lines offers a powerful vehicle for passionate and often frustrated emotion because, without sacrificing regularity, it strongly emphasizes variation and movement. It varies both speed and metre. Hugo uses it to powerful effect in *Paroles sur la dune*. Baudelaire, in *L'Irréparable*, alternates long and short lines to produce a restless emotional tone and a song-like lyricism. In this poem, the long line concludes the stanza, so we do not have the poignant effect characteristic of the short-line ending; instead, he mutes his ending by adding a metrically superfluous line, a kind of approximate refrain. If we compare this rhythm with the same poet's *Spleen* poems—so similar in theme— we notice not only the difference in lyrical quality but also the sense of agitation, of varying tension, produced by the alternation of the lines, which is in marked contrast with the sustained despair which the poet's uniform lines express in these other poems.

238   Pouvons-nous étouffer le vieux, le long Remo.rds,
         Qui vit, s'agite et se torti˙lle,
    Et se nourrit de nous commĕ le ve.r des mo.rts,
         Commĕ du chê˙nĕ la cheni˙lle?
    Pouvons-nous étouffer l'implaca˙blĕ Remo.rds [?]

In *Paroles sur la dune* Hugo uses quatrains which alternate twelve- and eight-syllable lines. The effect is both disturbed and lyrical.

239   Où donc s'en sont allés mes jou.rs évanou:is?
         Est-il quelqu'un qui me connai˙sse?
    Ai-je encore quelquĕ cho.se en mes yeux éblou:is
         De la clarté de ma jeune˙sse?

    Tout s'est-il envolé? Je suis seul, je suis las;
         J'appe˙llĕ sans qu'on me répon.de;
    O vents! ô flots! ne suis-je aussi un souffle, hélas!
         Hélas! ne suis-je aussi qu'une on.de?

    Ne verrai-je plus rien de tout ce que j'aimais?
         Au dedans de moi le soir tom.be.
    O te.rrĕ, dont la brume effa˙cĕ les sommets,
         Suis-je le spectre, et toi la tom.be [?]

The fact that the poem is written in stanzas is important. After each one, the rhetorical question is answered by silence, a pause which reinforces the impact of the stanza on the mind and imagination. These recurring silences make reflection possible. And they also serve to set off each stanza as a margin and a frame serve to set off a picture.

André Chénier, in his *Iambe XI*, uses the same metre and rime-scheme but without the stanza divisions. The reflective, lulling quality is lost. In its place we have a cumulative effect, a torrent of words, and a powerful sustained emotion which moves ceaselessly forwards. The emotion in this case is anger, and the alternate expansion and contraction of the lines expresses this by disturbing speed and tension. But the rhythm is still lyrical. This is indignation transformed into beauty. There is nothing incongruous in the fact that this violent protest against the Revolutionary Terror which destroyed the poet should possess an unexpected elegance, for the poem represents the triumph of a civilized mind over mindless brutality. There is no introspection, no pathos: in his closing lines it is not we whom the poet asks to weep for him, but Virtue herself, violated by his death. The fury is sustained, disciplined, carved for ever in words more lasting than any monument. The lyrical rhythm of the alternating lines makes their rhetoric more moving than it would have been in a uniform metre.

240   Nul ne restĕrait donc pour attendri.r l'histoi.re
         Sur tant de ju˙stĕs massacrés!
     Pour consoler leurs fils, leurs veu.vĕs, leur mémoi.re!
         Pour que les brigands abhorrés
     Frémi˙ssĕnt aux portraits noi.rs de leur ressemblan.ce!
         Pour descen.drĕ jusqu'aux enfe.rs
     Nou:er le triplĕ fouet, le fouet de la vengean.ce
         Déjà levé sur ces perve.rs!
     Pour cracher sur leurs noms, pour chanter leur suppli˙ce!
         Allons, étou˙ffĕ tes clameu.rs;
     Souffre, ô cœur gros de haine, affamé de justi˙ce,
         Toi, vertu, pleu.rĕ si je meu.rs [.]

The arrangement of the lines within a poem, in terms of their rime-scheme, relative length, and distribution in stanzas, is therefore a feature of much greater significance than is commonly realized, and deserves our careful attention. Certainly, not all the features we have discussed will be of importance in the case of every poem. But some of them will be. We began this chapter by stressing that a poet does not first of all decide to write on a subject and then sit down to think what to say. Whatever thought, emotion, or incident may start the creative process, the poem first assumes tangible form as fragments of language possessing both meaning and rhythm, and also, in all the cases we have considered, rudimentary rime. On this material the poet works. But he is unlikely consciously to choose his metre and stanza form: these will to some extent at least be chosen for him by the words, images, and accompanying emotion which present themselves to his mind. The stanza form is from the beginning not merely convention (although of course it will contain a degree of conventionality: rimes will be introduced now and again just because they have to be there in the finished article) but a necessary part of the substance of the poem. It is for this reason that, in preparing to read a poem, we should give some thought to these features, and bring out in our rendering those which make a positive contribution to its meaning.

Chapter Six
THE RULES OF RIME

WE HAVE all been familiar with rime since infancy. When we speak
of 'nursery rimes' we are in fact referring to verses, rime being only
one of their characteristics, and the expression serves to remind us
that in the popular imagination the essential feature of verse is that
it rimes. Even today one would find, among those who do not read
verse, a significant number, perhaps a majority, who would assume
that rime is a necessary feature of verse and the one by which it is
recognized. It is so much a part of our awareness of language that no
one, not even the least linguistically-minded, can fail to recognize it
when it occurs, and when we first make the acquaintance of French
verse it presents us with none of the difficulties and snares of metre.
Indeed, if we find ourselves unable to respond mentally to syllable-
count, it is by the occurrence of a rime-word that we recognize the
line as a metrical unit. It is a characteristic of rime that it falls in
stressed positions at fixed intervals. In contemporary verse it may
well not occur at all, since irregular phrasing has largely replaced
isometric lines, and the need for the regular beat contributed by
rime no longer exists; but it remains an integral part of traditional
verse and almost every line which we have so far had occasion to
quote has contained a rime-word. Since we are so familiar with the
phenomenon of rime, we may perhaps assume that it functions in
French in just the same way as in English, and that there is very little
to be said about it. But this is not the case. In fact, although it is
certainly true that we can recognize French rime when we hear it
without much specialized knowledge, we do require such knowledge
if we are to respond to it as does the French reader. Rather more
than most features of verse rime is governed by rules, many of which
are purely conventional; and though these may be the concern of the
poet rather than the reader, the latter is unlikely to enjoy the sound
of rimes fully unless he has some knowledge of them.

The manner in which rime works is basically similar in both
French and English. The poet places at the end of one line a word or
words which constitute, in my terminology, the *proposal* of a rime:
this creates in the reader a certain subdued anticipation which is
only satisfied when, in a corresponding position at the end of a

later line, the *answer* is heard. This answer resembles the proposal in having an identical final vowel and, if that vowel is followed by a consonant, that consonant must be identical too. If there are other phonemes in common, the rime is strengthened. This similarity is (with an exception which we shall discuss later) limited entirely to *heard* sound, and is unaffected by differences of spelling. And it is effective only if the two rime-words are unrelated in meaning. A word cannot rime with itself. In French theory, the maximum degree of phonetic resemblance produces the 'richest' rime: but this sensuous similarity should be accompanied by a difference of meaning and, if possible, grammatical function. Thus rime appeals both to the senses and to the intellect. For this reason, we cannot really appreciate it when we hear it in verse of a language which we do not understand. In such a case, all we hear is the repetition of sound. But when the poet proposes a rime in a language we do understand, our mind is prepared for an answer which will not be grammatically related to the proposal. If the answer is false—i.e. does not match the proposal phonetically—we feel let down; and we would feel the same if the answer and the proposal were not sufficiently dissimilar in meaning. Riming, in even the most serious verse, has all the characteristics of a game, and as is the case with all serious games we do not expect it to be too easy. The rimes fly to and fro like the ball on a ping-pong table, and we expect each rime-word to be skilfully returned. The rules of the game are in fact rather more difficult in French than they are in English, and one must know them in order to appreciate the skill of the player. This does not mean that in reading great verse our mind will be much preoccupied with assessing the quality of the rime. But it does mean that we should be sufficiently familiar with the technique of riming to feel its effect as if by instinct, so that the pleasure resulting from a skilful answer to a rime becomes part of our experience of a poem.

Rime plays a more important part in French verse than it does in English. For one thing, it is an obligatory feature of regular, or isometric, verse. French has no equivalent to English blank verse, in which the lines do not rime at all; or to that very popular English stanza form in which only two of the four lines rime, the first and third being 'blank'. The French quatrain contains two rimes, each with two rime-words. The reason for the insistence on rime is that, without it, the terminal stress of the line is not felt to be clearly enough marked: French lacks the tonic accent which falls on individual words in English and so beats out a clear metrical pattern, and the stresses it does possess are not particularly forceful. Even Verlaine, who experimented extensively with modifications of rime, believed that it could not be sacrificed because without it the French language was 'sourd à l'accent'. But in the twentieth century poets have quite often abandoned rime, a tendency encouraged by the development of free verse expressed in cadenced prose. When there is no regular recurring stress to run with or against the natural rhythm of the words rime becomes largely superfluous.

The importance which the French mind attaches to rime in regular verse is apparent in that the reader is conscious not only of the fact of phonetic correspondence within a rime but also of the degree of that correspondence. The greater the number of repeated phonemes, the stronger the rime. There is no real equivalent to this awareness in the field of English prosody, and the student therefore has to acquire it, just as he must acquire sensitivity to French metrical rhythm. An English rime is simply a rime, and unless it is either faulty or, for one reason or another, self-conscious and possibly humorous, we do not distinguish between one rime and another. French prosody takes account of the *quality* of a rime.

The basis of rime lies in the repetition of a vowel, but this by itself is not sufficient. Certainly this effect sometimes takes the place of rime, but the term used for it is *assonance*. We hear it in the first stanza of the poem by Henri de Régnier which we quoted early in this book:

241   Un petit roseau m'a suffi
        Pour fairĕ frémi.r l'herbĕ haute
        Et tout le pré
        Et les doux saules
        Et le ruisseau qui chante aussi [;]

In these lines the words *haute*, *saules* and *aussi* do not rime, but they (and for that matter *'roseau'*, *'ruisseau'*) all contain the vowel [ó] and this produces assonance. In the same way combinations such as *rite/rime*, *mètre/terre*, *entendre/chante* are assonant. They fail to qualify as rimes because in each case the stressed vowel is followed by one or more non-identical phonemes. Rime requires that the final phoneme must be identical, and if that phoneme is a consonant, the vowel which precedes it must also be identical. If the final phoneme is a vowel, it is sufficient by itself to produce a true rime. Thus *sceau* and *l'eau*, occurring on the line-ending, produce not an assonance but a *rime faible* or *rime pauvre*. The adjectives used to describe it indicate clearly enough that this type of rime is regarded as satisfying only the minimal requirements. It provides just enough similarity of sound for us to feel that the proposal of the rime has been adequately answered, and no more. However, to the English-speaking reader such a feeling may not come spontaneously. Since in English verse the words *so* and *lo!* form quite a strong rime, his natural tendency will be to hear *sceau* and *l'eau* as doing the same; but this is not the way in which the French ear hears them. The weak rime is a perfectly valid one, but lacks sensuous appeal. Words which on the line-ending produce weak rimes are, for instance, *tu/nu, vous/fous, son/bon, vie/nie, tombeaux/sanglots, au dessus/attendus*. As always in the case of rime, we are concerned with sound, not with spelling. The *s* of *vous* and *fous* is silent and does not contribute to the richness of the rime: nor does the *e* of *vie* and *nie*. There is no similarity of spelling between *tombeaux* and *sanglots*, but the final sounded vowel is identical and it is this which constitutes the rime. We shall see in due course that unsounded final vowels and consonants do affect the validity of the rime, but they never override the principle that rime is based on sound, and so for the moment we shall ignore them. It must also be borne in mind that the single vowel which produces a weak rime may be, and often is, represented in French orthography by two or more letters, but this again does not affect its quality as a rime. The riming is weak in Gautier's stanza

242   Fais les sirè˙nĕs bleu˙es,
        Tordant de cent façons
           Leurs queu˙es,
        Les mo˙nstrĕs des blasons [;]

since, despite the number of letters the rime-words have in common, the sounds they represent are [blœ̈/kœ̈] and [fá sò/blá zò], in which only the final vowel is identical. We shall, however, have more to say about this second rime.

The standard French rime is called *rime suffisante* and it involves two phonemes on the line-ending. One of these must be the terminal vowel; the other must be the sounded consonant that follows it if there is one, for if this was not identical there would be no rime. Examples of this form of sufficient rime are *vide/ride, choses/roses, fils/lis*. The consonant [r], which English-speaking readers sometimes overlook because in English it is silent in a terminal position, is in French very strongly pronounced and so must be taken into account. It often ends a sufficient rime, as in the combinations *fleur/sœur, sur/pur, cor/d'or, tir/souffrir*. When the terminal vowel is not followed by a sounded consonant, then sufficient rime requires that the preceding consonant, if there is one, shall be identical. This consonant is called the *consonne d'appui*, and its use produces what is felt to be the most satisfactory form of sufficient rime, since it causes the whole of the final syllable to correspond. Thus *ami/endormi, embrasés/baisers, tombeau/flambeau* form sufficient rimes in this class. The following stanza demonstrates the use of the *consonne d'appui*:

243   Le crépuscule ami s'endo.rt dans la vallé ̓e,
Sur l'he.rbĕ d'émĕraude et sur l'o.r du gazon,
Sous les timi ̓dĕs joncs de la sou.rce isolé ̓e
Et sous le bois rêveu.r qui trem.ble à l'horizon [,]

with which we may compare

244   Est-il possi ̓blĕ, – le fût-il –
Ce fier exil, ce triste exil?

Mon â.mĕ dit à mon cœu.r: Sai ̓s-je
Moi-mê ̓mĕ, que nous veut ce piè.ge [?]

in which the riming is sufficient but without the *consonne d'appui*.
(In the last couplet it will be noted that two words are used to
propose the rime, which is between 'Sais-je' [sè.j] and 'piège'
[pўè.j].) A third type of sufficient rime is possible in which the
terminal vowel is preceded not by a *consonne d'appui* but by another
vowel. We hear this in the riming of [re mü é] with [nü é] in

245   Je regarde, au dessus du mont et du vallon,
Et des me.rs sans fin remu:é ̓es,
S'envoler, sous le bec du vautou.r aquilon,
Toutĕ la toison des nu:é ̓es [;]

In this category one would include rimes formed with semi-consonant
+ vowel, such as *pieds/oubliez* [pўé/ú blўé], *sien/lien* [sўё/lё],
luit/nuit [lŭi/nŭi], *loi/foi* [lwá/fwá], *oui/enfoui* [ŭi/à fŭi]. As we
saw in a previous chapter, these semi-consonants may often be
treated as full consonants, and only the scansion of a particular line
will give guidance on the matter. Sufficient rimes may sometimes be
found in which, in either the proposal or the answer, a full vowel is
matched against its equivalent semi-consonantal form. Thus Musset
in *Souvenir* rimes *oubliez* [ú blí é] with *pié* [pўé], counting the first
word as three syllables, the second as one; and Baudelaire, in *Le
Cygne*, rimes *cieux* [sўœ] with *silencieux* [si là sí œ]. Of the semi-
consonants, only [ĭ] or *yod* can occur after the terminal vowel, and
in this position it can contribute to a sufficient rime, as in *réveil/soleil*
[ré vèў/sò lèў] or *taille/faille* [tà ў/fà ў].

In any of these forms, *rime suffisante* is satisfying to the French
ear, both in reinforcing the line-ending and in sensuous effect. The
poet has skilfully fulfilled the tacit undertaking he gave in proposing
his rime; the ball has been firmly lobbed over the net and the point
scored without ostentation. But if the poet fulfils the requirements
of sufficient rime and in so doing extends the sound correspondence
still further by including more identical sounds than the two required,

the result is termed *rime riche*. We are, of course, still thinking strictly in terms of sound. The fact that some phonemes—*ch, th, ll* for instance —are written with more than one letter does not affect the richness of the rime. *Penchants* forms a sufficient, not a rich, rime with *champs*, as they have two sounds in common [ʧɑ̀]; and *rive* forms a sufficient rime with *pensive* since the final *e* is ignored. Rich rime occurs when the stressed terminal vowel is preceded by a *consonne d'appui* and followed by another consonant, as when *correspondances* rimes with *cadences*, the common elements being [dà.s], *tonnerre* with *lunaire* [nè.r], *des îles* with *exiles* [zí.l], *puce* with *capuce* [pü.s], *frère* with *contraire* [rè.r]. If no consonant follows the stressed vowel, the rime may be enriched by including the vowel or consonant which precedes the *consonne d'appui*: thus *maison* constitutes a rich rime with *raison*, having in common [è zò], *chemin* with *demain* [e mě], *tourment* with *charmant* [rmà]. A rich rime may also use a single consonant with two vowels: *plié* riming with *oublié* [lí é] or *paria* with *s'écria* [ri á]. The similarity may be carried still further with effects such as the riming of *pâture* with *nature* [a tü.r] or *navrantes* with *enivrantes* [vrà.t].

There is no standard term to describe riming of greater richness than the minimum requirement for rich rime; but it is possible, though exceptional, for four or more elements to correspond. The effect may be sumptuously musical, as in Racine's

246   Arianĕ, ma sœu.r, de quel amou.r blessé ˙e,
Vous mourû ˙těs aux bo.rds où vous fû ˙těs laissé ˙s [ ]

where the four phonemes [-lè sé] produce a very strong correspondence of sound. A rime such as this, or the [á kà.t] correspondence of Banville's

247   Qu'autour du va.sě pu.r, trop beau pour la Bacchan.te,
La vervei ˙ně mêlée à des fleu.rs d'acan.the
Fleurisse ...

is sensuous in its effect: we are conscious of the actual sounds used in the rime, not merely of the fact that they match. We may describe it as *abundant*, or *sumptuous*. When the effect is deliberately startling or humoristic, ironical adjectives such as *acrobatic* or *millionaire* are appropriate, since we are conscious of excessive richness and verbal agility. Sometimes such riming can be extremely skilful without being sensuously strong, as Mallarmé demonstrates:

248   Gloi.rĕ du long dési.r, Idé ˙es
Tout en moi s'exaltait de voi.r
La fami.llĕ des iridé ˙es
Surgi.r à ce nouveau devoi.r [,].

In this stanza, *désir, Idées* is perfectly matched by *des iridées*, giving an eight-element correspondence; while *de voir* is similarly answered by *devoir*, repeating six elements. This may be described as a *punning* or *self-conscious* rime. This last example draws attention to the fact that riming is not limited to single rime-word, but takes in all elements on the line-ending which are common to both proposal and answer. When Baudelaire writes:

249   ... Nous avons vu des aˑstres
           Et des flots; nous avons vu des saˑblĕs aussi;
           Et, malgré bien des chocs et d'imprévus désaˑstres,
           Nous nous sommĕs souvent ennuyés, comme ici [.]

he is matching *vu des astres* in [1] against *d'impré-vus désastres* in [3]—an eight-element correspondence of which the first term involves three words, the second two. In lines we quoted earlier from Gautier,

250   Et moi, je regardais toujou.rs, ne songeant pas
           Que la nuit étoilée arrivait à grands pas [.]

the rime is in fact rich, since it takes in the second syllable of *songeant* answered by *grands*. The rime between *amer* and *la mer*, which proved a reliable stand-by for nineteenth-century poets, takes in both syllables, and in the case of

251   ... et que l'âˑ prĕ rafaˑle
           Disperse à tous les vents avec son souffle ame.r
           La laiˑnĕ des moutons siniˑstrĕs de la me.r [.]

it also includes the [l] of 'souffle' which gives us [lá mè.r] in both proposal and answer. In *Booz endormi* Hugo rimes *dans son aire* with *sa place ordinaire*, the common element being [-nèr], and *économe* with *jeune homme*, producing a rich rime on [-nòm]. This means of reinforcing the rime by taking a *consonne d'appui* from the word preceding the rime-word can change an apparently weak rime into a sufficient one, an effect heard in Musset's stanza

252   C'était, dans la nuit bruˑne,
           Sur le clocher jauni,
              La luˑne,
           Comme un point sur un i [.]

where the rime is on [-ni], and in Verlaine's *Mon rêve familier* where the poet, riming *exila* with *elle a*, expects us to hear the answer as [lá] which gives two elements in common where the eye might expect only one.

Before leaving this aspect of riming, the reader must be warned that although there is universal agreement on the facts and terminology which have been set out here, one does find a certain amount of inconsistency in the way in which the terminology is applied to the facts. This does not affect the appreciation of verse, and involves only theoretical distinctions. Even so, some mention must be made of the differences in usage which the reader is liable to find in books on French prosody. The main ones are as follows:

(*a*) The weak rime, having only one vowel in common between proposal and answer, is sometimes described as an *assonance*. It has been suggested above that this usage is unsatisfactory, since the only assonance which can form a weak rime is one which conforms to the basic rules of rime (some of which we have still to discuss). Thus *ville* and *riche* assonate but do not rime, and the same is true, for reasons shortly to be considered, of *beaux* and *sot*. Other theorists take the more logical view that since a weak rime is clearly a rime, it must be *sufficient*, and anything more than this must be *rich*. However, both these interpretations lead to a less adequate terminology than the one described here, and so neither is to be recommended.

(*b*) Some theorists hold that no rime can be considered rich if it does not include the *consonne d'appui*. According to this view, consonants following the stressed vowel cannot enrich the rime: they must of necessity be identical, since without this there is no rime, and so they are not felt to contribute anything to raise the rime above minimal requirements. This means that *cendre/fendre* [-à.dr] is heard merely as a sufficient rime; and the same would be true of *foudre/poudre*, *ombre/sombre*, *table/sable* etc. Only when the *consonne d'appui* is identical does the possibility of a rich rime arise. What is involved here is something more than a difference of definition: it is a question of the degree of satisfaction to be derived by the French ear from a correspondence in which an important element is lacking. This is not a matter on which the foreign reader of French verse can have any valid opinion. What is clear is that we do hear the correspondence of the terminal consonants, and this must contribute to the sensuous effect of the rime. It does not much matter what we call the rime so long as we recognize the effect and are consistent in our terminology.

We pass now to a feature of French rime which the theory of prosody does not recognize at all, but to which our empirical approach to the sound of French verse compels us to give attention. The classification of rimes as weak, sufficient, or rich adequately describes their impact on us in the majority of cases. But there are other cases in which the effect of rime is strengthened by its association with phonetic effects which do not technically form part of it. This can occur, for instance, when the *consonne d'appui* of proposal and answer is not identical and yet creates a certain feeling of equivalence. Thus we find Baudelaire, in one of his *Spleen* poems, riming *traînées* with *araignées*, an effect which we must describe as a weak rime if we apply the rules of rime rigidly, since the only terminal phonemes common to both is the final [é]. The *consonne d'appui* in the proposal is a dental [n] and in the answer is a palatal [n] which causes the interpolation of a *yod* sound. Once the chain of identical sound, running back from the end of the line, is broken, any earlier elements are considered as lying outside the rime. Yet the fact remains that to describe this rime as weak would be unrealistic: we do in fact hear a correspondence in [rè né] even though the two *n*'s are not identical. Again, in *Le Cygne* Baudelaire very frequently matches [l] with [r], and the question arises as to whether these sounds, when they constitute the *consonne d'appui*, are not felt to be equivalent even though not identical. If the effect had occurred once we might have been justified in saying that the *consonne d'appui* did not form part of the rime: but repeated as it is, we are less sure. To describe *mélancolie* and *allegorie* as a weak rime, having only the final [í] in common, would again be unrealistic, though technically correct. In practice, I think we hear a correspondence between [kò lí] and [gò rí]. We can explain this by saying that [k] is the voiceless form of [g] and the liquid [l] is often closely associated with the vibrant [r]. If we accept that non-identical but similar consonants may correspond in a rime, then we will recognize that it is equally unrealistic to describe Gautier's riming of *façons* with *blazons* as weak, since [s] is the voiceless form of [z] and the actual correspondence that we hear is between [-á sò] and [-á zò]. In the same poem he rimes *cisèle* with *se scelle*, giving the correspondence [s-zè.l/s-sè.l], and again *raison* with *frisson* [r-zò/r-sò]. In the case of the riming of *cieux* [sy̆œ́] with *silencieux* [si là si œ́] we recognize another type of approximate equivalence, in this case between the semi-consonant [y̆] and the vowel [i].

I shall call rimes such as these *amplified*. All such rimes must be valid according to the generally accepted criteria: e.g. *riche* cannot rime with *érige* even though [ʧ] is the voiceless form of [j]; *rose* cannot rime with *chausse* nor *sonne* with *cogne*, because in these cases the non-identical consonant occurs in a position which invalidates the rime. Such effects would be mid-way between assonance and rime. An amplified rime is one which does not violate the traditional requirements but which offers a degree of correspondence over and above that which can be accounted for in terms of those requirements. If we describe *traînées / araignées* as an amplified rime we mean that, although technically it is weak, its effect is much richer than such an interpretation would suggest. The examples we have quoted suggest a certain equivalence between non-identical but related phonemes in the position of *consonne d'appui*. But there are also cases in which the interpolation of a completely dissimilar phoneme does not much damage the opulence of a rime. Here are some examples of amplified rimes, culled from a variety of poets, each of which contains a dissimilar phoneme (represented by a hyphen) which does not disrupt the rime:

détordre / désordre	[dé-ò ˙ rdr]
formé / fermé	[f-rmé]
confondus / fendus	[f- dü]
arome / atome	[á-ò ˙ m]
fanal / fatal	[fá-àl]
renaît / reconnaît	[rĕ-nè]
appétit / est petit	[péti / é p-ti]
sommeil / soleil	[sò-è.y̆]
déplace / n'est lasse	[é-lá ˙ s]
étrange / dérange	[é -rà.j]
étude / élude	[é-ü ˙ d]
dorades / dérades	[d-rà ˙ d]
profond / plafond	[p--fò]
étendu / répandu	[é-à dü]
ses restes / célestes	[sé-è ˙ st]
dormi / demi	[d-mi]
quelqu'un est / le connaît	[k-lk-né / l-k-né]
nuit d'automne / bruit monotone	[ŭi ó tò ˙ n / ŭi ò tò ˙ n]
visqueux / visibles qu'eux	[vis kœ́ / viz- kœ́]
Syracuse / s'accuse	[s-á kü.z]
donnerai / anneau doré	[dòn-ré / - nó dó ré]
odieux / aux doux yeux	[ò dy̆œ́ / ó d- y̆œ́]
ses fers / soufferts	[s-fĕ.r]
luisants / les ans	[l-zà]
vers Harfleur / bruyère en fleur	[èr - flœ̀.r]
assassine / bassĕ cuisine	[á sá si ˙ n / ás - zi ˙ n]

In some cases, we may say that the rime is amplified by phonetic patterning. We have already quoted Baudelaire's riming of *cieux* with *silencieux*, which is technically weak but in fact rich since we regard the *consonne d'appui* as equivalent even though in the proposal it is a semi-consonant and in the answer it is a vowel. But the actual amplification, when this rime occurs in *Le Cygne*, is stronger than this. The proposal takes the form of '... à l'heure où sous les cieux' which is answered two lines later by 'dans l'air silencieux'. In both *sous les cieux* and *silencieux* we hear the same consonantal sequence: [s l s], following an [l r] correspondence heard between *l'heure* and *l'air*. We may note a similar free association of sound between the rimes of [1] and [3] in

253   Des baisers et des frissons d'ai˙les
        Sur les dô.měs aux bou˙lěs d'o.r,
        Et les molécu˙lěs fide˙les
        Se che.rchěnt et s'ai˙měnt enco.r [.]

The rime between *d'ailes* and *fidèles* is in any case rich [-dè.l], but is further amplified by an association between the 'fi-' of *fidèles* and the corresponding sounds in *frissons*. A similar effect is heard in

254   Et, parmi sa pâleu.r, écla˙te
        Uně bouche aux ri˙rěs vainqueu.rs;
        Piment rou.gě, fleur écarla˙te,
        Qui prend sa pourpre au sang des cœu.rs [.]

The first rime is clearly amplified, and we may represent the common elements as [é k-lá˙t]. But in fact the rime goes further back into the line than this, for we also hear the correspondence of *pâleur* and *fleur*, giving us the sequence [lœr é k-lát], a very sumptuous example of reinforcement. Nor does this quite exhaust the effect, since the [p-rmi] of *parmi* is echoed in the [pim r] of *piment rouge*.

In Lamartine's lines

255   Enfin un sol sans om.bre, et des cieux sans couleu.r,
        Et des vallons sans on.de!—et c'est là qu'est mon cœu.r [!]

the rime is sufficient. But it is supported by a similar phonetic pattern in both proposal and answer. In the proposal we have

        … cieux sans couleu.r [,]
          s   s   k   l

and in the answer:

        … c'est là qu'est mon cœu.r [!]
          s   l k   k

This does not enrich the line or add to it in the way amplified rime does, but it strengthens the correspondence between proposal and answer and so makes some contribution to our aesthetic satisfaction. Rime is a specific and strictly controlled application of the poet's tendency to think in phonetic clusters, and it is not surprising that he occasionally allows controlled effects to be enhanced by free ones.

The proposal of a rime creates in us a certain expectation of an answer, and if the rime is good we derive satisfaction from the poet's skill. The difficulty of riming is an important part of its appeal: we derive no satisfaction from facile and obvious rimes, nor from invalid rimes which suggest incompetence on the poet's part. We may respond with greater pleasure to rich riming than to its weak equivalent because it demonstrates greater verbal dexterity. In so far as this is all that is involved, the precise nature of the phonemes is of no importance; we are concerned only with the number of them which are effectively matched between proposal and answer. But if the riming is rich, aesthetic factors of a less calculable nature become involved, for we respond sensuously to the sounds themselves. In this regard we may make some distinction between rich and amplified rime. Since reinforced rime does not conform to the rules of prosody, we are less likely to regard it as a demonstration of verbal agility: all that is involved is an augmentation of the sensuous power of the sounds. From this it follows that the value different poets and periods set upon rich or amplified rime will depend on how sensuous or sumptuous they wish their verse to be, and the use of rich rime and of phonetic patterning will go together. The medieval *chanson de geste* did not use rime at all—assonance was quite sufficient to reinforce the stress of the lines; for these served simply to narrate adventures, and such aesthetic appeal as they had derived from the chant in which they were delivered and the musical phrases which accompanied them. In the seventeenth century rime was obligatory and governed by strict rules: but the verse of classical tragedy rarely sought sumptuous sensuous effects, and certainly it was no part of the dramatist's function to draw attention to his own verbal dexterity. Hence riming is modest and on the whole has little intrinsic interest: it is a form of metrical punctuation, a gesture of polite conformity to convention like taking one's hat off to a lady. 'La rime est une esclave et ne doit qu'obéir,' declares the theorist Boileau. But in the previous century lyric poets had awakened to the sensuous delights of language, and had delighted in rich and often self-conscious riming. Ronsard's dictum, 'Que la rime soit toujours résonnante, et d'un son entier et parfait' made it clear that in lyrical verse rime had a function to fulfil which went far beyond the marking of metre and the satisfying of convention. It was a source of aesthetic delight. Some sixteenth-century poets, the *rhétoriqueurs*, took pleasure in verbal acrobatics which modern taste finds excessive, and against which the more sober theory and practice of classicism was to some extent a reaction. The cult of lyricism among nineteenth-century Romantics naturally encouraged an interest in the melodious qualities of good riming, and Hugo's virtuosity set a high standard which influenced the Parnassians and Symbolists who followed him. Their feeling for poetry as a craft and ultimately as a semi-mystical activity led them to think of rime not merely as a source of sensuous pleasure but also as an aesthetic and imaginative discipline; and, indeed, as an inspiration. In lines that we have already quoted (page 7), Baudelaire makes it clear that for him rime is no docile slave but a source of inspiration; in his struggle to yoke words together according to chance associations of sound, he brings together new ideas and images. But rich riming, while it offers a stimulating challenge, can also be restrictive in that the number of such rimes is limited. Verlaine sought to develop the sensuous qualities of riming while lessening its rigidity, and more recent poets have responded each in his own way to the love–hate relationship which they felt for this medium which both restricts and stimulates. Many have abandoned both rime and regular metre. The function of rime, and the value attributed to rich riming, is therefore not a constant feature of verse, but one which can be assessed only in the context of the individual poet's work and that of his age. Such matters lie largely outside the scope of this book, but need to be mentioned in order to dispel any impression that richly-rimed verse is necessarily the hallmark of the good poet. Outside the field of comic verse we are not impressed by mere verbal cleverness; but we value the rich resources of sound which the poet can command when we feel that they are an integral and significant part of his work.

One example of the difference in taste between the French and the English tradition is the case of the *punning rime*, which may often be rich and yet strike the English ear as extremely weak. The punning rime is one in which the answer consists of exactly the same word as proposed the rime, but used in a different sense. We have already quoted a striking example from Gautier:

256   ... et la va ˙ gue
        De la vie ˙ illĕ cité berçait l'ima ˙ gĕ va ˙ gue;
        Et moi, je regardais toujou.rs, ne songeant pas
        Que la nuit étoilée arrivait à grands pas [.]

Here *vague* in [1] is a noun, entirely dissimilar in meaning and grammatical function from the adjective *vague* in [2], yet identical in form; *pas* is a negative particle in [3] and a noun in [4]. Hugo uses *tombe* as a verb in [1] below and as a noun, completely unrelated in meaning, in [3]:

257   Je ne regarderai ni l'o.r du soi.r qui tom.be,
        Ni les voi ˙ lĕs au loin descendant sur Harfleu.r;
        Et quand j'arriverai, je mettrai sur ta tom.be,
        Un bouquet de houx ve.rt et de bruyè.re en fleu.r [.]

Likewise a poet may rime *il porte* with *la porte*, *je cours* with *les cours*, the pronoun *lui* with *lui*, past participle of *luire*, the preposition *vers* with the plural noun *vers*. Effects such as these are pleasing to the French ear because they combine complete identity of sound with dissimilarity of meaning and grammatical function. But in English verse a rime of this kind would be unacceptable and would produce the same emotional deflation as if the poet, failing to find a rime, had answered his proposal simply by going back to the same word. The skill of riming lies in the combination of similarity with dissimilarity, and here it would be felt that the latter was lacking. But it is not, in French. In the punning rime the dissimilarity is apparent if we do not think of the answer simply in terms of its sound. According to the traditions of French verse, the poet has acquitted himself well.

In French, a rime is always felt to be stronger if proposal and answer use words having a different grammatical function, so that a verb answers an adjective, and so on. In cases where it does not, and the poet rimes a noun with a noun, a verb with a verb, the effect is termed a *rime banale*. According to the theory of prosody such rimes are to be discouraged, but this is a theory which has little effect on practice. There are simply not enough useful rimes in the French language for a poet to conform to this restriction, and the structure of the ordinary sentence makes it likely that words of similar grammatical function will occur fairly frequently on the line-ending. The poet will seek to differentiate his rimes, but not at the expense of other more important considerations. He cannot, however, use identical grammatical suffixes such as verb-endings to establish a rime. *Porté* does not rime with *donné*, nor *portais* with *donnais*: to make a rime of this kind effective he must include other elements belonging to the root of the verb. *Donner* makes an acceptable rime—though not a strong one—with *traîner*, or better still with *sonner*. Nor could one rime *bleuâtre* with *rougeâtre*. The rime between *volonté* and *volupté* would be valid, since the [-té] is no longer felt to be a suffix, but in a case such as this its banality is not merely theoretical but felt by the reader as a factor which deprives it of some of the contrast which good riming demands.

Similarity of sound coupled with dissimilarity of meaning is the basis of all French rime. This means that the matching and contrast involved is partly sensuous, partly intellectual. It would be perfectly reasonable to suppose that in the appreciation of rime the intellect is concerned solely with meaning and the senses with sound. But in practice this is not entirely true, and the fact that it is not makes the business of riming a good deal more complex than would otherwise be the case. In English, the sound of a rime is judged simply by what we hear, and we might reasonably expect this to be true of French also: but in fact it is not. By what today must appear no more than a rather bizarre convention, the reader of traditional French verse, and above all the poet himself, is required to take some account of the final unsounded phonemes of his rime-words. It is a familiar feature of the language that at the end of a word a neutral [e] becomes mute and more often than not a consonant is silent. This development has happened over the centuries. But, as we have already seen in considering the behaviour of the neutral [e] in the interior of the line, French versification shows considerable resistance to change and is prone to act as if change had not occurred, or had been much less radical than is in fact the case. Thus the concept of sound, so far as rime is concerned, involves not only what is actually heard but also what would have been heard at earlier epochs before the silent letters had been eliminated. This does not mean that the silent letters are pronounced, but simply that they are taken account of. The most immediately obvious example of what I call *fossilized sound*—i.e. sound which is embedded in the language but is no longer functional—is the rigorous distinction which has long been made between masculine and feminine rimes.

The terminology is unfortunate, since it has nothing to do with grammatical gender. The rime-word may be a verb or an exclamation, which has no gender; and a masculine noun may well give a feminine rime, as does *père*, while a feminine word, such as *sœur*, gives a masculine one. However, the distinction between masculine and feminine rimes is so well established that we have no alternative but to use the accepted terminology. A feminine rime is any one which ends in a mute [e] or a syllable containing a mute [e]. All other rimes are masculine, and end either in a vowel other than a mute [e] or in a sounded consonant. Now the reason this distinction must be interpreted in terms of fossilized sound is that the mute [e] is no longer pronounced, when it occurs on the line-ending. And yet it must be taken into account in riming. The fossilized phonemes cannot make a rime, for this depends on correspondence between heard sounds, but they can make a rime invalid. To the ear *fils* and *fisse* rime perfectly, but in verse they do not rime at all, since there is nothing in the proposal to match the fossilized [e] which concludes the answer. For the same reason *rendue* does not rime with *entendu*. Certainly the feminine ending of *rendue* is not pronounced, but it is a survival of a phoneme which was once sounded: it remains as a phonetic fossil which, in a valid rime, must be matched by a corresponding fossilized phoneme. A 'masculine' rime-word can be coupled only with another 'masculine' rime-word, and a 'feminine' one only with a 'feminine'. However similar the sound, rime between a 'masculine' rime-word and a 'feminine' one is impossible.

Another important effect of fossilized sound is to make it virtually impossible to rime a singular with a plural. *Vent* rimes with *chant* but not with *chants*, since the final [s] is not matched. When Baudelaire writes

> **258** Voilà que j'ai touché l'autom˙ně des idé˙es,
> Et qu'il faut employer la pelle et les râteaux
> Pour rassembler à neuf les te.rrěs inondé˙es,
> Où l'eau creu.sě des trous grands commě des tombeaux [.]

he finds himself obliged to put *râteaux* in the plural not because the image requires it—after all, one rake is as good as several—but because the singular *râteau* could not rime with the plural *tombeaux*. However, a plural word may rime with a singular one if the latter ends in an [s]. Thus *mes pas* makes a good rime with *trépas*. Rimes between different parts of speech likewise require the matching of the [s]: *finissons* rimes richly with *frissons* but not at all with the singular form *frisson*. The range of available rimes is slightly increased by the fact that, when they occur as fossilized sound, [s], [x], and [z] are considered equivalent and match each other. The reason for this will be apparent if we consider what happens to them in ordinary speech when we make a liaison. In liaison, fossilized phonemes are still pronounced: and in these circumstances both [s] and [x] are heard as [z]. We write *grands hommes* but we say [grà zòm]: we write *dix ans* but say [di zà]. Following this principle, *sanglots* makes a good rime with *tombeaux* and *chantez* rimes with *tentés*.

It is a general principle that the sound attributed to fossilized phonemes is that which they would have in ordinary speech if liaison was made with a vowel following. This is why it is legitimate to rime *sanglots* with *tombeaux* even though the *t* is not matched, the point being that it would not be heard in liaison. Words such as these rime in the plural though not in the singular: for *sanglot/ tombeau* is invalidated by the unmatched *t*. An exception is however made in the case of nasal vowels, which may be followed by any non-matching consonant other than *s* without any account being taken of it. So *sang/ comment* and *loin/ rejoint* are valid rimes: but *son/ ballons* is not. .

Faulty riming is much more unthinkable in French verse than in English. Whether it be rich or weak, a rime must be correct, and can never be approximate. However, two types of irregular rime are occasionally found and are sanctioned by poetic usage. The first of these is termed the *rime normande* since its validity rests on an archaic pronunciation which lingered in the provinces long after it had been abandoned in standard speech, and involves the matching of two words ending in -*er* which are no longer heard as identical in sound. Here are two examples:

259   Qu'une â.me ainsi frappée à se plain.dre est suje˙tte,
                Que j'ai pu blasphémer,
            Et vous jeter mes cris comme un enfant qui je˙tte
                Unĕ piè.rre à la me.r [.]

260   Il est ame.r et doux, pendant les nuits d'hive.r,
            D'écouter, près du feu qui palpite et qui fu˙me,
            Les souvĕni.rs lointains lentĕment s'élever,
            Au bruit des carillons qui chan.tĕnt dans la bru˙me [.]

The *rime normande* matches a word ending in [é]—usually a first conjugation infinitive—with one ending in [è.r]. It derives from the fact that by the fifteenth century all final *r*'s in spoken French had become mute, following the general tendency of the language to 'lose' consonants in this position: *la mer* was pronounced [lá mé] and *hiver* was [í vé]; and in the same way *finir* was indistinguishable from *fini* and *dur* from *du*. The resultant confusion was such that a conscious effort was made to bring the final [r] back into ordinary speech. This was, on the whole, successful; but the habit of pronouncing first conjugation infinitives (and some other words such as *dernier* or *sentier*) as if they ended in [é] proved irradicable, and so we still make no distinction between *donner* and *donné*. The result of the reformed pronunciation was that many words which had previously rimed no longer did so, and it was difficult to find rimes for first conjugation infinitives other than words of the same class. Poets, with their natural tendency towards conservatism in language, simply chose to ignore the changed pronunciation, and went on riming as before. The name *rime normande* suggests that the original intention was to give both proposal and answer their archaic pronunciation: but by the nineteenth century, when our two examples were written, it may have seemed more acceptable to give both words the pronunciation [èr], since infinitives were generally given this ending when liaison was made with a vowel following. But today stylization of this kind would hardly be acceptable, and the reader may give both proposal and answer its accepted modern pronunciation, resigning himself to the fact that the rime thus made is purely theoretical.

The second case of irregular but valid riming involves the matching of a sounded final *s* or *t* with an equivalent fossilized one, which is permitted in the case of a few words, or classes of words, which it would otherwise be difficult or impossible to match. The word *tous* [tús] is an example, since it calls for a masculine rime-word, whereas a terminal [s] is normally heard only in feminine ones (e.g. *douce*). This is how Vigny avoids the difficulty:

261 Aussi, loin de m'aimer, voilà qu'ils trem.blĕnt tous,
   Et, quand j'ouvrĕ mes bras, on tom.be à mes genoux [.]

In the same way we find Lamartine riming *crucifix* with *fils*, a practice which could perhaps be justified on historical grounds, since the archaic pronunciation of *fils* was [fí]. A similar situation arises with classical names ending in *-us*, for which no masculine rimes are available. In such cases the sounded [s] will be answered by a fossilized one:

262 Je sais qu'en vous quittant le malheureux Titus
   Pa˙ssĕ l'austérité de tou˙tĕs vos vertus [,]

In *Booz endormi* Hugo rimes *Judith* with *descendit*, and, in *La Rose de l'Infante*, *zénith* with *s'aplanit*. That he considered such rimes perfectly acceptable is clear from the fact that, as we have seen, he invented the name *Jérimadeth* as a rime for *se demandait*.

To these examples we may add the small number of cases in which an unfamiliar spelling of a word may be used in order to facilitate rime. Thus we may find *pié* for *pied*, *remord* for *remords*, *je croi* for *je crois*, and *encor* for *encore*. (The last of these alternatives is also useful for saving a syllable in the interior of a line.) In these cases the rime is perfectly regular but is conventional in that it involves the use of an archaic or 'poetic' form which would not be acceptable in prose usage.

It must be stressed, however, that these conventional rimes do not invalidate the principle that rime is based on sound and not on spelling. The point needs to be made because one sometimes hears rimes such as *s'élever*/*la mer* or *Vénus*/*nus* described as 'eye rimes', presumably because it is thought that it is their appearance which makes them acceptable. There is no such thing as an 'eye rime' in French, and even if there were it would not explain combinations such as *crucifix*/*fils*, *tous*/*genoux*, or *Jérimadeth*/*se demandait*, which neither look nor sound right. So it is not a useful hypothesis. Similarity or identity of spelling can never produce a rime. What could be more alike to the eye than *est* (= is) and *est* (= east)? But since one is pronounced [è] and the other [èst], they cannot rime. Nor can *fils* (= son) and *fils* (= threads), pronounced [fís] and [fíl] respectively; nor *le piment* [pí mà] with *ils briment* [brím], nor *présent* [pré sà] with *pèsent* [pè.z], nor *le couvent* [ku và] with *ils couvent* [kú.v]. It is equally true that dissimilarity of spelling never prevents a rime if the sound and fossilized phonemes are right. Thus *sais-je* rimes with *neige*, *rang* with *comment*, *héros* with *barreaux*, *temps* with *gants*, and *fin* with *faim*. A striking example of a rime which involves no visual similarity at all is Hugo's

263   On me tordait, depuis les ai˙lĕs jusqu'au bec,
       Sur l'affreux chevalet des X et des Y [.]

which is recognizable only when the last letter is given its French name of *i grec*. It is also true to say that from the end of the nineteenth century onwards sound has become to an ever increasing extent the sole criterion by which rime is judged. The contemporary poet is unlikely to take advantage of the irregular forms which we have considered above, and is very likely to ignore even such fundamental concepts as the alternation of masculine and feminine rimes or the matching of fossilized consonants. He is free to do as he wishes. In the following stanza, Jules Laforgue respects alternation, but rimes singular nouns with plurals:

264   Ils vont, se sustĕnant d'azu.r,
       Et parfois aussi de légu˙mes,
       De riz plus blanc que leur costu˙me,
       De mandari˙nĕs et d'œufs du.rs [.]

In Laforgue's time an effect such as this would be somewhat self-conscious, whereas today it would be accepted as perfectly normal.

Laforgue's stanza is also unusual in that his consecutive rimes are assonant: i.e. based on the same vowel. Although there is no strict rule on the matter, the writer of traditional verse is expected to use contrasting rimes, so that each one stands out firmly from the one which precedes and the one which follows. An example of good riming in this respect is heard in the opening lines of Hugo's *Pasteurs et troupeaux*:

265   Le vallon où je vais tous les jou.rs est charmant,
       Serein, abandonné, seul sous le firmament,
       Plein de ron.cĕs en fleu.rs; c'est un souri.rĕ tri˙ste.
       Il vous fait oubli:er que quelquĕ cho.se exi˙ste,
       Et, sans le bruit des champs remplis de travailleu.rs,
       On ne saurait plus là si quelque'un vit ailleu.rs [.]

Here we find the avoidance of banality (each noun rimes with a word of different grammatical function) and vowels and consonants change with each rime. Although this is not obligatory, it is a feature of good craftsmanship. On the other hand, a poet may choose deliberately to violate the principle, as Laforgue does in the example quoted. His intention, in this case, is to produce a humoristic effect. Baudelaire saw monotony as a positive feature of riming which could on occasions be used purposefully, and so did Verlaine after him. Even earlier, we have Lamartine expressing *ennui* by the use of identical sounds in consecutive rimes:

266 Quand je pourrais le sui.vre en sa va˙stĕ carri:è.re,
Mes yeux verraient partout le vide et les dése.rts;
Je ne dési.rĕ rien de tout ce qu'il éclai.re;
Je ne deman.dĕ rien à l'immen.se unive.rs [.]

Mallarmé produces a similar effect by using assonant rimes through-out his *sonnet du Cygne* and, in the opening lines of *L'Après-midi d'un faune* (page 104) blurs his alexandrine with the rime-sequence *clair/l'air, réve/s'achève, vrai/offrais*, all based on [è] and mostly involving [r].

There is however one principle regarding consecutive rimes which is invariably respected by poets using traditional verse-forms. This is *alternance des rimes*, which requires that consecutive rimes must never be of the same gender. If the first rime proposed is masculine, the second must be feminine. This applies whatever form of verse is used. It applies in passing from one stanza to the next, and in classical drama from one Act to another: if Act I ends on a masculine rime, Act II begins on a feminine one. In lyric verse, it must be observed even if there is a complete change of metre within the poem, as for instance in Musset's *Nuits*, where he changes from alexandrines to octosyllabics. The obligation to alternate the gender of rimes has been respected since the fifteenth century.

The importance attached to this rule is somewhat surprising. As we have seen, a feminine rime is one which ends in a mute [e] which is not counted in scansion; therefore, the distinction between a masculine and feminine rime is simply not heard. In the following stanzas by Gautier there is correct alternation of rimes, and yet we do not hear any real difference of sound between rime *b* and rime *c*:

267 Et la méda.ille austè.re
Que trou.ve un laboureu.r
Sous te.rre
Révèle un empĕreu.r.

Les dieux eux-mê˙mĕs meu.rent,
Mais les ve.rs souvĕrains
Demeu.rent
Plus fo.rts que les airains [.]

It is strange that so much importance should be attached to the distinction between two types of rime which, in practice, are often indistinguishable to the ear, and rely for their differentiation solely on fossilized sound. The most obvious heard effect of the feminine ending is that it lengthens the vowel that precedes it. But this is not really a distinguishing feature, since masculine rimes may have naturally long vowels. A final sounded consonant often indicates a feminine rime (e.g. in *sot* the *t* is silent, in *sotte* it is heard); but a final consonant is also heard in rimes such as *sec/bec*. In some cases it may be claimed that the final [e] of a feminine rime is actually heard (as in *admirable* or *saigne*); but is not some such terminal sound also heard in *sec* and *bec*? Although it is true that some consonantal groupings occur more readily in feminine rimes than in masculine ones, I think it must be recognized that the essential difference is conventional.

The reader will doubtless be aware that when French verse is sung, a final neutral [e] is always pronounced and quite clearly heard. Thus the ten-syllable line

268　　　Chagrin d'amou.r durĕ toutĕ la vie [.]

is heard, when sung, as having eleven syllables:

Chagrin d'amou.r durĕ toutĕ la vi:ĕ [.]

In this way, when any poem is set to music, the difference between its masculine and feminine rimes becomes a real one. Until the fifteenth century the terminal neutral [e] which is so commonly found in French was sounded in normal speech, so that French did possess two types of rime, one ending on a stressed syllable, the other on an unstressed one, even though the latter was not counted in scansion.

It was at this period that the rule of alternation was established. When it ceased to be pronounced in ordinary speech, the syllable disappeared also in verse in those positions in which it did not effect scansion. So the custom of alternating masculine and feminine rimes became generalized just at the time when the real distinction was being lost. It is therefore reasonable to think that the purpose of this rule was to preserve in the hearer's mind a distinction to which his ear no longer responded. The reader thus maintained his response to sound even after it became fossilized. He is still trained not to hear a feminine ending as a possible match for a masculine one, and he recognizes the existence of a final [e] as clearly when verse is spoken as when he hears it sung. And it may be relevant to mention that even today the ordinary French schoolchild is taught that, for instance, the word *village* has three syllables [ví lá jĕ], even though he pronounces only two of them.

What is normally meant by alternation has been illustrated in the examples quoted. A rime of one gender may be proposed in the first line and answered in the second, upon which a rime of the other gender will be proposed in the third line and answered in the fourth and so on. Or [1] may propose a rime of one gender, [2] propose one of the other gender, after which [3] and [4] will answer them either in the same or in reverse order. However, Verlaine experimented with other possibilities which still respected alternation, though in unusual ways. In the following example he uses masculine rimes in the first stanza, feminine ones in the second, and so on.

269   Je ne sais pourquoi
            Mon esprit ame.r
     D'une aile inquiète et fo˙llĕ vo˙lĕ sur la me.r.
            Tout ce qui m'est che.r
            D'une ai˙lĕ d'effroi
     Mon amour le couve au ras des flots. Pourquoi, pourquoi?

            Mouette à l'esso.r mélancoli˙que,
            Ellĕ suit la va˙guĕ, ma pensée,
            A tous les vents du ciel balancée,
            Et biaisant quand la marée oblique,
            Mouette à l'esso.r mélancoli˙que.

            I.vrĕ de sole.il
            Et de liberté
     Un instinct la guide à trave.rs cette immensité.
            La bri.sĕ d'été
            Sur le flot verme.il
     Doucĕment la po.rte en un tiè˙dĕ demi-somme.il [.]

Elsewhere he experiments with a pattern in which a rime proposed in one gender must be answered in the other—an arrangement which goes completely contrary to tradition since words of different gender cannot rime together, but which nevertheless creates a new kind of alternation.

270   C'est le chien de Jean de Nive˙lle
          Qui mo.rd sous l'œil mê˙mĕ du guet
          Le chat de la mè.rĕ Michel;
          François-les-bas-bleus s'en égaie.

          La lune à l'écrivain public
          Dispen.sĕ sa lumière obscu.re
          Où Médor avec Angéli˙que
          Verdi˙ssĕnt sur le pau.vrĕ mu.r.

Verlaine even occasionally produced poems entirely in feminine rime:

271   Dans l'intermina˙ble
          Ennui de la plai˙ne
          La neige incertai˙ne
          Luit commĕ du sa˙ble.

> Le ciel est du cui.vre
> Sans lueur aucu˙ne
> On croirait voir vi.vre
> Et mourir la lu˙ne [.] ...

In such a case alternation has been abandoned, but the difference of gender is still respected. There is no random mixture of rimes of different gender. The fact that in the context of French versification such limited variations appear quite revolutionary gives some indication of the hold which the convention of alternating rimes has on the French mind.

Chapter Seven
SOUND AND SENSE

EVERYTHING that has been said so far in our discussion of verse has been concerned in one way or another with the relating of sound to sense, for all good poetry involves the skilful union of these two concepts. But we have deliberately postponed, until this final stage in our investigation, any consideration of whether linguistic sounds can, in themselves, suggest to the intellect the meaning of the words of which they form a part. We have done so because this is undoubtedly the most controversial of the various issues involved in the reading and writing of verse. The fact of onomatopoeia (i.e. the suggestion of meaning through the use of appropriate phonemes) is not in question: words such as *cuckoo* or *splash* in English, or *murmure* and *siffler* in French, demonstrate it clearly. It is a feature of language, and therefore of verse, and all theorists have long recognized the possibility of *harmonie imitative*. What is in question is not the thing itself but rather its importance, and the manner in which its works. Is it an occasional ornament, a sort of phonetic flourish, or is it to a greater or less degree a feature of all good writing?

The general tendency among linguists has been to minimize the importance of onomatopoeia. Languages as we know them have developed by processes of evolution which have been studied in detail and found to take little account of the meaning of words. From generation to generation and from region to region, the sounds of which language is composed change according to principles which are unaffected by meaning, so that it seems on the face of it unlikely that, in the twentieth century, the pronunciation of a word in French or English or any other language should be directly related to its sense. In the case of certain words we may recognize a relationship between sound and sense, but these may be held to be exceptional. However, verse raises special problems, in that it differs from ordinary speech in two important respects. In the first place, we listen consciously to its sound, which is brought out forcibly in any good reading, and it is impossible for us to consider sound as being irrelevant to meaning. Secondly, we have already observed that by the use of phonetic clusters the poet may cause certain phonemes to predominate within a line or phrase in a manner which would be most unlikely to happen in ordinary speech. In that case, it is at least theoretically possible that onomatopoeia may be a feature not merely of the occasional word but of verse as a whole.

However, this possibility must be viewed with caution. The fact that a good line of verse strikes us as being absolutely right in its manner of expression may lead us to attribute to its phonemes qualities of suggestion which in fact they do not possess. A commentator on Baudelaire's *Les Aveugles* once drew attention to the [p v t] cluster heard in the lines

272   [...] on ne les voit jamais vers les pavés
                      v   v   p v
            Pencher rêveusĕment leur tête appesanti˙e [.]
            p   v   p
                              t t   t

which to him suggested an effect of heaviness. But this effect derives not from the sounds themselves but from the meaning of the words *pavés*, *pencher* and *appesantie*. The cluster merely reinforces their association, and it could equally well be used to suggest qualities of lightness, as Gautier demonstrates in his description of a girl on a Chinese vase:

273   Par son treillis ellĕ pa˙ssĕ la tê˙te,
            p   t   p   t t
            Que l'hirondelle, en volant, vient toucher [,]
                              v   v   t

Again, in another commentary on a Baudelaire poem, a particularly sinister quality was attributed to the repeated [bl] of

274   Il arri.vĕ souvent que sa voix affaibli˙e
                                              bl
            Sem.blĕ le râle épais d'un blessé qu'on oubli˙e [ ]
            bl   bl   bl

but any such quality can hardly lie in the sounds themselves, which occur with quite different associations in the same poet's description of the travellers who set out

275   ... cœur léger, sembla˙blĕs aux ballons [;]
                              bl bl   b l

A good deal will depend on the way in which we read the lines. The prevailing cluster in [r] produces a crisp and pleasing effect in

276 Harmonie et parfum, cha ˙ rmĕ, grâ ˙ cĕ, lumiè.re [,]
     r   r   r r   r

which bears little resemblance to what we hear in

277   Pour que des brigands abhorrés
         r   r   r
    Frémi ˙ ssĕnt aux portraits noi.rs de leur ressemblance [;]
    r   r r   r   r

Of course, it may be validly objected that in **277** other phonemes are involved, particularly the repeated [s]. But even so, the combination [s r] can be perfectly tranquil, as in

278 Sous la sérénité des som.brĕs a ˙ strĕs d'o.r [!]
    s s r   s   s r   r

If we describe the [r] as 'harsh' in **277**, we cannot do so in **276** or **278**. We are more likely to speak of its as 'soft and soothing'. And yet onomatopoeia seems necessarily to imply that phonemes possess constant qualities. Otherwise any such effects must be purely subjective. Commentators are only too prone to use phrases such as 'We can almost hear the poet spitting out his anger' in speaking of a line such as the one we have quoted from Chénier, but in doing so they throw very little light on how the line achieves its effect, since they establish no clear relationship between sound and meaning. How indeed can sound which expresses anger also express the serenity of a starlit night?

In an earlier chapter we examined the phenomenon of the phonetic cluster, and it is surely significant that we were able to do so without attributing any particular quality to the sounds of which these clusters are composed. A cluster is a phonetic rhythm, and may use any sounds. But the universality of phonetic clusters has not been generally recognized, whereas the phenomenon of *harmonie imitative* has been. In fact, onomatopoeic clusters are often the easiest to recognize: and from this follows a natural tendency to attribute onomatopoeic qualities to any cluster which happens to be recognized. What is merely a general tendency to organize sound is interpreted as an attempt to represent meaning in phonetic terms. To the more traditional critic, a phonetic pattern which had no onomatopoeic function would be a blemish. I hope that our consideration of the matter will have shown that no such conclusion is justified. Phonetic patterning does not necessarily, or even normally, imply onomatopoeia.

But we cannot be satisfied with such a negative conclusion. However limited its scope, onomatopoeia is a fact of language, and must therefore be a feature of verse. How can this be so if phonemes do not have a constant suggestive value? Or, to put the question in another way, can we convincingly deny that, despite the difference in meaning of the lines we have quoted, their meaningful content is in some way suggested to us by the phonemes which the poet uses? Whether we are expressing anger or tranquillity, do we not feel that these sounds are 'just right' for the purpose and are not chosen at random?

A partial answer to this question would be to say that the phonetic form of a word cannot by itself suggest anything: but, provided the meaning is understood, it can be used to intensify our awareness of the meaning. Thus a phoneme may change its value according to its context. This may in some cases involve an actual change in sound: for instance, in reading Chénier's line we shall hiss our [s]'s, which we shall certainly not do in reading the other lines. But such an answer gives us little indication of why a poet uses one particular group of phonemes rather than another in order to suggest his meaning. And if we are to understand this, we can hardly do better than turn our attention to some unquestionable examples of ono-matopoeia in ordinary language. These we find in common words which are obviously intended to imitate non-linguistic sounds—for instance, in English, *cuckoo, tick-tock,* or *plop.* Now the first thing we note is that these are not really imitations at all. When someone names the cuckoo, we do not think that we hear the actual bird, and when we listen to its song we hear nothing in it which resembles the word. Nor could we confuse *tick-tock* with the sound of a clock. The point becomes all the clearer if we recall that it is perfectly possible for those so talented to imitate these and indeed almost any sounds—a train leaving a station, a creaking gate, water gushing from a tap—using the human voice alone, and to do so with such realism as to deceive us completely. Some entertainers have earned their living doing just that. Yet clearly this is not what language does, nor does it attempt to do it. When we represent a non-linguistic sound in ordinary language, we do so within the conventions of that language. We do not imitate: rather, we suggest. In listening to the clock, we hear no sound corresponding to the [t] of *tick-tock* or *tic tac,* and yet there are very good reasons why we do not represent the sound as *bing bang.* Such a representation would be a false or inadequate translation of the sound heard.

The English language offers us one familiar example of an unsuccessful attempt at imitation. The expression *Tut tut!* was originally intended to represent the sound produced by the rapid withdrawal of the tongue from the palate, which was at one time commonly used to indicate disapproval. Sounds such as this, called *clicks*, are common in the Bantu languages but unknown in English, even though English people are obviously perfectly capable of making them. But there is no way of representing such a sound in English spelling, and so it was represented, as a matter of convention, by what was felt to be its nearest equivalent, i.e. by [t]. The original intention was that it should be read as a click, but in the course of time spelling has affected the pronunciation and it is now usually read as written. Language tends to reject any sound which does not belong to its own linguistic conventions, and it is in terms of these that it imitates non-linguistic sounds. Certain linguists have attempted to discredit the idea of onomatopoeia by pointing to the difference between the English *cock-a-doodle-doo!* and the French *cocorico!* —but common sense leads to the opposite conclusion. What is striking is the similarity of the words: and they are both clearly 'imitations' within different linguistic conventions of the same familiar sound. They are imaginative translations. I am, of course, labouring the obvious, but I do so because the point we are now examining is one which generates much heat and controversy. I hope we may agree that although language does not reproduce non-linguistic sounds, it can on occasions suggest them. It would be absurd to say that Vigny's line

279   Roulaient et redoublaient les fou ̆ drĕs de l'ora.ge [,]

sounds like thunder, and equally absurd to deny that it suggests it in its sound, and does so quite consciously and successfully.

The question of how this is done is a complex one, and we are unlikely to be able to explain it fully. Within the limited scope of this book, our object is twofold. First, the negative one of resisting the only too common tendency to explain the effect of a line by attributing purely subjective values to the sounds of which it is composed; and secondly to establish what phonetic features of a line may be considered genuinely suggestive, and, as far as possible, how and why this is so. We must begin with some consideration of the nature of linguistic sound. The study of phonetics has in our time become a highly sophisticated science, and judged by professional criteria what we have to say about it here will be very elementary indeed, for we are concerned with the mechanics of speech only in so far as they are relevant to verse. For the most part I shall treat phonemes as if they were constants, though they are not; and I shall accept the traditional assumption that long vowels have twice the length of short ones, though experiment can easily demonstrate that vowel-length is variable over a very wide range. In other words, I shall simplify. The reader will be aware that any competent ventriloquist can produce recognizable sound in apparently complete violation of the principles of phonetics: he can, for instance, make us hear labials without using his lips. He will also take into account that when we read verse to ourselves we create sound mentally, without the use of the vocal organs. Speech involves not merely a mechanical operation but also use of the imagination. But we must begin by looking at its mechanical basis.

Speech results from forcing air from the lungs out through the mouth (and to a certain extent the nose), so setting up vibrations which impinge on another person's ear and occasionally on his mind and intellect. If all the speech organs are relaxed and inoperative there is no vibration and so no significant linguistic sound. Vibrations may be caused by tensing the membranes in the larynx which we call the *vocal cords*. When these are tensed, the throat and mouth cavity function in a manner similar to a musical wind-instrument such as a recorder or a clarinet. In these, air is set in motion by striking a sharp edge or a vibrating reed. The body of the instrument then amplifies the sound, gives it a particular tonality (for no two types of musical instrument sound alike) and can also vary its pitch. Keys or holes enable us to vary the length of the tube which is actively used in producing the note: and the shorter the effective tube, the higher is the note. A tiny instrument such as the piccolo produces a higher and shriller note than a large one such as the tuba. When we sing, the mouth actually is a musical instrument. In ordinary speech the volume of air is insufficient, and too inconsistent, to produce a firm musical note, but it does produce a recognizable sound which can be modified at will by movement of the tongue and of the facial muscles. Any sound which results from the uninter-rupted flow of breath set in motion by the tensed vocal cords is termed a *vowel*. It is a musical sound of limited tonality which can, by an increase in the volume of air, be converted into a real musical sound, so that any vowel can be sung. Speech consists basically of a long and constantly-modified vowel. But the flow of air may be partially or completely interrupted or obstructed by muscular move-ments at various points in the vocal cavity which extends from the throat to the lips. Such interruptions produce non-musical noises which are called *consonants*. A consonant cannot be pronounced, and certainly cannot be sung, by itself, but must always be accom-panied by a vowel. If we try to pronounce [k] in isolation, only the opening part of the sound we make represents the consonant, what follows being a neutral vowel necessary to make it audible. All linguistic sounds are classed as either vowels or consonants, apart from a small in-between class called *semi-consonants*. Any sound characteristic of a language (i.e. necessary to its pronunciation) is called a *phoneme*. As we have seen, phonemes are only imperfectly represented in normal spelling by the letters on the printed page, and for this reason it is convenient to represent them by the symbols we use in our phonetic transcript.

The different vowel-sounds are produced by restricting the effective air-flow to particular parts of the mouth, which is done largely by movement of the tongue. (The word 'mouth', in this discussion, refers to the buccal cavity, and not as in ordinary speech to the lips.) The tongue forms the floor of the mouth. It may be raised towards the roof of the mouth at the back, in the middle, or towards the front, and in any of these cases only that part of the mouth which is in front of the raised tongue effectively amplifies sound. The degree to which the tongue as a whole is raised may also vary, thus increasing or decreasing the degree of amplification. At the back the roof of the mouth is soft: at the front it is hard, which causes the tonal quality of a back vowel to differ from a frontal one. In pronouncing a vowel the lips may be either slack or rounded. In the latter case the facial muscles are taut and the sound is more firmly musical. Vowels which use the mouth alone are described as *oral*, but French also makes use of a number of *nasal* vowels, in the formation of which the buccal and nasal cavities are joined together to give added resonance to the sound. Nasal vowels are always *open* (i.e. pronounced with the lips well apart, an effect indicated in our phonetic transcript by the use of a grave accent); oral vowels may be either open or *closed*, the aperture between the lips being restricted in the latter case (which we indicate by the use of the acute accent). Varying combinations of the features that we have here listed give the different vowels of French their characteristic sounds.

The poet will naturally make use of this range of sound. Here is Baudelaire using a sequence of closed middle and frontal vowels to suggest the toneless hissing of damp wood on a fire:

280   D'écouter, près de feu qui palpite et qui fu˙me [,]

and Hugo using open back vowels and nasals to suggest the deep murmur of the sea:

281   Qu'igno.rĕ l'Océan grondant à l'horizon [.]

If these lines are declaimed aloud, the difference in sound will be immediately apparent. Lines of verses are not meant to be skimmed like those of a newspaper. They must be savoured. Obviously, if we are to 'feel' the meaning of these lines and not merely comprehend them with the intellect, then we must respond to the sound. What is involved is not merely an isolated onomatopoeic word, but a grouping of a series of sounds in such a way as to affect the imagination. When we pronounce the sequence *qui palpite et qui fume* [í á í é í ü] we are using vowels formed in the front of the mouth with the lips in a comparatively closed position: the sounds are brilliant, being formed against the hard palate, but thin and lacking in resonance. On the other hand, in *grondant à l'horizon* [ò à á ò í ò] the lips are open and rounded, most of the vowels are formed in the back of the throat, and half of them are nasals: i.e. use the nasal cavity to produce added resonance. The effect is sufficiently striking to justify an attempt to make some kind of classification of vowels so as to bring out their effect on the imagination. I would suggest that the following groupings are worthy of attention:

1. The constricted vowels [i], [ü], and [u], as heard in *fit, fut*, and *fou*. These I describe as *constricted* because all are formed with the tongue in a raised position, thus leaving only a narrow passage in which the sound can be formed. Both [i] and [ü] are frontal sounds, having minimal amplification and therefore thin, but bright because they are formed against the hard palate. Both are closed vowels. The difference between them is that [i] is pronounced with the lips slack, whereas [ü] is rounded and consequently more musical. [u] is also a rounded, thin sound, lacking in resonance, but it differs from the other two in that it is pronounced further back in the throat. This gives it greater depth, and it is altogether a more pleasant sound to listen to. These vowels often occur together in clusters, of which the following are examples:

282   Tout m'affli.ge et me nuit et conspi.re à me nui.re [.]
         ú   í   ŭi   i.   ŭi

283   Revole, et puis si tristĕment cri˙e [!]
         ŭi i i   i

284   Quand du stérile hive.r a resplendit l'ennui [.]
         ü   i   i   i   ŭi

All these lines have the same emotional tonality. They suggest weariness and frustration: and this will generally be found to be the case when this combination of sounds occurs. The line from Baudelaire quoted at **280** is introduced by the words 'Il est amer et doux ...', and there can be no doubt that the line expresses the sense of *amer* rather more than *doux*. The fire is not warm and cosy, but damp, spluttering, and smoky. The reason that these vowels carry with them a certain emotional association is, I would suggest, twofold. In the first place they are thin sounds, without much body, and the [i] in particular, being unrounded, is not musically satisfying. Secondly, because of the constricted form of the mouth, they require a certain muscular effort to produce. We are not physically relaxed. [i] suggests the minimum of sensuous pleasure. Of the three vowels, [u] is the most musical, being rounded and also a back vowel: it is sonorous, but, as it is made against the soft palate, lacks the brilliance of the other two. We notice this different tonality in the following lines, in which the sharp [i] of [2] is very striking:

285   Pouvons-nous étouffer le vieux, le long Remo.rds,
             u   u   u
                 Qui vit, s'agite et se torti.lle,
                  i i   i   i
             Et se nourrit de nous commĕ le ve.r des mo.rts [,]
                  u   i   u

Because of its musicality, [u] is more suggestive of melancholy than of frustration, as Lamartine reminds us:

286   Ainsi, toujours poussés vers de nouveaux riva.ges,
                 u   u   u   u
             Dans la nuit éternelle emportés sans retou.r
                  ŭi   u
             Ne pourrons-nous jamais, sur l'Océan des â.ges,
                  u   u   ü
                 Jeter l'an.cre un seul jou.r [?]
                                      u

These three constricted vowels in French differ from all others in two respects. They have no nasal form. (The nasal vowel which is written *in* is in fact related to [e], not [i].) And secondly, presumably owing to their lack of body, they are very prone to change into semi-consonants when immediately followed by another vowel. This we have already discussed on p. 39. The combination [ŭi] occurs very frequently in clusters suggestive of melancholy frustration.

2. The vowel [a] is usually frontal and unrounded, and appears as [á] in our phonetic script; but it does also have a back form which is open and therefore represented as [à]. These two sounds are different in quality. Frontal [á] differs from [i] and [u] in that it is not constricted but is pronounced with the tongue in the low position. It therefore has much more volume and is strong, even aggressive in

quality; and being made against the hard palate, is bright and clear. Its self-assertive quality can be heard in

287   Dans sa flamme implacable abso ˙ rbĕ-toi sans fin [;]
            á   á á   á   á

and in the long interlinear cluster heard in

288   Et, martelant le front massif des cachalots,
            Seul, le Roi de l'espace et des me.rs sans riva.ges,
            Vo ˙ lĕ contrĕ l'assaut des rafa ˙ lĕs sauva.ges.
            D'un trait puissant et sû.r, sans hâ.tĕ ni reta.rd,
            L'œil dardé par delà le livi ˙ dĕ brouilla.rd [,]

It may be noted that ordinary spelling is not a very reliable guide to the occurrence of [á]. It frequently appears in the form *oi* as in *noir* [nwá.r]. On the other hand, in combinations such as *au* and *ain* the written symbol *a* does not represent a phoneme at all, and so it should not be counted as contributing to clusters.

In contrast, back [a], which is open and rounded, is one of the most melodious of vowels. It is formed at the back of the mouth with the tongue in the low position and the lips wide open (which is why the doctor tells you to say 'Ah!' when he wishes to examine your throat). It is therefore a very full and strong sound making the greatest possible use of the vocal organs, and the easiest sound to sing. It is comparatively rare in French, but when it combines with frontal [á] to produce clusters, it results in a much more pleasing effect than does [á] by itself. Examples of this are

289   Votre â.me est un paysa.gĕ choisi [ ]
                à   á   w̆á

and

290   Le froid scintillĕment de ta pâ.lĕ clarté [ ]
                w̆á   á à.   á

Like all back vowels, [à] is made against the soft palate, and so does not have the brilliance of the frontal [á].

3. The back vowel [o] is rounded and soft and strongly heard since it makes full use of the cavity of the mouth. Its sound is often enhanced by its tendency to combine with the consonant [r], as in

291   Toutĕ sono.re encor de vos derniers baisers [;]

Particularly when mingled with its nasal equivalent [ò] this sound can suggest depth and darkness, and also deep sound. Baudelaire is suggesting sound when he writes

292   Commĕ de longs échos qui de loin se confon.dent [,]
           ò   ò   ó   ò ò

but his choice of vowel is also explained by the fact that in the next line he uses the word *ténébreuse*. In Vigny's well-known opening line to *Le Cor*:

293   J'ai mĕ le son du co.r, le soi.r, au fond des bois [;]
            ò   ó   ó ò

to me at least his words conjure up the darkness of the woods in the evening rather than the shrill note of the hunting-horn. In analysing the effect of this vowel within a line, the reader should bear in mind that it is often lengthened by a following [r], and also that in conventional spelling it may be represented by the letters *au*.

4. The remaining oral vowels, which are based on [e] or [œ], are formed in the middle of the mouth, and are rather neutral in quality and unobtrusive. Thus we are not really very conscious of the eight occurrences of [e] in

294   Et, malgré bien des chocs et d'imprévus désa˙stres [,]
        é   é ë é   é   é   é

Perhaps the very frequency of this sound in French militates against its effectiveness. However, [è] can form strongly-heard doublets and triplets when heard in association with a following [r], as in

295   Ce fe.r que le mineu.r che.rche au fond de la te.rre [,]
       è.r   è.r   è.r

and the same can be said of [œ]. These vowels + [r] were much used by Symbolist poets to conjure up an atmosphere of restrained melancholy, and their very tonelessness can be effective. This, indeed, is demonstrated by the closing line of Chénier's *Iambe XI*:

296   Toi, vertu, pleu.rĕ si je meu.rs [.]

5. All open vowels have nasal forms which possess the qualities of the oral vowel but also have an added power and resonance due to the fact that in pronouncing them the cavity of the nose is used as well as that of the mouth. The importance of the nasal cavity can be

easily demonstrated if we attempt to pronounce the word *bon* while pinching the nose between the fingers. Under these circumstances oral vowels such as that of *beau* [bó] present no difficulty, since they use only the mouth; but a nasal vowel cannot be pronounced with the mouth alone. Nasal vowels are so common in French that we may expect to find them in most lines of verse, without having any particular effect on its sound. However, when used in clusters they can produce a very marked resonance. It is not surprising that they are often used to suggest musical sound. In the following lines by Baudelaire, we note how the poet stresses nasal vowels in [1A] to suggest the deep tolling of the bell, and then passes to closed frontal oral vowels to suggest the hissing fire and the toneless tick of the clock:

297   Le bourdon se lamen.te, et la bûche enfumé ˙e
      Accompagne en fausset la pendule enrhumé ˙e [,]

The nasals of the second clause of the sentence carry no stress, and the dominant effect is achieved by the oral vowels. Hugo uses a similar transition in

298   J'entends le vent dans l'ai.r, la me.r sur le récif [,]

in which the four-times repeated [à] of [A] suggests a strong and musical sound—the humming of the wind—while the less sonorous oral [e] of [B] suggests a quieter, more distant sound. We have already made it clear that any such interpretation must be rooted in the meaning of the words. Apart from this, we cannot attribute a specific value to sound, and nasals will frequently occur without any such association. But, where the meaning encourages such interpretation, we may even give a different value to different nasals: thus, by varying his nasal vowels, Baudelaire is able to evoke bells of varying pitch:

299   Les souveni.rs lointains lentĕment s'élever
      Au bruit des carillons qui chan.tĕnt dans la bru ˙me [.]

When the poet wishes to suggest resonant sound, he will almost inevitably use nasals. Hugo expects us to hear the [à] of *retentis-santes* as a clanging in

300   Comme un guerrier qui pend aux pou ˙très des plafonds
      Ses retentissantĕs armu.res [.]

Baudelaire uses the same word to suggest a duller sound, isolating it amid oral vowels:

301   Le bois retentissant sur le pavé des cou.rs [.]

In these cases, the repeated nasal carries with it the suggestion of an echo. But where a sound is specifically non-resonant (as in Baudelaire's evocation of a spluttering fire), the poet will use oral vowels, probably frontal ones, and will also rely heavily on consonants, as Hugo does when he suggests the powerful flapping of sails:

302   Les voi˙lĕs font un vaste et sourd battĕment d'ai˙les [;]
      w̆á   á   á
  é   é u   è

To explain the full suggestive power of any of these lines it will be necessary to consider the nature and quality of consonants, and it is to this matter that we shall now turn our attention.

Consonants are for the most part non-musical sounds which impinge on vowels in a number of ways. As is the case with vowels, phoneticians classify them according to the manner in which they are produced. They may be divided in the first place into two main categories, according to whether they are voiced or voiceless, the difference being that the vocal cords vibrate when a voiced consonant is produced, whereas they are slack and unused in the case of a voiceless consonant. The vocal cords act like the reed of a musical instrument, causing the air which is passed between them to vibrate and so producing the basic sound which is modified to form vowels. If the vocal cords are relaxed when a consonant is produced, it loses musical quality but often becomes more forceful, since it interrupts the continuous vibration of the breath. When we say [d] we use the vocal cords, and if we relax them the sound becomes [t], which is voiceless. Most consonantal phonemes have both voiced and voiceless forms, but some are always voiced.

A consonant involves the use of the throat, tongue, teeth, or lips to interrupt the continuously varying vowel-sequence, or to introduce a greater or less degree of hiss or variation. This may be done in several ways.

When the column of air is completely interrupted, the consonant is called a *stop*. (The terms *occlusive* and *plosive* are also used.) Stops may be produced in different parts of the mouth. [p] and [b] are produced by cutting off the air-stream with the lips, [t] and [d] by blocking the air-flow with the tongue against the teeth, and [k] and [g] by interrupting it briefly in the throat. In each case, the first phoneme of these pairs is voiceless; the vocal cords are relaxed and the vibration of the breath ceases. The second phoneme is voiced: i.e. the vocal cords remain taut, and so the interruption is less complete. A voiced stop is therefore less obtrusive than a voiceless one. With these six stops we may associate the two nasal consonants [m] and [n], which are always voiced. These result from an interruption of the airflow in the mouth, but both also involve the use of the nasal cavity, so the interruption is not complete. Like the nasal vowels, these nasal consonants have a marked resonance.

A second class of consonant, known as a *fricative*, is produced when the air-flow is restricted to the mouth and is only partially obstructed. These sounds lack the suddenness of the stops, and involve hiss or vibration. Voiceless fricatives are [f], [s],and [ʧ], and their voiced equivalents are [v], [z], and [j]. The pair [f/v] is frontal and results from contact between the lips and teeth; [s/z] is a hiss (or, in the voiced form, a buzz) which results from restricting the air passage and the forcing the breath through a narrow space between the tongue and the roof of the mouth. [ʧ/j] is a similar effect produced further back. The fricatives which involve a high degree of hiss—[s/z] and [ʧ/j]—are known as *sibilants*. Thus in Mallarmé's

303   Sur maints chaˑrmĕs de paysa.ge [   ]
     s   ʧ   z j

the consonants indicated, though different, have the common feature of being all sibilants, the last two being the voiced equivalents of the first two. Consonants having similar characteristics may often be grouped effectively in this way.

The French [r] is a voiced fricative made in the throat, and, being in a class by itself, it is called a *vibrant*. The reader will hardly need reminding that it differs from any of the sounds given to this phoneme in English. What may usefully be stressed, however, is that this phoneme, which in English is self-effacing, is very strongly heard in French. Its presence in a line frequently gives rise to effective clusters. It occurs both singly and in combination with stops or fricatives, as in *arbre* and *sinistre*. These are characteristics which it shares with the consonant [l]. This latter phoneme is not classed as a fricative, and unlike most of this latter class it cannot be prolonged. It is termed a *liquid*. It is formed by a turning movement of the tongue. The phonemes [r] and [l] have a good deal in common, and speakers of some languages find it very difficult to distinguish between them. In French, they are very frequently associated in clusters.

The common feature of all consonants is that they are noises rather than musical sounds, and this fact gives them considerable suggestive potential. It is therefore important to distinguish between their qualities. The *voiceless stops* [p], [t], and [k] are crisper and firmer than their voiced equivalents, for reasons that we have already mentioned. (In fact, such words as *staccato* and *stop* suggest their meaning by the use of voiceless stops.) Although these consonants have no musical quality in themselves, their crispness can be very pleasing, as in Baudelaire's

304   Et mon esprit subtil, que le roulis care ́sse [,]
             p   pt k   k

and in the following lines by Leconte de Lisle the adjective *crystalline* may well serve to sum up the limpid effect of these sounds:

305   Si mon berceau, flottant sur la Thétis anti ́que,
                           t   t t   t k

             Ne fut point caressé de son tiè ́ dĕ cristal;
             p   k   t   k t

             Si je n'ai point prié sous le fronton atti ́que,
             p   p   t   t k

             Beauté victorieu.se, à ton autel natal [;]
             t   kt   t   t   t

But this is not only the kind of effect that can be produced by voiceless stops. When pronounced with force they can be extremely obtrusive. Indeed, when reading

306   Et les peu ́plĕs, d'un bout à l'au ́trĕ de l'empi.re,
                    p   p   t   t   p

             Tremblaient [...]
             t

or Lamartine's aggressive

307   Pourquoi le prononcer, ce nom de la patri ́e?
             p   k   p   p t

we may feel that we are dealing with an entirely different kind of sound. For voiceless phonemes are particularly sensitive indicators of tone of voice, however paradoxical that may seem. In a quiet passage, a brief interruption does not disturb the flow of words. But in a passage which implies agitation or great determination, such an interruption will be much more forceful. So we cannot attribute to stops any invariable emotional quality. They can indeed be aggressive, but only if we make them so: and good reading requires that we attribute to them the value which is appropriate to the sense. The English-speaking reader should however note that even when voiceless French stops such as [p] are not accompanied by the explosion of breath which is characteristic of their English equivalent.

Voiceless fricatives are equally variable. [f], [s], and [ʧ] resemble stops in that they can be pronounced lightly, in which case they are quite soft, or violently, in which case they hiss. They do not have the crispness of stops, for fricatives are not instantaneous, and can in fact be prolonged. In practice, [f] can only be lengthened when it occurs in combinations such as [fl], [fr]—as it often does—but the sibilants [s] and [ʧ] may always be hissed if we so desire. We shall not wish to take advantage of this possibility in a line such as

308   Sur son festin de mo.rt il s'affaisse et chance˙lle [,]
s   s   f   f   s   ʧ   s

since the effect is already very strong, and suggests a soft and yielding collapse, very different from the firmness produced by voiceless stops in the lines quoted above from Leconte de Lisle. However, some degree of lengthening would be very natural in reading

309   Frémi˙ssĕnt aux portraits noi.rs de leur ressemblan˙ce [;]
f   s   s   s
  r   r r   r   r

since the words are charged with violent emotion. Likewise in

310   Cependant que grossit et durcit ton éco˙rce [,]
s   s   rs   rs

In lines such as these, one naturally does not recommend a melo-dramatic rendering: what is required is a strong but natural articulation of the sounds offered by the poet. The same may be said of the use of voiceless stops and fricatives in the line:

311   Un sou˙fflĕ rauque et bref, d'unĕ bru˙squĕ secou˙sse [,]
s   f   k   f   sk   s k   s
  r   br   br

in which the consonants, combined with closed vowels, suggest the forceful breathing of a jungle animal.

The range of intensity available from voiced phonemes is much less. The reason for this, I suppose, is that they cannot stand out so markedly from adjacent vowels, which are necessarily voiced. If we compare two lines from Baudelaire:

312   Une oasis d'horreu.r dans un dése.rt d'ennui [!]

and

313   Nous voulons voyager sans vapeu.r et sans voi˙le [,]

I think we shall conclude that, while the clusters in [d] and [v] are clearly heard, the fact that one is a stop and the other a fricative is of no great importance.

From our point of view, perhaps the most interesting of voiced phonemes are those which have no voiceless equivalent—[r], [l], [m], and [n]. As we have seen, both [r] and [l] frequently combine with fricatives and stops. [r] has a range of tonal variation equal to that of any voiceless phoneme, and, being of indeterminate length, it can be given whatever prominence we desire. Its effect may be extremely light, as in

314   Le Printemps adorable a perdu son odeu.r [.]
                r   r   r   r

or

315   Tant son tim.bre est ten.dre et discret
                         r   r   r

in both of which lines it is associated particularly with voiceless stops of the crisp, restrained variety. Or it may be aggressive, as we have already heard in

316   Frémi˙ssent aux portraits noi.rs de leur ressemblan.ce [;]

The two effects may indeed be combined in the same line. In Hugo's

317   Pendant que l'om.brĕ trem.ble et que l'â˙prĕ rafa˙le [ ]

there could be no possible case for giving a violent pronunciation to the [r] of the first hemistich, whereas we shall certainly do so to that of the second. This change is reinforced by the dominance of nasal vowels in [A] and of oral ones in [B], as well as the absence of voiced consonants from [B]. We hear a correspondence between *l'ombre* in [A] and *l'âpre* in [B]: but the former is resonant—a nasal vowel followed by a voiced consonant—while the latter is abrasive rather than musical, having a strong unrounded oral vowel followed by a voiceless consonant. And this unrounded oral vowel is further extended in the forceful terminal triplet in [á] offered by *âpre rafale*.

The phoneme [r] readily combines with [l] to great musical effect, as in Leconte de Lisle's

318   Au tintĕment de l'eau dans les porphy.rĕs roux
       Les rosiers de l'Iran mê˙lent leurs frais murmu.res,
       Et les ramiers rĕveu.rs leurs roucou˙lĕments doux [.]

In such cases, the [r] is normally soft. However, the same poet offers a striking example of the use of the strong [r] in a similar combination:

319   Dans l'immen.sĕ largeu.r du Capricorne au Pô.le
       Le vent beu˙glĕ, rugit, si˙fflĕ, râle et miau˙le,
       Et bondit à travers l'Atlanti˙quĕ tout blanc
       De ba.vĕ furieu.se. Il se rue, éraflant
       L'eau bleu:ĕ qu'il pourchasse et dissipe en bué˙es;
       Il mord, déchi.re, arrache et tran.chĕ les nué˙es,
       Par tronçons convulsifs où sai˙gne un brusque éclai.r [.]

In passages such as this the [r] may be described as *strongly vibrant.* There is therefore no inconsistency in attributing to it qualities quite different from those heard in lines such as

320   Harmonie et parfum, cha˙rmĕ, grâ˙cĕ, lumiè.re [,]

or

321   Et mon esprit subtil, que les roulis care˙sse [,]

in which we give it the soft pronunciation. One difference which we may note between [l] and [r] as we read these examples is that the former, unlike the latter, is invariable in length and quality. This is not strictly speaking true, since the phonetician distinguishes more than one form of [l], but the distinction seems to have no significance in the reading of verse. If we attempt to stress [l], the effect is absurd, as Verlaine demonstrates when he parodies his own fondness of phonetic clusters in the line

322   Et de ces lu˙nĕs, l'une après l'u˙ne [.]

Quite apart from the comic effect of the play on words, here the [l] is too aggressive to be taken seriously. The point is that whereas [r] is a phoneme which requires little muscular effort to produce, [l] is quite literally a 'tongue-twister', produced by twisting the tongue. To give it prominence would require considerable physical gymnastics.

What [l] and [r] have in common is an ability to effect a smooth transition between other consonants and vowels. They regularly attach themselves to stops and fricatives to produce phonetic groupings such as [fr], [pl] etc. Only when [l] or [r] is involved does it become possible, in French, to pronounce three consonants in series, as we do without difficulty in words such as *arbre* or *splendide*. Although [l] is unquestionably a consonant it is remarkably close to the vowels, and in the course of the evolution of the French language it has frequently changed into one: thus *castellum* has become *château* and *chevals* has become *chevaux*. It is perhaps because of this quality that it strikes us as a particularly musical phoneme. The ease with which it blends with vowels is demonstrated by the fact that *la-la-la* is the most natural of all sound-sequences to sing.[r] also blends easily with vowels but in an entirely different way: it extends vowels by prolonging them as a vibration, providing a sort of purring accompaniment.

The vowel which most frequently benefits from association with [r] and [l] is the open [e]. In our consideration of vowels, it was suggested that [è] was the only middle vowel which held much phonetic interest for the reader of verse. The reason for its good fortune may well be the ease with which it combines with liquids and vibrants, which provide this unrounded frontal vowel with much-needed musical support. Combinations of these phonemes were much used by Baudelaire and his followers to produce an effect of pleasing but weary monotony. Here is a somewhat extreme example from Mallarmé:

323   Des crépusculĕs blancs tiédi˙ssĕnt sous mon crâ˙ne
       Qu'un ce˙rclĕ de fer se.rre ainsi qu'un vieux tombeau,
       Et, tri˙stĕ, j'e.rre après un rê.vĕ vague et beau,
       Par les champs où la sève immen.sĕ se pavane;
       Puis je tom.be énervé ...

The suggestion of monotony is achieved by constant repetition of the same sound. If the sound chosen had been musical, as [à] and [o] are, the effect would have been quite different. [è] is an open vowel which is not in itself particularly pleasing, but the overall effect becomes musical because it is a perfect vehicle for [l] and [r]. More moderate examples of the same thing are heard in

324   S'envo˙lĕnt un moment sur leurs ai˙lĕs blessé˙es [,]

and

325   J'ai˙mĕ de vos longs yeux la lumiè.re verdâ˙tre,

In both these examples [m] plays a small but significant part, and it is clear that the nasal consonants [m] and [n] have a great deal to contribute to the musicality of verse. [m] is in fact an exception to the general principle that one cannot sing a consonant without vowels. We have only to close our lips, and we can reproduce a melody easily by humming. The only phoneme we are using is the nasal consonant [m]. This is produced by closing the lips as for a labial stop, but bringing the nasal cavity into operation so that the sound is not interrupted but emerges from the nose. It is the use of the two cavities, oral and nasal, as amplifiers which give this conso-nant its resonance and musical quality. [n] is produced in a similar manner but further back in the mouth, where the tongue is brought into contact with the teeth. Of the two, [n] is the less common and the less important, not very frequently forming significant clusters, though it can mingle effectively with [m]. But [m] is very important among the phonetic resources of verse. It is not a mere interruption of the air-flow, but a tuneful sound which continues and links vowels. When used with [l] or [r] it gives a strong sense of continuity and form, as in *calme* or *charme*. At the same time, if we choose to pronounce it forcibly it can have the same effect as a stop, since, so far as the mouth is concerned, that is what it is. So we can say of [m] as we said of [r] that it has two different qualities according to the force with which it is uttered. We may distinguish between the two forms of [m] by describing one as *forceful*, the other as *musical*; but it must be made clear that these terms are not vague and subjective attributes but refer to a specific difference of sound. [m] is forceful when it is read with strong movement of the lips, as in

326   Et, martelant le front massif des cachalots [,]
            m   m

327   Ma maison me regarde, et ne me connaît plus [.]
            m m   m   (m)

It seems likely, in practice, that the forceful [m] will only occur as the initial consonant of a word, whereas musical [m] can occur anywhere. The sound is musical in

328   Et pourtant aimez-moi, ten˙drĕ cœu.r! soyez mè.re
                              m   m   m

        Mê˙mĕ pour un ingrat, mê˙mĕ pour un méchant;
        m   m   m   m   m

        Amante ou sœu.r, soyez la douceu.r éphémè.re [ ] ...
        m   m

and in

329   Perle ou ma ˙ rbrĕ, fleu.r ou ramier [?]
                    már   rám
       rl   r   l   r

The conclusions which may be drawn from our comments on consonants may be summarized as follows:

(*a*) Most consonants may be pronounced vigorously or otherwise, and this will affect their sound and our reaction to it. The adjectives *strong* and *soft* may be used to make the distinction, so long as it is made clear that these are not vague terms but refer specifically to the manner in which the sound is produced. Vigorous consonants, whether stops or fricatives, are most effective when they are voiceless.

(*b*) The voiceless stops [p], [t], and [k] are short, clear and decisive. In their strong form they are obtrusive sounds; when soft, they are crisp, firm, and pleasing.

(*c*) The voiceless fricatives [f], [s], and [ʧ] are equally variable. When strong they hiss; when soft they rustle pleasantly. Unlike the stops they are of indeterminate length and (particularly in the case of the sibilants) may be prolonged to 'colour' the line.

(*d*) [r] is a voiced vibrant which can make a marked contribution to the musicality of a line. When strong it dominates other clusters; when soft, it blends smoothly with other consonants and vowels, tending to prolong the latter as a vibration. [l] is a voiced liquid having similar qualities but for all practical purposes existing only in the soft form, in which it mingles easily with [r] to produce musical and satisfying effects.

(*e*) [m] is a nasal consonant which shares the musical qualities of [r] and [l], at least in its soft form in which it combines easily with these consonants to produce an effect of smooth continuity and also forms powerful clusters in its own right. It is voiced and resonant owing to the use of the nasal cavity. When strong, [m] sounds like a voiced stop. [n] also is a nasal, but has not strong form and is less versatile.

(*f*) The voiced stops [b], [d], and [g], together with the voiced fricative [v], are less obtrusive than their voiceless equivalents. They are generally soft sounds and effective vehicles for [r] and [l].

(*g*) The voiced fricatives [z] and [j] are necessarily soft, easily prolonged, and may add appreciably to the musicality of a line.

We noted at an earlier stage in our study that consonants in French do not bear metrical stress. This stress falls on the vowel alone. However, there is one circumstance in which a consonant may be stressed, in verse as in speech; and this occurs when we single out a word for especial emphasis. This *accent d'insistance* is quite different from normal stress which occurs on the last syllable of a syntactically-linked group of words. When, for instance, we hear the expression 'C'est f´ormidable!' pronounced with some excitement, we recognize two stresses: the normal syntactical one which falls on the final [á], and an *accent d'insistance* which leads us to stress the initial consonant of *formidable*. If we say: 'On l'a t´ué?' we express incredulity at the idea: whereas 'On l'a tué?' with normal stress merely queries fact. An effect of this kind is almost bound to happen, I should think, when a very long word is used to suggest massive power, as in

330   Un navi.re y passait, m'ajestueu.sĕment [;]
                                      m

in which the *accent d'insistance* may even be thought of as supplying the subsidiary stress of [B]. Emphasis of this kind may also be given to shorter words when appropriate.

With stress we may associate the concept of length. As we have seen, in scansion consonants are reckoned as having no length, for this aspect of metre depends solely on the number of vowels. But metre is a somewhat abstract concept. If we consider the actual time taken to read a word or a line, we note not only that this time is affected by the number of consonants present, but also that some consonants take longer to pronounce than others. For instance, [ʧ] necessarily takes longer than [p]; and the length of sibilants and vibrants is variable, whereas that of stops is not. This is often of no importance at all, but obviously if a large number of fricatives and vibrants occur within a particular line, this could have the effect of influencing not the scansion but the temporal length of that line. For instance, when we read

331   Les cocotiers absents de la superbe Afri˙que,
        Derriè˙rĕ la mura.ille immen.sĕ du brouilla.rd [;]

we recognize that the use of voiceless stops in [1] and of voiced nasal consonants and vibrants in [2] is one of a number of contrasting phonetic effects which cause [2] to sound heavier and longer than [1].

But the concept of length is of greater general interest in its application to vowels. Most students of French verse are aware that a line may contain both long and short vowels, and that when long vowels predominate the musical quality of the line is likely to be enhanced (since vowels approximate to musical sounds). We have already considered one form of lengthening which occurs only in verse: i.e. the slight extension of a vowel which occurs in a syllable followed by a neutral [ĕ]. But French also has *naturally* long vowels: i.e. vowels which are long in normal usage, and by convention these are regarded as being twice as long as the normal short vowel. We must be able to recognize them when they occur.

The best way to recognize a long vowel is to hear it as long, as will the student who has learnt to speak French correctly. For this reason we have indicated them in our quotations. But in practice some additional guidance is likely to be necessary, and so we shall attempt to summarize the conditions under which, in French, a vowel becomes long. In the first place it must be recognized that the vast majority of vowels are short, and that long ones are exceptional. In the second place, length is not indicated by spelling. It is tempting to think that vowels such as *eau* and *ai* are naturally long because more than one symbol is used to write them, but this is not the case: the final vowel of *tombeau* [tò bó] is short, as is that of *fait* [fè]. All vowels are basically short, and only become long under specific circumstances; indeed, the same word may have at one time a short vowel and at another a long one. In the line

332   Ainsi, toujours poussés | vers de nouveaux riva.ges [,]

the only long vowel is that of the rime-word; but in

333   Cettĕ chanson d'amou.r | qui toujou.rs recommen.ce [?...]

the final vowel of *toujours*, as well as that of *amour*, is long. For a vowel to be long, two conditions are necessary: it must be stressed and it must be blocked. The *toujours* in 332 does not bear stress, which in [A] falls on the final syllable of *ainsi* and *poussés*; whereas in 333 it bears a subsidiary stress. The second condition, that it must be blocked, requires some explanation. A vowel is *free* when it ends a word, and *blocked* if the word ends in a sounded consonant, as is the case with *toujours* and *amour*. In the first line, the final syllable of *toujours* meets the requirement of being blocked, but it is not stressed; whereas in the second line, it is both blocked and stressed. The final vowel of *poussés* is stressed, but it is free, and so must be short.

However, the fact that a vowel is both stressed and blocked does not necessarily make it long. These merely constitute the conditions under which it *may* be long, but whether it in fact is will depend upon the consonant or consonants that follow it. A stressed vowel will be long under the following conditions:

(*a*) If it is followed by [r] and no other sounded consonant in the same word. If the [r] is attached to another sounded consonant, then the vowel is short. Thus *vert* [vè.r] has a long vowel, since the *t* is silent; but the vowel of *verte* [vèrt] is short. Likewise *mort* [mò.r] and *morte* [mòrt]. When the [f] of *cerf* [sè.r] is silent, the vowel is long, but it is short if the word is pronounced [sèrf]. In the case of a double [r], this is sounded as a single phoneme, and so we have *terre* [tè.r] and *tonnerre* [tò nè.r].

(*b*) If followed by any *voiced* fricative: i.e. [v], [z], [j]. Thus we have: *livre* [li.vr], *rouge* [ru.j], *rose* [ró.z], and *heureuse* [œ̀ rœ.z]. It should be noted that [l] is not a fricative, and the vowel which precedes it, as in *zèle* [zèl] or *calme* [kálm] is naturally short.

(*c*) If followed by *yod*, i.e. the phoneme represented in our phonetic transcript as [ỹ], and which in this position on the word-ending is written in ordinary spelling as *-il* or *-ille*. Thus: œil [œ̀.ỹ], soleil [sò lè.ỹ], travaillent [trá và.ỹ].

In addition to the above general rules, applicable to all vowels, the following special cases should be noted:

(*d*) A nasal vowel, which of course is short when free, is always long if it is stressed and blocked, whatever may be the sounded consonant that follows it. Thus the vowel of *grand* [grà] is short, but that of *grande* is long. So also *longue* [lò.g], *chambre* [chà.br], *blanche* [blà.ch], *ronce* [rò.s], *prince* [prë.s].

(*e*) The three oral vowels [œ̀], [ó], and [à] follow the same rule as nasals: i.e. provided they are both stressed and blocked (by any consonant or consonants) they are long. Thus: *émeute* [é mœ̀.t], *jaune* [jó.n], *âme* [à.m]

Since the alexandrine normally has four stresses, it cannot contain more than four naturally long vowels, and it may have none at all. But as we have seen, even under circumstances other than those listed above, a vowel may be slightly lengthened by a following neutral [ĕ], and this will always happen on the stressed syllable of a feminine rime. If we apply these principles to the line

334   Le monde est som.bre, ô Dieu! l'immuable harmoni˙e [ ]

　.　　.　　.　　..　　　.　　...⏐.　　.　..　　.　　.　...

we find that the nasal of *monde* is short, being unstressed, while that of *sombre* is long, since it is blocked and bears a subsidiary stress. This greatly affects its prominence in the line. The vowel of *Dieu* on the caesura is free and short. The stressed [á] of *immuable* is also short, since it is not followed by a voiced fricative and the following neutral [ĕ] is elided. The final vowel of *harmonie*, being free, is naturally short, but will be slightly lengthened by the feminine ending.

If we bring to our consideration of this line the various points which we have discussed, we note the following:

(*a*) The prominence of [o], occurring in both nasal and oral forms: *monde, som.bre, ô, harmonie*. This is a musical sound. This musical quality is enhanced by three occurrences of the nasal consonant [m] spread throughout the line, and also by the vibrant [r] and three occurrences of the liquid [l]. There is also a nasal [n]. There are only four stops, and these are all voiced. Hence the line flows smoothly and its general effect is sonorous. As we have suggested, [o] in its oral and nasal forms can suggest darkness and depth, and it will certainly take this colouring from the word *sombre*.

(*b*) [A] is strongly dominated by the repeated nasal [ò], and this effect is intensified by the long vowel of *sombre*, as well as by the semantic importance of the words in which the vowel occurs. However, the vowel on the caesura is closed and comparatively toneless, and those of [B] are all closed and with one exception frontal. So the deep resonance with which the line opens fades away into thinner, less musical sounds. This prepares us for the antithesis of the line following:

335 Se compo.sĕ des pleu.rs aussi bien que des chants [;]

Hence the tone of the first line is not merely musical and satisfying, but also follows the meaning of the words, with their implications of frustration.

I am not suggesting that in all cases we should expect to find such a close association between sound and sense: nor would we generally wish to analyse lines in such detail. This example does however illustrate the way in which sounds will tend to suggest themselves to the good poet and so give his lines that sense of 'rightness' which changes verse into poetry. Nor will such effects be limited to the single line. In this particular case we may note how the vowel [o] is continued throughout the stanza, both to musical effect and also to prolong the sense of darkness:

336 Le monde est som.bre, ô Dieu! l'immuable harmoni˙e
     ò   ò ó   ò
   Se compo.sĕ des pleu.rs aussi bien que des chants;
     ò ò.   ó
   L'hommĕ n'est qu'un atome en cette om.bre infini˙e,
     ò   ò   ò.
   Nuit où mon.tĕnt les bons, où to.mbĕnt les méchants [.]
     ò.   ò   ò

To sum up this part of our investigation, I would say that we may legitimately and conveniently use certain specific terms to qualify

sequences of sound, and that these terms will not be merely subjective but will throw light on the phonetic substance of a line or
stanza.

(*a*) We may describe a line as *resonant* if it is dominated by nasal
vowels, probably associated with strong oral ones; and such lines
may often suggest musical sound. Strong oral vowels may be described as *sonorous*.

(*b*) We may speak of it as *musical* if dominated by nasal vowels
and consonants, or open back vowels, perhaps supported by clusters
of liquid and vibrant consonants. Stops and fricatives will generally
be either voiced or, if voiceless, lightly pronounced. The constricted
vowel [u] may also contribute to such lines.

(*c*) It may be *toneless* if middle vowels predominate, or closed or
unrounded ones.

(*d*) It may be potentially *harsh* or *aggressive* if strong stops and
hissed fricatives predominate, perhaps supported by the strong [r]
and unrounded vowels, particularly [á]. If we use terms such as
these, it must be made clear that we are referring to the manner in
which we think the line should be read, rather than to any inherent
quality in the sounds themselves; though some sounds do lend
themselves more readily than others to particular renderings.

(*e*) It may be *constricted* if dominated by [i], [ü], and [u], this
effect often being associated with the expression of frustrated
melancholy.

Many other terms will suggest themselves in connexion with
particular lines; but the above, it seems to me, are of general
application.

The question remains as to whether we can go further in our
relating of sound to meaning: or rather, how much further we can
go, since I take it for granted that since onomatopoeia or *harmonie
imitative*, in a more specific sense than we have so far discussed, is a
fact of ordinary language, it must also be one of the resources of
verse. We have already drawn attention to the caveats which must
be borne in mind in approaching this subject. But we have, I
believe, demonstrated that phonemes do have characteristics which,
in suitable circumstances, may be interpreted meaningfully; and the
possibility that such characteristics may be felt to relate to the
phenomena of ordinary life—specifically to the sounds that we hear
around us, though we are not limited to that field—remains to be
investigated.

We began our chapter with reference to the bird which the
French, like the English, name after its call: *coucou*. This does not
really sound like the cuckoo's call, and no one could guess its
meaning from sound alone: however, it is equally true that if the

hearer was told it referred to a bird with which he is familiar, he would be able to identify it without difficulty. The same phonemes occur in *roucouler*, with the addition of a vibrant and a liquid; and if the hearer unfamiliar with French was invited to choose between *roucouler* and *siffler* as words representing the song of doves and, say, the whistling of a thrush, it would be unwise to offer a substantial prize for a correct answer. Why is this? Surely because the constricted frontal vowel of *siffler* suggests a shrill sound, while the [u] of *roucouler*, though constricted, is deep, being made in the throat, as is also the consonant [k]. Apart from its brilliant vowel, the word *siffler* is not onomatopoeic in this application, and it represents very inadequately the music of birdsong; but it is truly onomatopoeic when applied to forceful human whistling, for then the [fl] combination suggests the expulsion of breath. Only by linguistic convention has this not very musical-sounding word been extended so as to apply to the song of birds. (It may be noted that if we change the vowel, as in *souffler*, we lose the brilliance of sound but retain the implication of breathing.) The word *roucoulement*, on the other hand, is applied only to the song of doves, and is fully onomatopoeic, the musical effects to which we have already referred being augmented by the addition of a nasal vowel and consonant.

Clusters in [r l m] are among the most musical in the French language. But the fact that [l] is termed a *liquid* suggests that, quite apart from its musical potential, it also has onomatopoeic force. It is heard in French in words such as *couler*, *glisser*, and in English in *flow*, *slip*, *slide*, *slither*. It may serve to suggest flowing or liquidity in the widest sense. Baudelaire uses it to this effect, with sibilants, to suggest the sunset and the sky blended with the sea:

337   La gloi.rĕ du sole.il sur la me῍r viole῍tte,
           La gloi.rĕ des cités dans le sole.il couchant,
           Allumaient dans nos cœu.rs une ardeu.r inquiè῍te
           De plonger dans un ciel au reflet alléchant [.]
           l   èl   lé   lé
             j   z   s   ʤ

The liquid, the guttural stop, and the closed vowel of *roucoulement* are all present in another onomatopoeic word, *glouglou*, which as every Frenchman knows represents the sound of a liquid emerging noisily from the neck of a bottle. Its phonemes are similar to those of *roucouler*, but the [k] is now voiced, and pronounced further back in the throat. The vowel is musical, rounded, and constricted. The [g] lacks the lightness of [k]. The liquid [l] is much more prominent. The word *glouglou* has a certain musicality as a result of its rounded vowel and voiced stop and liquid, although the tongue-twisting effect of the repeated [gl] is what catches the imagination. Both the [g] and the vowel are produced in the throat; the vowel suggests constriction, and the [l] suggests flow. The 'real life' sound represented by *glouglou* is quite different from that represented by *roucoulement*, and the two could not possibly be confused.

Glouglou leads us to *engloutir*. Again we have the same sense of throatiness and constriction, but we do not have the self-conscious repetition which is a frequent characteristic of onomatopoeia. And indeed *engloutir* does not suggest a sound at all. But the act of swallowing is associated with the throat, with constriction, and with flowing movement. The association of [g] with the throat—deriving from the physical action required to pronounce it—is apparent in words such as the English *guttural* or the French *gorge*. In combination with the liquid [l] it gives us *sanglot* and *étrangler*. The poet of course can use phonetic qualities of this kind to suggest meaning through sound. Thus Gautier writes

338   Et l'engloutit dans un sanglot [.]

in which the voiced consonants are supported by a triplet of the back nasal [à]. But even when immersed in other patterns, the word still retains its onomatopoeic qualities, as Lamartine demonstrates:

339   Vaste océan de l'être où tout va s'englouti.r [!...]

It is thus clear that even in verse onomatopoeic effect is not totally dependent on clusters, though it may be reinforced by them.

In *étrangler* and *sanglot* the [gl] suggests an obstruction in the throat, just as in *glouglou* it suggests the obstruction offered by the neck of the bottle; but whereas this last word has a closed vowel, in pronouncing the other two the mouth is wide open. But if we compare *étrangler* with *étouffer*, we note that we now have a closed vowel and the voiceless fricative gives us the hiss of breath passing through a constricted space between the teeth and lips. This word has no resonance at all: it is not only cognate with, but also similar in quality to, the English *stuffed up*. We have lost not only the resonant vowel but also the liquid and the voiced stop. All of which, of course, is perfectly appropriate to the sense.

A 'throaty' effect of a different kind is offered by the French *bâiller* and the English *yawn*, both of which use the *yod* sound which is produced in the throat. The muscular effort required to produce this sound is not dissimilar to yawning. Baudelaire demonstrates that in this case too onomatopoeic effect can be independent of patterning:

340   Et dans un bâîllĕment avalĕrait le mon.de [;]

In cases such as this the onomatopoeic effect is meaningfully restricted to one word, and the effect would be lessened if it was spread throughout the line.

It seems that when onomatopoeic words are created, the phonemes express certain qualities which are felt and not necessarily heard in the original. There is nothing in the original sound equivalent to the [k] of *coucou* or *tic tac*, or even to the [gl] of *glouglou*. [k] gives the call a crisp beginning and associates it with the throat; [gl] being voiced blends more fully with the vowels, is not at all crisp but more melodious, and it is not a mere play on words to say that the [l] gives the combination a liquid quality. But the twisting of the tongue required to produce [l] also suggests obstruction (and, as we have already suggested, this sound becomes absurd if we attempt to stress it. It is ideal for tongue-twisters). In both *coucou* and *glouglou* the vowel is constricted, velar, closed, and rounded, as indeed it is in *étouffer*, but not in *étrangler* in which an open mouth is implied, and so the vowel is open and unrounded. Words such as *engloutir*, *étrangler*, *étouffer*, and *bâiller* are not representations of sound; and even those which are, seem to interpret the qualities of sound rather than to imitate it. Hence the onomatopoeic process is not limited to suggesting sound; it can use the muscular movements that we make in pronouncing phonemes to suggest concepts having nothing to do with sound, such as openness, closedness, depth, lightness, liquidity, vibration, and so on. The words we have considered represent a first stage in this kind of development, since they all refer to actions of the mouth and lips (or in one case, by extension, to the neck of a bottle) so that they can easily be represented by sounds which require a similar muscular movement of the mouth. But once this development has occurred, the next, which is a kind of metaphorical extension of the same principle, may be expected to follow automatically. In words such as *coucou*, duplication of sound is used in order to bring out the onomatopoeic function of the word. In the case of other words less obviously onomatopoeic, but nevertheless constructed in such a way that the phonemes are suggestive of their meaning, the poet can achieve an effect similar to duplication by associating these words with others also containing the relevant phonemes. Here, for instance, we have the use of [l] and [r], together with some other phonemes, to suggest liquidity and vibration:

341   Au tintĕment de l'eau dans les porphy.rĕs roux
              l   l   r   r   r
       ó   ó   ò

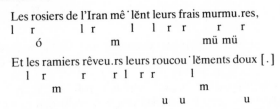

Here Leconte de Lisle is representing sounds—the tinkling of water, rustling of leaves and cooing of doves. However, his words, when read aloud, do not sound even remotely like the non-linguistic sounds which they evoke. Their effectiveness depends upon the fact that the sounds [l] and [r] are formed in the mouth by a muscular effort which suggests a glide, and hence flowing liquidity, and also vibration. These qualities of the phonemes intensify the meaning of the words and enable them to appeal more directly to the imagination. In this case, it is true, the combinations of phonemes are selected mainly with the object of achieving musicality of sound, and the fact that they suggest other sounds is in a sense incidental: the adjective *frais* in [2] conveys nothing to the intelligence and is where it is simply to enhance the phonetic pattern. The functions of musicality and onomatopoeia are often blended in this way.

Since [l] and [r] do not copy non-linguistic sounds but rather suggest sensation by the way in which they are pronounced, it is perfectly possible to use them to appeal to senses other than hearing. When Lamartine writes

342   Et dans leurs frais vallons, au sou˙fflĕ du zéphi.r [,]
        l   r fr   v l   fl   f   r
                         z   s   z

what he is suggesting is not specifically associated with sound. In addition to [l] and [r] the poet uses the voiceless fricative [f], formed by blowing between the lower teeth and upper lip, as well as voiced and voiceless sibilants. This does not reproduce the hum of the breeze but rather the sensation of vibrant movement, of blowing. Hugo associates a similar combination of phonemes not only with the breeze but also with perfume:

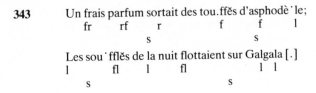

So does Baudelaire: and we have suggested that the image

344   Il est des parfums frais commĕ des chai.rs d'enfants [,]
            rf   frè   èr   f

derives as much from phonetic association as from any other source.
It seems, then, that [r] and [l] can be used effectively in images
derived from various senses—hearing, touch, and smell. And the
effect is partly visual in

345   Pendant que l'om.brĕ trem.ble, et que l'â˙prĕ rafa˙le [ ]
            l   br tr   bl   l   pr r f l
         à à   ò   à   á   á á

as is made clear by the use of the word *ombre*. The fact that the
essence of the image is vibration is also established by *tremble*. In
[A] the sound is rich and resonant, as the result of the use of four
nasal vowels (all velar) and mainly voiced consonants: in [B] the
effect is much thinner, for the vowels are oral, the consonants
voiceless, the vibrants will be vigorously articulated, and there is a
strong terminal triplet in the unrounded consonant [á]. What is
suggested in [B], one may think, is tactile rather than visual. We
return to an unquestionably visual effect in Verlaine's

346   L'om. brĕ des a˙rbrĕs dans la riviè.re embrumé˙e [ ]
            l   br   rbr   l r   r   br

where the vibrant, coupled with voiced stops, suggests the blurring
of an image reflected in flowing water. One may speak less cate-
gorically of the stanza following: but here it seems to me that the
vibrant suggests two effects: a visual one, a sort of brilliant sheen or
miroitement, and an oleofactory one—the perfume of flowers and
amber.

347   Des meu˙blĕs luisants
                    m   l l
                Polis par les ans
                   l   r l
            Décoreraient notre cham.bre;
                 r r   r   r
                Les plus ra.rĕs fleu.rs
                l   l r r l   r
                Mêlant leurs odeu.rs
                m l   l r   r
            Aux va˙guĕs senteu.rs de l'am.bre.
                       r   l   r

Les ri.chĕs plafonds,
  l   r   l
Les miroi.rs profonds,
  l   mr r   r
La splendeu.r orienta˙le
l   l   r r
Tout y parlerait
      rl r
A l'â.me en secret
  l   m   r
Sa dou˙cĕ lan˙guĕ nata˙le [.]
       l   l

One of the most remarkable effects of *miroitement* is that obtained by Hugo in his description of moonlight sparkling on seabirds' wings:

348   Sont-ce des cormorans qui plon.gĕnt tour à tou.r
           Et cou˙pĕnt l'eau, qui roule en pe˙rlĕs sur leur ai˙le [?]
                l   r l   èrl   rl r èl
         ku   p   k   u   p

Here the effect is heightened by the modulation of vowels from [1] to [2]. The first of these lines opens with a series of back vowels, some of them nasal and therefore sonorous and resonant:

Sont | – ce des cormorans | qui plon.|gĕnt ...
 ò | ò ò   ò
   | à | |

These are associated with the impact of the birds; there is an impression of power, size, and possibly darkness—all of which concepts can be suggested by [ò]. While still remaining in the back of the throat, the vowels then change to [u], a lighter sound to express a change of movement:

..... tour à tou.r,
       u   u
Et cou˙pĕnt l'eau, qui roule ....
   u   u

while the actual reflection and sparkle is expressed by thin frontal vowels:

..... en pe˙rlĕs sur leur ai˙le [?]
       è   ü œ è

To this may be added the change in rhythm from the binary to the ternary alexandrine:

> Sont-ce des cormorans | qui plon.gĕnt tour à tour,
> Et coupĕnt l'eau, | qui roule en per | lĕs sur leur aile [?]

A feature of interest in these two lines is the use of repetition or phonetic parallel to an end which, if not strictly onomatopoeic, is closely related to the point we are considering. We have *Sont-ce* [sò.|sĕ] answered by *plongent* [plò.|jĕ], the first two syllables of *cormorans* [kòr mòr], *tour à tour*, the neat balance of the doublet in [kupl]:

> Et cou῾ pĕnt l'eau, qui roule en pe῾ rlĕs ....
> k up l   k   ul   p

which is continued by the more complex mirror effect of

> ... roule en pe῾ rlĕs sur leur ai῾ le [?]
> r l   è rl   r l   êl

There is a general effect of massive and complex phonetic reduplication which is so strong, I would suggest, as to have the effect of blurring our vision. *En perles sur leur aile* gives us a kind of echo which is both visual and phonetic, and it is the culmination of a series of such reduplications. This is an application, or extension, of the ordinary echo as used, for instance, by Baudelaire:

> **349** Commĕ de longs échos qui de loin se confon.dent,
>   ò fò d
> Dans unĕ ténébreu.se et profon.de unité [,]
>   òfò d

(lines in which, of course, the other [o]s, both oral and nasal, play their part). In this case the actual sound of an echo is suggested, as it is, with much greater dramatic effect, in Vigny's

> **350** Roulaient et redoublaient les fou῾ drĕs de l'ora.ge [,]
>   rul   r u l   l   u r   l r
>   d   d d

But it is also possible to suggest an echo by the mere fact of repetition, even if the words themselves are not onomatopoeic. This, I believe, is what Hugo does in

> **351** J'entends enco.re au loin dans la plaine ouvriè.re
> Chanter derrièrĕ moi la dou῾ cĕ chevriè.re [,]

where the sequence *ouvrière, derrière, chevrière* expresses by a sort of echo the prolongation of the singing in the poet's mind. It is not onomatopoeic, except to the extent that the light vowels suggest a girl's voice, but the fact of repetition expresses meaning. In the same way a mirror image can be expressed by repetition:

352   Combien, ô voyageu.r, ce paysa.gĕ blê˙me
            Te mira blê˙mĕ toi-mê˙me [,]

Thus in the case of repetition, as in that of the other devices we have considered, the effect which the poet achieves may be audial, visual, or tactile at will. We have quoted lines from Hugo's *Clair de lune* (**348**) in which the peculiar ambiguity of moonlight was expressed by a reduplication of sounds, associated with the liquid and vibrant effects of [l r] to suggest the sparkling of the water. Since it was this example which launched this short divagation on the poet's capacity to make us see double, we may conclude it with a comparable technique used by Gautier in *Soleil couchant*. In this case there is no sparkle on the water and the [l r] effect is not present, save in [2] below which refers specifically, though not vividly, to the river. For the rest, what is desired is a shadowy vagueness, an uncertainty of vision; and to achieve this Gautier makes use of the repetition of identical words with different stress, or different meaning, as well as of enjambement on both line-ending and caesura in order to soften or blur the outline of the metre:

353   …. L'air était doux; les eaux
            Se plaignaient contrĕ l'arche à doux bruit, et la va˙gue
            De la vie.illĕ cité berçait l'ima.gĕ va˙gue;
            Et moi, je regardais toujou.rs, ne songeant pas
            Que la nuit étoilée arrivait à grands pas [.]

In [1] the adjective *doux* is stressed. It recurs, unstressed, in [2], as a contrapuntal echo. *Vague* is stressed at the end of both [2] and [3] and gives the impression of repetition: but in the first case it is a noun, in the second an adjective, and the two words have nothing other than their form in common. It is a punning rime. And it so happens that the first occurrence of *vague* in [2] calls for a good deal more stress than does its recurrence in [3], an effect contrary to that normally found in rime. Identical rime-words are again used in [4] and [5]. In this case they are truly identical, at least so far as origin is concerned, for the negative particle *pas* derives from the identical word meaning *a step*. The effect of this repetition throughout the passage is one of deliberate monotony, but also of ambiguity;

suggesting the uncertainties of half-light, in which things are not always what they seem, and one object merges with another.

From this highly sophisticated use of suggestive sound, I propose now to return to a simpler level: in fact to the one line which all readers of French verse will admit is onomatopoeic, however much they may dislike such frivolities. I refer to Racine's

354   Pour qui sont ces serpents qui si ˙fflĕnt sur ma tê ˙te [?]
            s   s s   s   s
            i   i i

which we may agree represents the hissing of snakes in a manner comprehensible even to the tone deaf. (The theatre, making allowance for human nature, has always had recourse to exaggerated and over-simplified effects.) We must note, in the first place, that even an effect as blatant as this depends on interpretation. If we read this line giving the sibilants their soft value, as in

355   Cettĕ chanson d'amou.r qui toujou.rs recommen.ce [?..]

it will be as soothing as any lullaby. Onomatopoeia can never exist effectively unless it is interpreted as such, which means that it can never be independent of the meaning of the words. In this case, the sounds are vigorous and fierce. The prevailing cluster is in [s] and [i], and we all know that snakes *sifflent* or *hiss*. In fact, snakes do not utter any kind of phoneme. When unintentionally trodden on or otherwise provoked they expel their breath violently (or so my limited experience leads me to believe), producing a sound which one might represent as [hhhhhh], though the constricted aperture through which the breath passes perhaps brings it closer to [ssssss] than these symbols indicate. The Greeks called the snake *herpa*, and English uses the [h] in *hiss*, but French lacks this sound. And English, even though it includes [h] among its phonemes, does not possess an extended [h], and so it is the [s] which we prolong. French must rely entirely on [s]. The essential points are (a) that the sound represents the friction of expelled breath, and (b) that the sound is voiceless, since the snake has no vocal cords. In theory there should be no vowel at all, but since this is contrary to linguistic usage, the problem is solved by introducing the most frontal and constricted, and hence the least sonorous or resonant, of vowels, which is [i]. When voiceless breathing is expelled between lip and teeth we obtain [f], which, with the 'flowing' effect of [l], gives us *siffler*. The only phoneme which *serpent* has in common with *siffler* is the initial [s]. So Racine has to bring this into prominence by the use of otherwise characterless words such as *sont, ces* and *sur*. The last also brings in the [r] of *serpent*; and in fact the [rp] of this word is pre-echoed by the [p-r] of *pour*. The importance of the [p] is that it can express the voiceless expulsion of breath which results from the rapid opening of the lips, as in the English *spit*. (Unlike Englishmen, Frenchmen apparently spit from the back of the throat, if *cracher* is any guide.) And so, with the addition of the only usable vowel [i] and the careful avoidance, as far as possible, of resonant or sonorous phonemes, we are given:

356   Pour qui sont ces serpents qui sifflent sur ma tête [?]
         　　i.. | s s s 　　 | 　si.. 　sü
         p　r　|　　r p　|　　　|　　r

All the vowels are constricted, with the exception of the unimportant [sò] and the very important but unavoidable [pà]; all the consonants are voiceless with the exception of [r] which adds vibration and [l] which prolongs [f]. So we are given, in fact, what we expect: an obvious translation of natural sound into a linguistic equivalent. We now compare this with Hugo's

357   Les cho.sĕs qui sortaient de son nocturne esprit
         Semblaient un gli˙ssĕment sini˙strĕ de vipè.res [.]

Again, we have onomatopoeia: and what is remarkable is that, although neither the word *serpent* nor *siffler* is used, the general phonetic quality is remarkably similar. There is a prevalence of voiceless stops, and the same [i], [s], and [pèr] as Racine used, now appearing in *glissement sinistre de vipères*. Here the [s] refers not so much to the hissing of snakes as to their slithering movement, which is soundless: but of course the mention of the word *snake* so easily conjures up the thought of hissing that this may be implied also. A comparison of the pitch-slopes of Racine's and Hugo's line may serve to remind us that some of the principles discussed in our first chapter are relevant to the representation of meaning through sound. In Racine's line the voice will tend to rise to indicate the rearing up of the snakes; it will fall in Hugo's line, for here they are slithering downwards:

[sà ^blè | tœ glí sĕ mà sí ní strĕ dĕ ví _pè.r]

A third approach to snakes is demonstrated by Musset:

358   Et c'est un frisson plein d'horreu.r
         Quand cettĕ vipè.re assoupi˙e
         Se dérou˙lĕ dans notrĕ cœu.r [.]

A new word is used to introduce the familiar [is] sound: not *siffler* nor *glissement* but *frisson*. The sounds of *cette vipère assoupi* need no comment; but we may note that the fierceness of the [i] is softened (for the snake is sleepy) by modulating, through a phonetic copula, to a more sonorous constricted vowel:

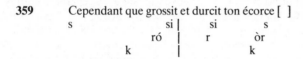

The association now is with slow movement and horror.

This raises a question. No one can doubt that all these cases are examples of onomatopoeia. But is something more involved? Is the poet representing the sound and movement of snakes, or is he expressing primarily that deep aversion which man has always felt for these beautiful and often harmless reptiles? Is his phonetic colouring governed by emotion? Consider how Baudelaire addresses the *grand arbre* Desire, for which he feels so much loathing:

359   Cependant que grossit et durcit ton écorce [ ]
        s   si | si   s
                          ró | r   òr
               k | k

The prevailing cluster is very familiar. We are no longer concerned with snakes, but the sibilants still produce a hiss which suggests revulsion. And this is also true of

360   Frémi˙ssent aux portraits noi.rs de leur ressemblan.ce [!]
                i | s | s   s
             r | p r r   r| r

Thus the sounds which we associate with snake-images can express an emotional reaction of the kind which these reptiles usually occasion, even in a phrase which has nothing to do with snakes. What then happens when a poet writes of snakes without aversion? First, an example from Lamartine which, although not about snakes, contains a sustained snake image:

361   Quelquĕs ceps dont les bras, cherchant en vain l'éra˙ble,
        Serpen.tĕnt sur la te.rre ou ram.pĕnt sur le sa˙ble; [....]
        Là, deux ruisseaux cachés sous les ponts de verdu˙re
        Tra˙cĕnt en serpentant les contou.rs du vallon:
        Ils mê˙lĕnt un moment leur on.de et leur murmu.re,
        Et non loin de leur source ils se pe˙rdĕnt sans nom [.]

We still have patterns in [s], [èr], [p], and [à]—the phonemes which form *serpent*—and an abundance of voiceless sounds; but they are now soft, and [i] is missing. Baudelaire gives us an image in which the snake is more vividly present:

362   A te voir marcher en caden.ce
           Be˙llĕ d'abandon,
           On dirait un serpent qui dan.se
           Au bout d'un bâton [.]

No horror at all, and to all intents and purposes no [i]. Next Rimbaud, full of bizarre wonder, but without fear or disgust:

363   Où les serpents géants dévorés de punai.ses
           Choient, des arbres tordus, avec de noi.rs parfums!

One's first inclination may be to say that none of these are as closely onomatopoeic as the earlier examples: but analysis would show that they all use sound-patterns or words to suggest certain qualities associated with snakes which are considered attractive: a graceful, quiet, sliding movement in Lamartine; rhythmic balance in Baudelaire; rich sensuous twisting in Rimbaud (for *tordus*, although it describes the trees, is imaginatively associated with the snakes). Rimbaud, in addition to his [s-j-ʧ] fricatives, actually gives all the phonemes of *vipère* with the conspicuous exception of [i] in his powerful phrase *dévorés de punaises*. In all these examples, [i] is avoided.

  These examples tend to confirm the view that when a snake is represented by a cluster in [is] and other associated sounds, what is expressed is not merely the sound or movement of the reptile but an attitude of revulsion towards it. When such an attitude is not implied, these phonemes are not in evidence. This is presumably only a specific application of what must be a general principle: that onomatopoeia may not only evoke the thing itself but also seek to make that thing pleasing or otherwise to the reader. On the whole the tendency will be to make it pleasing, since onomatopoeia favours the creation of phonetic clusters which enhance the texture of the line and bring it nearer to music. But the phonetic cluster can also produce tongue-twisters and other exaggerated effects, though these must be used with caution if the poem is not to suffer. An example of successful cacophony is heard in the contemptuous reference of the Travellers, in Baudelaire's *Le Voyage*, to the albums in which the stay-at-homes, avid for novelty, store other people's souvenirs of foreign parts:

364   —Pourtant nous avons, avec soin,
               Cueilli quelques croquis pour votre album vora˙ce [.]
               k   k   k   k k

                              vò r a   vòra

I am assuming that [k], [v], and [r] will be pronounced vigorously. If
they are not, there is nothing either harsh or comic about the line,
and it could indeed be quite melodious. This qualification must
likewise be borne in mind when we speak of a cluster in [is] implying
revulsion. Certainly it is apt to do so, but only if our reading
encourages such an interpretation.

But it is perfectly possible for a sentiment which is not in itself
pleasing to be expressed in a pleasing and musical manner. If we
analyse Racine's line

365   Tout m'affli.ge et me nuit et conspi.re à me nui.re [.]
                    i   ŭi   i   ŭi
               m   m n   m n
                                          r   r

we note that the thin and constricted vowels which so admirably
express discontent are supported by a cluster of nasal consonants
which greatly enrich the tonality of the line. It is well known that
nasal consonants can in themselves suggest musical sound, when
pronounced softly, as in Lamartine's allusion to streams running
through a valley:

366   Ils mê˙lĕnt un moment leur on.de et leur murmu.re [,]

an effect to which the nasal vowel of *onde* makes a discreet contribution. As we have suggested, it is the nasal vowel which is the
prime resource of the French language for suggesting musical sound.
A comparison of two of Hugo's lines

367   J'entends le vent dans l'ai.r, la me.r sur le récif [,]
                    à à   à   à
                        l   l   l   l
                                    èr   èr   r   ré
                                          s   s

and

368   Pendant que l'om.brĕ trem.ble et que l'â˙prĕ rafa˙le
                    à à   (ò)   à
                        l   r r   l   l   r r   l
                                          á   á á

will show that in the first case the melodious sound of the wind is suggested by the use of nasal vowels; in the second unrounded oral vowels and voiceless consonants are used to suggest its blustering force without any musical quality. Both lines show a modulation from nasal vowels in [A] to oral ones in [B]. In [1B] the lack of resonance may well suggest the distance of the sea and the fact that it is not heard as a musical hum. In [2A] the nasal vowels do not suggest sound at all, but offer a sumptuous richness of phonemes which makes all the more effective the transition to the bleakness of [2B]. Gautier offers an interesting example of wilful lack of musicality in the last line of one of his stanzas to the monks painted by Zurbarán:

369 Et vous vivez muets, inclinés sur vos bi˙bles,
Croyant toujours enten.dre aux plafonds entr'ouve.rts
Éclater brusquĕment les trompe˙ttĕs terri˙bles [!]

Since the sound of trumpets is musical, we might well expect nasal vowels to dominate the line. But the two which actually occur are quite insignificant. What we have is a series of stops, most of them voiceless, supported by a cluster in [r]. This is an effective representation of the sound in that it reproduces the tonguing of the instrument. The reason Gautier has chosen this form of expression is that the theme of his poem is the monks' total insensitivity to beauty. To them, the last trumpet is the harbinger of divine vengeance, not a musical sound. Thus here, as in previous examples, we find that onomatopoeia suggests not only the thing itself but an emotional attitude towards it.

Modulation from nasal to oral vowels, and vice versa, can be a very effective means of intensifying meaning. Thus Vigny, in the following lines, gives phonetic expression to disillusion by opening with an apparently self-confident assertion of man's achievement, expressed in resonant nasals, and following on with a second line of oral vowels which express the self-defeating nature of that achievement:

370 La distan.ce et le temps sont vaincus. La scien.ce
Trace autou.r de la te.rre un chemin triste et droit [.]

A similar though inverse effect is obtained by Baudelaire when he evokes, with a series of voiceless stops, the vain day-dream of her native continent cherished by the negress exiled in northern Europe, only to overwhelm it by a resonant combination of nasal consonants and vibrants (strengthened by enjambement on the caesura) compared with which the first line seems fragile indeed:

371   Les cocotiers absents de la superbe Afri˙que
         Derriè.rĕ la mura.ille immen.sĕ du brouilla.rd [;].

The possibilities of yoking sound to meaning are so extensive and
so varied that in a study of this kind one can do no more than call
attention to some of the methods adopted by poets to this end, and
endeavour to understand some of the principles upon which this
aspect of poetic creativity rests. This is a field which can be but
incompletely comprehended, since so little is known about our
response to language, and it is perhaps as well that it should be since
here lies the mystery of poetry. One cannot avoid some subjectivity
of judgement, and the reader will not necessarily agree with some of
the claims I have made. However, the attempt at comprehension is
well worth while, since it opens to us great riches of imaginative
potential which lie within language, to which we shall remain deaf if
we do not give some thought to the matter. It is not to be supposed
that the mere pronunciation of the words of verse will enable it to
communicate its overtones. A quick and superficial reading may
yield up all that is necessary for intellectual comprehension, but
only careful and thoughtful preparation—indeed, rehearsal—will
enable us to uncover those levels of imaginative and emotional
meaning which are characteristic of great verse, in which the poet
has used his words in the only way which could fully communicate
his thought. The impossibility of translating poetry does not spring
only from the difficulty of matching rimes and metre, but also from
the fact that words and combinations of words act on so many
different levels. The approach here adopted can be of value to the
student if it frees him from the hypocrisy of pretending that he
responds to effects which he does not hear, and encourages him to
consider carefully what he does hear. Only too frequently does one
encounter, in commentaries on poems, sweeping generalizations
which suggest that the student has recognized that a particular line is
doing more than make an intellectual statement, but that he lacks
the method to understand what it is in fact doing. We are told 'You
can almost hear the wind ....' or 'The sharp consonants bring out the
poet's despair ....', and we know that the student has anaesthetized
himself to the true magic of the words by convincing himself, or
attempting to convince the examiner, that he has felt something
which he thinks he ought to feel but in fact does not.

   If our present study has succeeded in its purpose, it will have
achieved three results. In the first place, it will have given the reader
greater skill and confidence in his ability to translate the words on
the printed page into what the poet actually created: a sequence of

visions and images embodied in linguistic sound. Secondly, it will enable him to participate in the poetic experience, which means reading with pleasure and enlightenment. Thirdly, it will give him a method by which he may examine the poet's achievement critically, applying to it standards applicable to all, or most, verse, and assessing his experience in a way which satisfies both his imagination and his reason. I hope it will have done these things. On the other hand, if it has the effect of exalting the technique of verse at the expense of the vision and pleasure of poetry, then it will have failed. In this book we have been concerned almost entirely with method because that is our subject, but no method exists for its own sake. It exists to be applied to some purpose. For this reason, although we have not attempted to discuss the wider implications of poetry, we cannot leave this examination of the poet's resources and craft without some demonstration of how they can be applied to the reading not merely of verse but of poetry. We shall now attempt to give such a demonstration.

COMMENTARIES

A NOTE ON THE COMMENTARIES

No commentary on a poem can be exhaustive. It represents, at the best, a personal reading. It should as far as possible be factual, but a fact can only be said to exist in so far as it is seen to be significant, and on this matter judgement will vary. Any commentary will aim at drawing attention to some facts which will be of permanent value to other readers in their interpretation of the poem.

It may be objected that to expose the mechanical structure of a work of art to too close a rational scrutiny is to destroy our appreciation of it. This is not so in the case of a poem so long as we bear in mind that our object is to prepare ourselves for reading the poem. Analysis is not the end but the beginning. The poems here examined do not exist on paper, but only in the imagination, and even then only to the fullest extent when re-created by the human voice. For the purpose of this re-creation, we need to be fully aware of the potential of the lines, which in the end will differ to some extent for each individual reader.

The reader of these Commentaries will make his own decision as to which of the facts I adduce are relevant to the interpretation which he himself would wish to give to the poems.

However dedicated a student of French verse the reader may be, he will not often find it possible to explore a poem as fully as has been attempted here. Most Commentaries written are merely short tests of knowledge and comprehension, and as such they can be very useful. Much of what follows could find no place in such an exercise. Even so, in a much shorter assessment, the same principles would apply. We have to restrict ourselves to fewer examples. But the recognition of a few important features of a poem, and the demonstration of their importance, is enough to indicate that we are capable of reading it. That, and not the reproduction of other people's views, is the purpose of a Commentary on a poem.

A SONNET BY RONSARD

Comme on void sur la bran.che au mois de May la ro.se

En sa be ́llĕ jeune ́sse, en sa premie.rĕ fleu.r,

Rendrĕ le ciel jaloux de sa vi.vĕ couleu.r,

4   Quand l'au.bĕ de ses pleu.rs au poinct du jou.r l'arro.se:

La gra.cĕ dans sa feu.ille, et l'amou.r se repo.se,

Embasmant les jardins et les a ́rbrĕs d'odeu.r:

Mais battue ou de pluye ou d'excessi.ve ardeu.r,

8   Languissan.te ellĕ meu.rt feuille à feu.illĕ déclo.se.

Ainsi en ta premie.re et jeu.nĕ nouveauté,

Quand la te.rre et le ciel honoroient ta beauté,

La Pa ́rquĕ t'a tuée, et cen.drĕ tu repo.ses.

12   Pour obse ́quĕs reçoy mes la ́rmĕs et mes pleu.rs,

Ce va.sĕ plein de laict, ce panier plein de fleu.rs,

Afin que vif et mo.rt ton co.rps ne soit que ro.ses [.]

IDENTIFICATION

This sonnet is by Pierre de Ronsard (1524-85), who is today known to all literate Frenchmen as the author of some of the finest short lyrics in the French language, and was celebrated in his own time as scholar, literary theoretician, and court poet. As arbiter of literary taste and one of the leaders of the group of poets known as the *Pléiade*, he had an enduring influence on the development of French verse by his blending of the classical influences generally associated with the Renaissance with the native French tradition so as to invigorate and renew the language and give it a literary standing previously enjoyed only by Latin. These influences came into France from Italy, and the sonnet was an Italian form. Ronsard's successful adaptation of this form was to no small extent responsible for the prestige it has subsequently enjoyed in French literature.

The sonnet is one of the twelve published in 1578 and written on the command of Henri III on the death of the king's mistress, Marie de Clèves, at the early age of 21. To this extent it may be considered an example of pure craftsmanship put at the service of the poet's royal patron. However, it does have personal relevance for the poet. In 1555 he had published his *Amours de Marie* addressed to a young woman he had loved, of whom little is known but who is thought to have been an Angevin peasant girl, and who herself died young. The coincidence of name and circumstances must surely suggest that something of the poet's own earlier experience passed into this present work.

The poem is reproduced here in its original spelling, which differs only in minor respects from modern usage. Spellings such as *void, pluye, embasment* (= embaumant) will cause the modern reader little difficulty: but it may be useful to note that the form *reçoy* in [12] is a singular imperative which today would be written *reçois*. The grave and circumflex accents were not in general use at this period.

THEME

[1-8] The poet takes as his symbol the rose, which reaches perfection in its first freshness but is soon destroyed by rain and the heat of the day.
[9-11] He tells of the early death of the young woman to whom the poem is addressed, and whose beauty has called up the image of the rose.
[12-13] He places an offering of milk and flowers upon her grave.
[14] He links the gift of flowers with the rose of the earlier stanzas. The reader understands his offering as being the poem itself, which will for all time associate his beloved with the beauty of the rose.

Although the poem is a tribute to a particular girl, its theme is the fleeting and fragile nature of beauty, the expression of grief, and the consolation offered by the poet's power to give immortality to that which life destroys. The personal element is discreet and muted. Love of nature and life and beauty, the assertion of hope which transforms grief, the absence of sentimentality and introspection, are features of the poem which may be felt to be particularly characteristic of the sixteenth century and of the Renaissance in Europe.

The rose has been used in literature since antiquity as a symbol of the ephemeral, but in general it has been associated with the passing pleasures of the senses. This is the value Ronsard gives it in his well-known lines:

Vivez, si m'en croyez, n'attendez à demain:
Cueillez dés aujourd'hui les ro.sĕs de la vi˙e [.]

which echoes not only the *carpe diem* of Horace but the apocryphal Wisdom of Solomon: 'Come then, let us enjoy what good things there are, and use this creation with the zest of youth [...] Before they wither, let us crown ourselves with roses.' But in this sonnet Ronsard renews the theme in that he writes not of carnal pleasures but of beauty, which is no less fleeting. And since he appeals directly to our senses with his image of the rose, it is no mere cliché or convention. Indeed, the rose is no less the subject of the poem than is the girl to whom it is compared. In this respect, it is closer to the nineteenth-century concept of the poetic symbol than to the traditional figure of rhetoric. It differs also from its predecessors in that we feel it is 'drawn from life'. However, we must not think of Ronsard as a Romantic *avant la lettre* turning to wild nature for consolation. As the use of *les jardins* in [6] reminds us, his rose is a cultivated one such as he would observe in the ornamental gardens of great houses and palaces. (The garden, although it had not developed in France as it had in Italy, was a feature of Renaissance architecture.) But it is definitely a real rose, and not merely a figure of speech.

The image of the second tercet is a classical and literary reminiscence. It is, however, skilfully tied into the theme of the quatrains. Its acceptability is increased by the fact that the offering of flowers to the dead, while here implying a classical and pagan rite, is nevertheless a universal one, and is readily assimilated to the Christian custom of placing flowers on a grave, which would be familiar to Ronsard's contemporaries as to us.

The opening lines, celebrating the beauty of the rose, make a vivid impression on the imagination, and the quatrains (together with the last line) are the most immediately memorable part of the poem. In comparison, the death of Marie is touched on only in the most abstract and general terms. (It is unfortunately true that poets rarely have anything interesting to say in their verses about the women they love.) The death of the rose is not introduced until [8], and that of Marie not until [11], while the poet's grief is disposed of in [12] in a single hemistich. Thus the overall content of the poem does not emphasize sadness: nor does the beautiful line with which it concludes. And yet, mingled with the theme of beauty there is pathos. This derives not merely from what is said, but from the fact that the poem is written *because the girl is dead*: and it is this fact that gives as it were an emotional and poignant echo to the sensuous beauty of the lines.

PRESENTATION AND STYLE

The poem reveals a mind steeped in classical literature and using as the natural medium of poetry the rhythm and imagery of rhetoric: but it does so with originality and naturalness. Its rhythms are French, its images unforced, its vocabulary that of normal literary usage. The use of *ardeur* in [7] in its literal sense of 'heat' was doubtless an archaism, but Ronsard sought deliberately a 'literary' style which would enable French to fulfil all the functions of the traditional language of literature and learning, which was Latin; he wished his language to be that of current usage, but nevertheless not commonplace. *Déclose* (= open, of a flower) is likewise a term of respectable ancestry. The use of *feuille* in [5, 8] to refer to petals, not leaves, is accepted poetic usage; and *cendre* [11] describing mortal remains is traditional (cf. the English *ashes to ashes*). In this line, *cendre* is of course used rhetorically in apposition to *tu*. The construction of [5], in which the singular verb *se repose* agrees with the second of two subjects, appears to be based on the model of Latin, its purpose being to make the rime.

The sonnet takes the form of a simile introduced in [1] by *comme*, the first term of the comparison extending through the octave and being answered in the sestet by *ainsi*. As the rose perishes in the first flush of its beauty, so has the girl to whom the poem is addressed. The extended simile is a familiar feature of rhetorical and *précieux* style. Although in the case of the rose personification is not specifically used as a figure of speech, it is implied by the choice of vocabulary: particularly *jeunesse* in [2], not normally applied to a plant, and *languissante* in [8]. Both *grace* and *amour* in [5] suggest human qualities, and in [3] the expression *rendre le ciel jaloux* treats the relationship between the sky and the rose as that between two women, one jealous of the other's beauty. The other term of the comparison, Marie, is likewise personified, in this case by apostrophe: i.e. addressing the dead as if she were living and present. This too is fully justified in poetic terms, not only because this manner of expression is readily acceptable in a situation of extreme emotion (cf. its very similar use by Hugo in *Demain dès l'aube* ...) but also because it serves to make her vividly present. Indeed, it is the only means used to this end, since we are told nothing of her save in the most general terms, and she would otherwise remain a very shadowy figure indeed.

Thus in both cases personification fulfils a genuinely poetic purpose, and contributes to the effectiveness of the comparison between Marie and the rose. We find it also in other cases where it is little more than a conventional feature of style: e.g. in [10] where *la terre* and *le ciel* are personified in a rather unimaginative hyperbole. But as we have seen, the poet has already personified the sky in [3], where it is apparently rather less ready to pay tribute to beauty than it is in [11]. The image of jealousy is the more interesting of the two. It is a typically *précieux* metaphor, and introduced for a purpose: to intensify our awareness of the vivid colouring of the rose by associating it with human emotion. But, we may object, would it not have been better if the poet had told us what colour the rose is, so that we could see it in imagination? I think in fact that he does. In the sixteenth century the choice would lie between red and white, since the multifarious development of colour and shape which has characterized the modern garden rose belongs to the nineteenth and twentieth centuries. *Sa vive couleur* does not, I think, describe a white rose. The word *rose* in French means pink (and—if the reader will pardon the irrelevance—one of the earliest paintings of this delightful flower is by a contemporary of Ronsard, Jacques de la Moyne de Morgues, and shows a beautiful red specimen). Here, one may think, lies the point of the poet's metaphor: for the dawn sky is red, but not so red as the rose.

In [4] the sky is again personified, but this time in the form of the dawn whose tears are the dewdrops. There is no attempt to sustain the previous metaphor: jealousy is forgotten, nor does the dawn weep out of pity for the rose, for such an interpretation would be contrary to the sense of [3]. The images are quite independent. That of [4] springs simply from the visual resemblance between a dewdrop and a tear (and also, as we shall suggest later, from the riming of *pleurs* with *couleur*). It is simply a charming, if rather *précieux*, ornament. But it has a definite poetic function, to suggest the cool dampness of the early morning in which the rose is seen in its splendour, as compared with the heat of the day in which it opens and its petals fall. In [11] we have a conventional classical personification: death represented by *la Parque*, one of the goddesses who wove and cut the thread of life. This is a slightly erudite flourish which would be accepted without comment in any literary work of the period—after all, there was no point in calling death Death if one could find a nobler expression—but, like the other ornaments, in the hands of a skilled poet this one has its purpose, for it leads naturally to the classical image of the last tercet, which suggests a sacrifice at an altar.

But, in contrast with these personified images, the death and destruction of the rose are presented in [7-8] in quite vividly realistic terms, with only the word *languissante* sustaining the tone of what has gone before. In their description, these lines revert to [l], which was clearly visual and apparently, as we have suggested, 'drawn from nature'. (In [1] it may be felt, such apparently realistic details as *sur la branche* and the specific *au mois de May* help in creating a feeling of realism.) But whereas in [7] the *battue de pluie* image is clear enough, that of *excessive ardeur* is perhaps a little less so. Admittedly we are speaking of the sixteenth century, when summer began on 1 May, and the weather was on the whole (I believe) rather better organized than it is today. But excessive heat in May? Perhaps the reader will object that I am being too prosaic, and that the poet should be allowed his sole privilege, which is poetic licence. But I think not. I do not think the poet is speaking of scorching heat at all. In the warmth of the sun the rose unfolds—*feuille à feuille déclose*—and its magic is gone. The heat is excessive simply from the point of view of the rose. We must remember too that the sun-worship of the twentieth century is a reaction against the growth of industrial cities. No lady of the sixteenth century would have welcomed a sun-tan. Half a century after Ronsard Shakespeare was writing 'Fear no more the heat of the sun ...' It is a simple fact that until fairly recent times heat was considered oppressive.

But if the destruction of the rose is described realistically, that of the girl is not. We need only compare the very specific imagery of [7-8]:

> Mais battue ou de pluye ou d'excessi.ve ardeu.r,
> Languissan.te ellĕ meu.rt feuille à feui.llĕ déclo.se [.]

with [11]:

> La Pa˙rquĕ t'a tuée, et cen.drĕ tu repo.ses [.]

to realize that we have passed into an entirely different dimension. Human physical death is never dignified. The medical report on a consumptive heroine of a Puccini opera who dies on stage in full song would not make edifying reading. Hence the euphemism.

Just as in the poem we have the parallelism of images—the rose and the girl—so we have the parallelism of phrase and cadence which is of the nature of rhetoric. The division of the alexandrine into hemistichs lends itself to such effects. Thus in [2] we have

> En sa be˙llĕ jeune.sse, en sa premie.rĕ fleu.r [,]

and in [13]

> Ce va.sĕ plein de laict, ce panier plein de fleu.rs [,]

There are other examples in [7] and [11]. In a similar way individual words are often balanced one against the other. In [5], *la grace, l'amour*; in [6] *les jardins, les arbres*; in [8] *feuille à feuille*; in [10] *terre et ciel*; in [12] *mes larmes et mes pleurs*, two words which mean exactly the same thing, as do *premiere et jeune* in [9]. So far as meaning is concerned these words are tautologous, but their function is to achieve a balance of sound. And the poem ends with the most effective antithesis of all, *vif et mort* in [14]

There are therefore two distinct elements in the poem. One is the direct appeal to our senses, with or without actual description. We see the rose in [1], are aware of its colour in [3] and its scent in [6]. We feel the cool of the morning [4] and the heat of the day [7]; the gentle moisture of the dew [4] and the beating of the rain [7]. The other element is rhetorical evocation and cadence, which avoids the specific and the real. We see not one rose but roses in general (hence *les jardins* in the plural in [6], and the ambiguity as to its fate in [7]). Hence, too, the predilection for abstractions rather than for concrete description: *jeunesse, grace, amour, nouveauté, beauté*, and for the transformation of reality by personification and metaphor. Although there is in the poem a real awareness of nature, its effect derives largely from the skilful use of rhetorical patterns. It is, in sum, a highly self-conscious literary creation. Those who consider poetry as a spontaneous out-pouring of emotion will consider this a damning judgement. Those who admire craftsmanship and vision will think otherwise.

VERSIFICATION AND SOUND

(*a*) *Metre*

The poem is written in alexandrines with regularly-stressed caesura, and all the lines save the first are end-stopped. On first reading, [1] may give the impression of being as syntacticaly complete as are the others, and therefore stable. This is because we take *la rose* to be the object of the verb *void*. The effect is subtle, since it accounts for a good deal of the immediate visual impact which the poem has on the reader. But in fact the poet is not showing us the rose: he is making a statement which we may summarize thus: *Comme on voit la rose rendre le ciel jaloux*. Admittedly, this has a much less forceful effect; and so, by interpolating [2], the poet isolates his first line. But grammatically *la rose* is attached to *rendre* in [3]. Thus [1B] is dislocated (*au mois de May | la rose*) and *la rose* is a *contre-rejet*. As a result the first line is unstable and should end at middle pitch, keeping the mind in suspense until the sentence is continued in [3]. This is the only example of enjambement in the sonnet. All the lines rounded off with commas or full stops are stable and will end at neutral or low pitch as the case may be. [4] and [6] seem likely to end at middle pitch.

Having said this, I must admit to a difficulty. The poem was probably written to be sung, and therefore has a melodic line in a quite literal sense. However, we are now considering it as a poem to be read, and the music with which we are here concerned is the music of words. We shall, however, have occasion from time to time to take into account its original intention: and all that we have to say will have some relevance to any possible musical setting.

For instance, the marked regularity of metre lends itself well to interpretation in a melodic line. Not only are the lines and hemistichs regularly stressed, but the subsidiary stresses conform to fairly regular patterns. None are eroded, and none are on isolated syllables. About half the hemistichs are divided 3:3 the others being in roughly equal proportions either 2:4 or 4:2. The two opening lines have an identical rhythm 3:3 | 4:2 though, as we have seen, they differ in pitch. The others are varied, but nevertheless within recognizable patterns. This is particularly important in [B], which governs the closing cadence of the line. The following is a summary of the rhythm of the closing hemistich of each line in the four stanzas:

	I	II	III	IV
1.	4:2	2:4		
2.	4:2	2:4	2:4	2:4
3.	3:3	3:3	3:3	3:3
4.	4:2	2:4	2:4	2:4

It will be apparent from this that the cadence of the line follows a pattern which is related to the form of the stanza.

In all cases, the short segment is likely to be lengthened in reading, and the long segment to be proportionately contracted. So in [1] we read *au mois de May* more quickly than the closing words *la rose*, on which the voice dwells. In the same way *rendre le ciel* in [3] will be read more quickly than *jaloux*. It will be noted that a high proportion of the stressed vowels in the poem are either naturally long or lengthened by a following neutral [e]. This effect lends itself well to singing, and when the poem is read it enhances its musicality. It is also likely to suggest a comparatively slow diction.

It will be noticed that Ronsard does not share the dislike of hiatus which, following Malherbe's strictures, was to lead to its virtual prohibiton in subsequent centuries. In [7] we have [bá tü u] followed almost immediately by [plŭi u], and in [11] the sequence [tü é é]. There is also hiatus in [ë si à] in [9]. This readiness to accept hiatus may have been affected by the fact that the words were written to be sung, since transition from one vowel to another is easy in singing. Even so, none of these effects strikes the modern ear as in the least offensive, and their use by an artist as conscious of sound as Ronsard should perhaps have given his successors food for thought.

(b) Verse-Form and Rime

The poem is a Petrarchan sonnet, which Ronsard uses with scrupulous regard for its form. The two quatrains present the theme of the rose, the first six lines being devoted to the beauty of the flower and the last two to its death. The tercets introduce a change of subject—Marie herself—and a change of style, since from this point on the poem is in the form of an apostrophe. The first tercet tells of her untimely death, concluding with [11] which provides a conscious parallel with [8]. In the last tercet the poet makes the offering which associates her with the rose, and in the closing line the two main themes are brought together. There is thus a perfect correspondence between the arrangement of the material and the verse-form.

The rime-scheme of the sonnet is AbbA AbbA ccD eeD (the capital letters indicating feminine rimes). There is no alternation between the first and second stanza since the rime does not change. However, while respecting this rime-scheme, the poet introduces an interesting variation, in that he re-uses rime-words from the quatrains in the last four lines of the poem. Thus, so far as the ear is concerned, only two alternating rimes are used throughout the poem, with the exception of the couplet [9-10]. However, on its recurrence each word is distinguished by the addition of a final *s*, and this use of fossilized sound makes it technically a new rime. Thus we have *rose* in [1] and *roses* in [14]; *fleur* in [2] and *fleurs* in [13]; *repose* in [5] and *reposes* in [11], these pairs forming a match to the ear but remaining metrically distinct. This effect demonstrates considerable virtuosity. The effect of continuity of rime is further emphasized by the fact that in the rime-scheme here used the last four lines constitute a quatrain of *rimes embrassées* [D eeD] and thus repeat the pattern of the quatrains. The more usual rime-scheme would use *rimes alternées* at this point, in which case the correspondence would not have been so exact.

One effect of this run-on rime is to isolate the couplet which introduces the tercets, thus reinforcing the form of the sonnet. The vowel of the rime-words in [9-10] is not only different from that of the others, but is also open and short, whereas all the other riming vowels in the poem are blocked and long. The fact that twelve out of the fourteen lines end in [z] or [r] has the effect of lengthening the lines, since the ear is very conscious of this final consonant, which is capable of some prolongation. This is not the case with the rime on the couplet. However, it must be said of words such as *nouveauté* and *beauté* that, in spite of theory, in practice the penultimate vowel is quite likely to receive the main stress, and this vowel [ó] is identical with that of the [A] rimes, so that a sort of off-beat continuity is obtained. The vowel [ò] also occurs in the rime-word *odeur* in [6]. The general effect is that in this poem we are extremely conscious of the sound of the rimes. They are by no means a mere metrical formality. We note also that all the three effective rimes are strongly contrasting in sound. This will be even more true when the poem is sung, in which case the mute [e] of the feminine rime is sounded, and the distinction between masculine and feminine rime then becomes a real one.

It is not surprising that the poem opens with a rime of resounding richness: *la rose* | *l'arrose* matches five phonemes, or indeed six when sung. Of the remaining rimes, all are rich (matching three phonemes) with the exception of [4, 8] and [11, 14], which are sufficient: though the [r] amplifies the rime [*rose*|*reposes*].

(c) Phonetic Patterning

1. We have already referred to the continuity of rime which in this poem goes far beyond the requirement of metre. With this we may associate the poet's habit of riming the caesura of the last line of each stanza save the fourth with the previous line-ending.

[3-4]   Ren.drĕ le ciel jaloux de sa vi.vĕ couleu.r,
           Quand l'au.bĕ de ses pleu.rs | ...
[7-8]   Mais battue ou de pluie ou d'excessi.ve ardeu.r,
           Languissan.te ellĕ meu.rt | ...
[10-11]   Quand la te.rre et le ciel honoraient ta beauté,
                                       tá   té

           La Pa.rquĕ t'a tuée, | ...
           tá t é

The regularity with which this terminal echo occurs makes it seem almost a feature of metre, particularly since in all other cases the syllables on the caesura are strongly contrasting in sound both with the line-ending and with each other. The run-on terminal echo does not occur in the closing line of the sonnet. Instead we have a linear contrapuntal echo:

[14]   Afin que vif et mo.rt | ton co.rps ne soit que ro.ses [.]
                              òr   òr

These are all contrapuntal effects but nevertheless tend to reinforce metrical rhythm.

2. The poet's use of run-on rimes and echoes is paralleled by his habit of repeating significant words, sometimes with slight variation, from one line to another. In addition to the rime-words *rose/roses, fleur/fleurs* and *repose/reposes*, we hear in different lines: *belle* [2], *beauté* [10]; *jeunesse* [2], *jeune* [9]; *premiere* [2, 9]; *ciel* [3, 12], *vive* [3] and *vif* [14]; *pleurs* [4, 12], *feuille* [5 and 8 twice]; *meurt* [8] and *mort* [14]. The wide spacing of these words makes it impossible to consider this strictly as either a phonetic or a rhetorical effect, but such extensive repetition in so short a poem must have significance. I would relate it to the lulling quality of the rime and rhythm. In addition it contributes to the general phonetic coherence of the poem as a whole. It is remarkable that the poet achieves this effect without giving us any feeling of tautology.

3. If we limit ourselves for the moment to consonantal effects, we note that the dominant interlinear clusters in the octet are (a) [l r], and (b) sibilants, which will naturally be given their soft sound. The [l r] cluster is in some cases supported by [m]. This combination of liquids, vibrants, and nasal consonants is one of the most musical effects of the French language.

```
          Comme on voit sur la bran.che au mois de May la ro.se,
            m               r l   r         m      m   l   r
                        s            ʤ                         z

          En sa be·llĕ jeunesse, en sa premie.rĕ fleur,
                    l                    r m   r  l   r
            s            s    s

          Rendrĕ le ciel jaloux de sa vivĕ couleu.r,
            r    r l   l   l                    l   r
                  s   j       s

  4       Quand l'au.bĕ de ses pleurs au poinct du jou.r l'arro.se [:]
                  l                l   r              r l  r
                        s                                      z

          La gra.cĕ dans sa feuille, et l'amour se repo.se,
            l   r                          l  m   r   r
                  s      s                      s      z

          Embasmant les jardins et les arbres d'odeu.r,
                m    l    r     l   r r              r
                          j         z

          Mais battue ou de pluie ou d'excessi.ve ardeu.r,
                              l                   r     r
                                            s  s

  8       Languissan.te ellĕ meurt feuille à feu.illĕ déclose [.]
            l                l   m                         l
                  s                                             z
```

It will be noted that this effect weakens in the last two lines. The average number of phonemes involved in these clusters in [1-6] is 9.5, whereas in [7-8] it is only six. This we may relate to the change in theme. The function of [1-6] is to evoke the beauty of the rose, while [7-8] tell of its destruction, and so other clusters become prominent.

In the first tercet, a new cluster is introduced. This is in [t], a phoneme which has hitherto only been heard twice—in *battue* and *languissante*.

Ainsi en ta premie.re et jeuně nouveauté,
    t   t

Quand la te.rre et le ciel honoroient ta beauté,
    t   t   t

La Pa.rquě t'a tuée, et cen.dre tu repo.ses [.]
    t t   t

The [t] cluster disappears entirely from the final tercet (apart from one minor occurrence in [14]). Other voiceless stops [p, k] dominate, with the voiceless fricative [f], and the [l r m] cluster and the sibilants return:

12   Pour obse˙quěs reçoy mes la˙rmes et mes pleu.rs,
    p   p k   p
      r   r   m l rm   m   l   r
          s   s

Ce va.sě plein de laict, ce panier plein de fleu.rs,
          p   p   p
           l   l   l   l   r
    s   z   s
                              f

Afin que vif et mo.rt ton co.rps ne soit que ro.ses [.]
    k   k   k
         m r   r   r
                   s   z
    f   [v] f

4. In the matter of vowels, we note that no significant use is made of nasals. Average occurrence is only slightly more than one per line, and with the exception of an unstressed [ò] in [1, 14] they are all either [à] or [ë]. Rare as they are, they occur in the first word of eight of the lines, and in two of these [6, 8] are doubled; however, I see no significance in this except perhaps as reflecting some underlying mental rhythm. Since nasals are an important source of musicality,

their lack in a poem such as this is a little surprising. Two comments may be made: the poem lacks aural imagery, which often generates nasals; and, more important perhaps, nasal vowels are not particularly effective in singing. For this purpose [a] and [o] are more useful in producing a satisfying musical effect, and these oral vowels abound.

5. In the poem as a whole, no individual vowels predominate, but there is an obvious modulation in quality between, for instance [1] and [2], or the dominant [a] of [5-8], and the middle vowels prominent in [9-10]. The main distinction seems to me to lie between strong vowels (back orals and nasals + frontal [a]) and comparatively subdued ones (middle and frontal). This corresponds to the distinction of the main rime-scheme, which uses [ó] and [œ]. Only in [1] do strong vowels predominate, in the ratio of 9:3. In six lines they are equally matched, and in the remaining seven subdued vowels predominate. Such a numerical analysis has little value in itself, since a good deal depends on how the phonemes are distributed among stressed and significant words. In [2] the four strong vowels are limited to the repeated *en sa*, which balances the line but is irrelevant to its imaginative force, which derives entirely from words using subdued vowels:

> En sa be˙llĕ jeunesse, en sa premie.rĕ fleur [,]
> è ĕ œ è   ĕ ў́é ĕ œ

A similar effect obtains in [9], where only the [á] of *ta* and the [ó] of *nouveauté* are strong. In both [7] and [12-13] the two strong vowels are heard to good effect among the ten weak ones:

> Mais battue ou de pluye ou d'excessi.ve ardeu.r [,]
> á   á
>
> Pour obse˙quĕs reçoy mes la˙rmĕs et mes pleu.rs [,]
> wá   á
>
> Ce va˙sĕ plein de laict, ce panier plein de fleu.rs [,]
> á   á

In [14] strong and subdued vowels are equally numerous, but even so it is the extremely sonorous triplet [òr|òr ró] which dominates its tonality. In the poem as a whole, we may say that the predominance of subdued vowels contributes to the quality of pathos, but that there is contrast between the lines and within them: and the use of [ó] in the rime-scheme gives it an importance far beyond that which the number of occurrences would suggest.

6. Apart from the general effects discussed above, we may call

attention to certain specific modulations. In [3] *jaloux* and *couleur* provide the doublet [lu|ul]. Phonemes from these words combine in [4] to give *jour*, which is echoed in [5] by *amour*. Also in [5] [a] becomes prominent in a very striking sequence: *la grace, l'amour*; *embasmant, jardins, arbres* [6], *battue* and *ardeur* [7]. The phonetic patterning of [7-8] is, I think, worthy of special attention. Here we have

> Mais battue ou de pluie ou d'excessi.ve ardeu.r,
>   ü   ŭi   s si
>   u   u
>
> Languissan.te [...]
>   is

This is the first of two occurrences in the poem of a cluster using constricted frontal vowels, in this case associated with [s]. We have suggested that in general this combination is prone to suggest frustration and melancholy. Its occurrence at this point is most appropriate, and I would suggest that unlike the other clusters, of which the function is musical and rhythmic, this one has an onomatopoeic quality. The other cluster based on [ü] occurs in [11], a line which has the same emotional tone as [8]: the one describes the death of the rose, the other the death of the girl. In [11] the [ü] doublet is not strong enough to have much effect on its own, but it forms part of an effective sequence:

> La Pa˙rquĕ t'a tuée, et cen.drĕ tu repo.ses [.]
> á á   á
>   t tü   tü
>   é é
>   p r   s   r   r p z

The liminal triplet in [a]—a strong vowel—modulates to the constricted [ü] and middle [é] which cannot be run on to [b], as in that case we would lose a syllable. There must be hiatus, and the voice stops, briefly, at the caesura. The effect is a strong start which becomes constricted and ends in unexpected silence. The consonants which lead up to the falling-away of the last two syllables of [A] can be pronounced very forcibly, as they are voiceless stops: from this point of view [p k t t] may be regarded as a single cluster. The hemistich can be violent in its sound, contrasting with what preceeds in [10]—where we shall pronounce the [t] crisply but quietly—and with the hemistich which follows, dominated by sibilants and vibrants. Since [8] and [11] are so similar in theme, the phonetic reminiscence of *battue* [8] which is heard in *t'a tuée* [11] may possibly reinforce the association.

7. We conclude our remarks on the poem with a few notes on the arrangement of linear clusters in some of the lines.

```
[1]     Comme on void | sur la bran. | che au mois de May | la ro.se [ ]
          m            |              |      m         m    |
                   wá  |     lá       |      wá             | lá
          ò            |              |      ó              |       ó.
                       |  r    r      |                     |    r
                       | s            | dʒ                  |       z
```

This is not so complicated as it looks: in fact, it is really rather elegant. We note the pleasing modulation from one cluster to another in *void| mois| May*: the blending of liquids, vibrants and sibilants in *sur la branche*, and the way in which all clusters but one culminate in the riming segment, *la rose*. This close integration of the rime-word into the linear pattern is a feature of the poem; and we shall note in the next example that the [l r] of *la rose* is featured also in the [b] rime, so that it runs through all the rime-words of the stanza. All clusters in [1] are in clear doublet or triplet form and are well spread through the segments, producing a rich and balanced sound.

```
[3]     Ren.drĕ le ciel | jaloux | de sa vi. | vĕ couleu.r [,]
          r    r         |        |           |            r
                 l     l |  lu    |           |       ul
                    s    |  já    |    sá     |
               d         |        |  d    v   | v
```

A strong defining doublet in [r], but the dominant effect is heard in the liquids and sibilants (here, one may think, quite harsh) of *le ciel jaloux*, echoed in the [ul] of the rime-word. The sequence *ciel, jaloux, sa vive* modulates through three clusters.

```
[4]     Quand l'au ˙ | bĕ de ses pleu. | rs au poinct du jou.r | l'arro.se [:]
          l ó        |                 | ró                    | r | l   ró
                     |       s         |                    j  |   |    z
                     |    d     p      |    p      d           |
```

As in [1], the main cluster is an extension of *la rose*: even more so if one makes the liaison between *pleurs au* so as to add a [z] to the pattern given above. The sibilants also closely follow the pattern of [1]. The dominant cluster is a triplet in [ó], the first and last elements forming a contrapuntal echo between the first subsidiary and the terminal stress; this pattern being associated with interlocking triplets in [l] and [r]. The [d p] doublet is minor, but adds to the

neatness of the line. Vowels are strong in the two outer segments,
mainly neutral in the inner ones. A beautifully balanced line.

```
[6]      Embasmant | les jardins | et les a˙r | brĕs d'odeu.r [,]
            bà     |     ár      |     á˙r    | br          r
                   | è  j        |lé lèz      |
                   |      d      |            |      d   d
```

The dominant pattern is the doublet in [ár] in the two inner segments, greatly enhanced by the other phonemes of *les jar-*and *les
ar-*: the word *arbre* being anticipated by [bà] in the first segment and
echoed by [r] in the last. The effect is very strong. We have noticed
elsewhere the tendency to associate the vibrant with perfume, even
though the word *parfum* is not used. The hemistichs are distinguished
in that [A] contains three nasal vowels and a nasal consonant: [B]
contains none of these. The nucleus of the [d|dd] triplet gives the
line a strong terminal cluster (cf. *d'excessive ardeur* in the next line).

```
[12]     Pour obse˙ | quĕs reçoy | mes la.r | mĕs et mes pleu.rs [,]
          p     p   |            |          |              p
             r   s  |    r s     |   l  r|              l   r
                    |     á      |   á  |
                    |            | m    | m    m
```

[p r] supported by a doublet in [s] provide the characteristic cluster
of [A], whereas in [B] we hear particularly a triplet in [m] interwoven with a doublet in [l]. These give a strong tonal contrast. The
line also has a liminal doublet in [p], and *pour* is answered at the end
of the line *pleurs*, thus giving a defining doublet in [p r]. In the inner
segments, the [á] of *reçoy* and *larmes* contrasts with the sequence of
middle vowels which surround them. Apart from the contrast of
hemistichs, the modulation of the clusters is rather pleasing: *pour
obseques* gives a doublet in [p] and introduces [r s] which is answered in *reçoy*; the [r] and [á] of this word are answered in *larmes*,
which introduces the [l m] cluster. The [á] doublet balances the line
well. In [A] the final consonant of each segment is [s]; in [B] the
segments end in [l r], giving a terminal echo which reinforces the
dominant [m l] cluster.

```
[14]     Afin que | vif et mo.rt | ton co.rps | ne soit que ro.ses [.]
                  |    ò.r       |    ò.r      |            ró.
              k   |              |      k      |       k
            f     | v f          |             |    s        z
```

The most striking effect is the sonorous triplet in [ò.r| ò.r ró], the vowels being long and situated on the stresses. *Mort* and *corps* provide a contrapuntal echo, and *corps* links the pattern with the other prominent cluster, the triplet in [k]. The fricatives and sibilants contrast [A] and [B]. The fricatives sequence has in fact already been introduced in the previous line by *vase* and *fleurs*, and *afin que* in [14] echoes the repeated *plein de* of [13]. But the most striking reminiscence of the previous line is heard in the last segment of [14], which redistributes the phonemes of *obsequĕs reçoy* in [13]. We hear the parallel between *reçoy* and *ne soit*; supported by other effects as follows:

```
obsequĕs reçoy |  ne soit que ró.ses
    s      ĕswá|   ĕ swá        z
      kĕ        |       kĕ
  ò      r      |           ró
```

The effect is not regular enough to be heard in its entirety as a phonetic cluster, occurring as it does in different lines, and it makes no very significant contribution to the linear pattern which we have set out for [14]—or for that matter for [13]. But it sets up a subdued though rich contrapuntal echo between the two lines. What is involved is doubtless more a reminiscence, a mental rhythm, than an effect of conscious art: it is one more expression of the tendency towards off-beat repetition which we have noticed throughout the poem, in its superfluous riming effects, word repetition, and abundant clusters. The patterning of these two lines, and the many run-on effects, leaves one with a powerful feeling of the oneness of the poem. The interlocking clusters, blending so perfectly with the form of the sonnet, and involving no greater liberties with standard language than the singular *se repose* of [5] and the tautology of *mes larmes et mes pleurs* in [12], well illustrate the capacity of the poet's mind to blend image, sense, and sound into a single whole which appeals both to the reader's emotions and to his sense of beauty. The poem also demonstrates how the form of the sonnet can be used creatively, both consciously (in the sustained comparison which forms the substance of the poem) and instinctively in its rhythms and the balance of its sound.

LE CYGNE

by Baudelaire

I

Andromaˑquĕ, je pen.se à vous!/Ce petit fleu.ve,

Pauvre et triˑstĕ miroi.|r où jadis resplendit

L'immen.sĕ majesté | de vos douleu.rs de veu.ve,

4   Ce Simoïs menteu.r | qui par vos pleu.rs grandit,

A fécondé soudain | ma mémoi.rĕ fertiˑle,

Commĕ je traversais | le nouveau Carrousel.

Le vieux Paris n'est plus| (la foˑrmĕ d'unĕ viˑlle

8   Chan.gĕ plus vite, hélas! | que le cœu.r d'un mortel);

Je ne vois qu'en esprit | tout ce camp de baraˑques,

Ces tas de chapiteaux ' ébauchés/et de fûts,

Les heˑrbĕs, les gros blocs | verdis par l'eau des flaˑques,

12   Et, brillant aux carreaux, | le bric-à-brac confus.

Là s'étalait jadis | unĕ ménageriˑe:

Là je vis, un matin, | à l'heure où sous les cieux

Froids et clai.rs le Trava'.il s'éve./ille, où la voiriˑe,

16   Pousse un som.bre ouragan | dans l'ai.r silenciˑeux,

Un cy/gnĕ qui s'était 'évadé de sa ca.ge,

Et, de ses pieds palmés | frottant le pavé sec,

Sur le sol raboteux | traînait son blanc pluma.ge.

20   Près d'un ruisseau sans eau | la bête ouvrant le bec

Baignait nerveusĕment | ses ai˙lĕs dans la pou˙dre

Et disait, le cœur plein | de son beau lac natal:

'Eau, quand donc pleuvras-tu?| Quand tonneras-tu, fou˙dre?'

24   Je vois ce malheureux, | mythe étran.ge et fatal,

Vers le ciel quelquefois, | commĕ l'ho˙mmĕ d'Ovi˙de

Vers le ciel ironi|que et cruellĕment bleu,

Sur son cou convulsif | tendant sa tête avi˙de,

28   Commĕ s'il adressait | des repro˙chĕs à Dieu!

II

Paris chan./gĕ! mais rien ' dans ma mélancoli˙e

N'a bougé!/ palais neufs, ' échafauda.gĕs, blocs,

Vieux faubou.rgs,/tout pour moi ' devient allégori˙e,

32   Et mes che.rs souveni.rs | sont plus lou.rds que des rocs.

Aussi devant ce Lou.|vre une ima.gĕ m'oppri˙me:

Je pen.se à mon grand cy|gne avec ses ge˙stĕs fous,

Commĕ les exilés, | ridicule et subli˙me,

36   Et rongé d'un dési.r ' sans trê./ve! et puis à vous,

Androma˙quĕ, des bras | d'un grand époux tombée,

Vil béta.il/sous la main ' du supe˙rbĕ Pyrrhus,

Auprès d'un tombeau vi|de en exta.sĕ courbée,

40   Veu.vĕ d'Hector, hélas! | et fe˙mmĕ d'Hélénus!

Je pen.se à la négre|sse, amaigrie et phtisi˙que,

Piétinant dans la boue, | et cherchant, l'œil haga.rd,

Les cocotiers absents | de la superbe Afri˙que,

44 Derriè.rĕ la mura.′ ille immen./sĕ du brouilla.rd;

A quiconque a perdu | ce qui ne se retrou.ve

Jamais, jamais!/à ceux ′ qui s'abreu.vĕnt de pleu.rs

Et te˙ttĕnt la Douleu.r | comme unĕ bonnĕ lou.ve!

48 Aux mai.grĕs orphelins | séchant commĕ des fleu.rs!

Ainsi dans la forêt | où mon esprit s'exi˙le,

Un vieux Souveni.r so|nne à plein soufflĕ du co.r!

Je pen.se aux matelots | oubli:és dans une î˙le,

52 Aux captifs, aux vaincus! | ... à bien d'au˙trĕs enco.r!

IDENTIFICATION

A poem by Charles Baudelaire (1821-67). One of a number of new poems included in the second edition of *Les Fleurs du mal* (1861) which replaced the first edition legally condemned in 1857. In his later years Baudelaire increasingly turned to Paris as a theme of his work (a collection of prose poems *Le Spleen de Paris* was published after his death) and in *Les Fleurs du mal* 'Le Cygne' is grouped with a number of other poems on this theme in the section *Tableaux Parisiens*. It was first published, with some minor differences in the text, in *La Causerie* in 1860, and was presumably composed in the previous year, when it had been offered to (and refused by) the editor of the *Revue contemporaine*.

The poem bears the dedication 'A Victor Hugo'. His relevance to the theme is that Hugo was in exile in the Channel Islands, where he had fled following Louis-Napoléon's *coup d'état* of 1851.

When first published in *La Causerie* the poem bore the epigraph *Falsi Simoentis ad undam* taken from the third book of Virgil's *Aeneid*. This makes clear the source of Baudelaire's material on Andromache, and was omitted from *Les Fleurs du mal* probably by oversight, as in one of his unpublished prefaces intended for the definitive edition of the book Baudelaire makes clear his wish to acknowledge his debt to Virgil.

SUBJECT MATTER

The poem develops a number of parallel themes of which the common element is exile.

(*a*) Andromache, princess of Troy, spent her life in exile following the death of her husband Hector and the destruction of her city. She was given as a concubine to Pyrrhus, son of her Greek conqueror Achilles, and after his death married Helenus [38, 40]. Virgil tells how she remained faithful to the memory of Hector, building him a tomb in Epirus—empty [39] since he had perished at Troy. She also re-named a local river 'Simoïs' after one of the rivers on which Troy stood [4].

(*b*) The poet himself feels an exile in Paris as a result of the transformation brought about by Louis-Napoléon's rebuilding of the city [II, VIII]. He stands in the Place du Carrousel [6], a great empty space which had once been a honeycomb of streets and houses, cleared to provide a vista on the Louvre [33].The completion of this great palace, which had been neglected since Louis XIV turned his attention to Versailles in the seventeenth century, was one of the major achievements of the Second Empire. It was part of a wider programme designed to make Paris an imperial capital and the commercial centre of Europe. But the poet, conservative by nature, indifferent to political grandeur, civic pride, or commercial success, shows no interest in its more positive aspects and offers no description of the new Paris. He views the changes with deep regret [7-8].

(*c*) His thoughts turn back to the Place as it was, and he recalls an episode which he had witnessed here some years previously. Early one morning he had seen a swan, a regal bird rarely seen in Paris, dirty and bedraggled and searching for water in the arid streets. It had escaped from a local menagerie. With Andromache in mind he now thinks of this bird as an exile, like her and like himself. He imagines the bird dreaming of 'son beau lac natal' to which it can never return [22], and protesting to God against its fate [28].

(*d*) He thinks of other exiles—a black woman in Paris longing for sunlit Africa [XI], orphans [48], marooned sailors [51], captives, and the defeated [52]. The list ends indeterminately—'à bien d'autres encor'—with the implication that it could be continued indefinitely.

Crépet has explained the reference to Ovid (who has a certain personal relevance to the theme, as he died in exile) as an allusion to lines from the *Metamorphoses*:

> Os homines sublime dedit caelumque tueri
> Jussit, et erectos ad sidere tollere vultus [.]

and Adam has drawn attention to Baudelaire's allusion in *Fusées* to 'le visage humain qu'Ovide croyait façonné pour réfléter les astres'.

In all these cases, the poet sees exile as the state of suffering of an individual whose natural development is stunted by loss of the environment in which it could flourish. The exile is a victim of circumstances for which he is himself not responsible. He contributes to his own suffering only by his refusal or his inability to adapt, and this is at one and the same time his weakness and his grandeur. The examples chosen are so varied that no common cause can be attributed to their situation. Although the poem is dedicated to Victor Hugo, the most outspoken critic of Napoleon III, Baudelaire draws no political or moral conclusions from the transformation of Paris, which he rejects simply from innate conservatism. Of course, it may be thought that this was due to political prudence: but Baudelaire was not prudent, as the banning of the first edition of *Les Fleurs du mal* demonstrates; and in any case the dedication to Hugo was, at this time, in the highest degree imprudent. His approach to his theme is simply fatalistic [24]. The exile is

> ... quiconque a perdu ce qui ne se retrouve
> Jamais, jamais! ...   [45–6]

To this situation he reacts with melancholy [32] and a sympathy which is apparent throughout the poem. At the same time he stresses the greatness of the exile, which lies in the refusal to accept circumstances even though they cannot be changed, as a result of which he is both 'ridicule et sublime' [35]. In the story of Andromache he admires her faithfulness to the dead Hector [39], and the swan he sees as a rebel against God [VII]. The negress gains not only pathos but also dignity from her memories of her homeland [XI]. In an image presumably based on the story of Romulus and Remus, he sees suffering as a life-giving force [49], though the shorter images of [XIII] do not carry this implication.

Baudelaire's use of the swan reminds us of an early poem, *L'Albatros*. In this a great bird, magnificent in flight, is helpless and indeed absurd when 'exilé sur la terre'. This is an allegory of the poet, incompetent in daily life because his gaze is directed on high. The swan is in a similar situation, though in the present poem Baudelaire forges no specific link between his melancholy and his role as poet.

PRESENTATION AND STYLE

In *Le Cygne* the poet does not, as a Romantic might, set out his own suffering as a spectacle to engross the reader. His art springs from his own suffering, but also from that of others. His achievement is to bring the images together into a poem. From this the poem gains, since it minimizes sentimentality and self-pity, two ever-present dangers in treating what may be seen as a theme of 'hard luck'. Although *je* occurs frequently it is not dwelt on, and almost always leads to something else which absorbs our attention. Thus the poem is built on *je pense à ...* [1, 34, 41, 51], reduced to the preposition *à* in [36, 45, 46, 48, 52], and on *je vois* or *je vis* in [9, 14]. In this respect, it may be said that the main unifying factor of the poem lies in the act of its creation. This occurs at a specific time and in a specific place, when the poet crosses the Place du Carrousel [6, 33] with Andromache in mind as a result of his reading of Virgil [1 + epigraph p. 212]. He is struck by the great emptiness of the square. (Originally he wrote *ce vaste Carrousel* in [2], but changed the adjective to *nouveau* in order to emphasize the theme of change.) His thoughts turn back to the very different scene he remembers there a few years previously [III, VIII] and in particular to the episode of the swan [IV-VII, 35]. Thus the poet's feelings of melancholy have three more or less simultaneous sources. This simultaneity does produce difficulties of expression. It involves the recapitulation in Part II, though in a different order (here it is the swan who leads the poet to Andromache) and with different emphasis, of the themes of Part I; and although the image of the negress in [XI] reinforces the unity of the poem by its close links with Paris, those of [XII, XIII] have no such links. Thus the formal unity of the poem is weakened. Even the poet separates himself from real time and place and is now *dans la forêt où [s]on esprit s'exile'* [49] (an allusion perhaps to the *forêt de symboles* of *Correspondances*). At this late stage he introduces an entirely new image in [50]:

> Un vieux Souvenir sonne à plein soufflĕ du cor [!]

which can only be understood as a reminiscence of *Les Phares*:

> Un appel de chasseurs perdus dans les grand bois [!]

That is, Baudelaire is associating himself with the *ardent sanglot* of the great artists who bear witness before God to man's suffering; and his memory of the swan is the trumpet-call by which he does this. The image is, therefore, directly associated with the act of creation of the poem.

However, there is undoubtedly a loss of tautness and cohesion at the end of the poem as a result of the disparate nature of the images and, indeed, their brevity. They are also less satisfying in that all are of apparently literary origin, and do not spring, as his more powerful images do, from the poet's personal experience. (No one reading [I|X] can doubt that Andromache had become very much a part of his experience.) The diffusion of force which results from these weaker images may be justified as leading naturally to the deliberately weak *à bien d'autres encor* with which the poem ends, but one may still think that the imaginative unity of the work suffers as a result of it.

If one may be allowed to pass briefly from fact to conjecture, I would suggest that the diverse images with which the poem ends are largely the result of what Baudelaire describes in *Le Soleil* as 'les hasards de la rime'. Having begun [XII] with the powerful 'A quiconque a perdu ce qui ne se retrouve' the poet found *louve* among the limited number of rime-words which presented themselves and so introduced the theme of Romulus and Remus, which he skilfully integrated into his stanza with the amplification '... à ceux qui s'abreuvent de pleurs [] Et tettent la Douleur ...' He then required a rime for *pleurs*. The choice of *fleurs* results from phonetic association with *orphelins* [rf l|fl r] which is itself a development of the idea of mothering in the previous line. The poet thus arrives at two images which he would have been unlikely to choose had he been writing prose.

The image of the hunting-horn in [50] may owe its origin to similar considerations. The unexpected last line of the poem is not the result of the poet's suddenly running out of ideas: and it may well be that he began the final stanza from this line. This is supported, though not proved, by the fact that the rime-word is included in the phonetic patterning, and indeed uses all its elements:

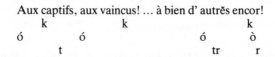

When the rime-word is only weakly integrated into the patterning (as in [50]) this often means that it is the answer to another rime-word and so, in the poet's mind, pre-exists the composition of the line as a whole. If this was so in the present case, the new image based on 'cor' enters the poem as a result of the poet's riming with 'encor'. The rime-word may have stimulated in Baudelaire's mind the same associations as it did in *Les Phares*, where it is sounded 'dans les grands bois', and this leads to the introduction of the word *forêt* into [49]. So we have another image which, splendid though it is, arises from phonetic and imaginative association rather than from any 'real life' link with the other themes of the poem. In a similar way, having proposed a new rime in [49] with 'où mon esprit s'exile', the poet answers it in [51] with *île*, and this naturally suggests marooned sailors. In good verse, riming is always part of the creative process, and the poet's skill enables him to integrate the answer to each rime into a new syntactical context. In the present case, Baudelaire has certainly maintained his theme of exile, but his ear for phonetic affinities has led him to the most diverse images.

In sum, we may say that the poem derives formal unity from (*a*) Andromache, whose tragedy is impressed on us by powerful rhetoric; (*b*) Paris seen as the source of the poet's melancholy, the negress's exile, and the swan's sufferings; (*c*) the powerful phonetic resonance of the language; and (*d*) the use of the actual genesis of the poem, closely associated with the Place du Carrousel—where Baudelaire saw the swan—as one of the main themes of the poem. And this same formal unity is weakened by (*a*) the difficulty of expressing simultaneous ideas, and (*b*) the failure to maintain the unifying factors in the last two stanzas.

We now turn to the language itself.

The style of the poem is rhetorical. This is seen in the extremely effective apostrophe of Andromache by the poet [1, 35] which introduces her as a living person. Apostrophe is also used, though, one may think, with less satisfying effect, in the case of the swan's appeals to the rain and thunder [23]: here we are rather too conscious of the literary device, which blends somewhat unhappily with the realism of the descriptions. Personification is also used. *Le Travail s'éveille* [15] seems a little archaic in its context, but *tettent la Douleur* [47] and *Un vieux Souvenir sonne ...* [50] belong naturally enough to their respective images. There is implied personification in [26], where the sky is described as *ironique et cruellement bleu*. Antithesis is also effectively used: in [I] the contrast between *petit* and *immense*; in [35] the juxtaposition of *ridicule et sublime*; in [37, 38] between *des bras* and *sous la main*, and in [40] between *veuve d'Hector* and *femme d'Hélénus*. (In this last case, we also note the rhetorical *hélas!*). Rhetorical repetition of *Là* occurs in [13, 14] and of *Vers le ciel* in [25/26]. Inversion is used in [4, 18, 37, 39]. The vocabulary sometimes shows Latin influences: *Simoïs menteur* [4] referring to the fact that the river was not really the Simoïs, and recalling Virgil; *superbe* used with the sense of 'proud' in [38]—though its meaning in [43] is not so precise. *Fatal* in [24] retains its early associations with fate. And Adam has pointed out the Latin origins of the construction *fécondé ... fertile* in [5], though this latter adjective has, as we shall suggest below, an importance in its own right. The most important feature of rhetoric, however, is its cadence, and this is apparent throughout, though nowhere more strongly than in [I].

Metaphor and simile are common features of poetry as of rhetoric. In [32] the description of the poet's memories as *plus lourds que des rocs* is given force by its association with *blocs* in [30] and the continuation of the idea of weight in [33] with the word *opprime*. In [38] *Vil bétail* powerfully conveys Andromache's servitude. In [46] tears become life-giving water drunk by life's victims, and in [47] they are the she-wolf's life-giving milk. The water image is continued in [48], where the orphans wither like flowers for lack of it. The most strikingly sustained rhetorical image is that of the river in [I]. In [2-3] it is presented as a mirror reflecting Andromache's sorrow ('pauvre' because it was merely an imitation of the real Simoïs). But it is also a watercourse which is so swollen by her tears [4—a *précieux* hyperbole] that it overflows in the poet's memory and fertilizes the dormant images which lie there [5]. (A similar metaphor is used by Baudelaire in *L'Ennemi*.) Other metaphors, less rhetorical, are used by the poet in association with enjambement to give a particularly vivid image of the ideas they represent: in [36] '*rongé* d'un désir sans trêve' and in [44] 'derrière la *muraille* immense du brouillard'. These are totally effective: but when in [16] the poet sees the dust raised by the road-sweepers as 'un sombre ouragan', we may feel that rhetorical hyperbole does not blend so easily with realism.

In contrast with the rhetorical style, and sometimes uneasily yoked to it, are images of contemporary life. Expressions such as *bric-à-brac* [12], *la voirie* [15] and *phtisique* [41] certainly do not belong to the world of Andromache. Oddly enough, Baudelaire does not describe the old Paris which for him is the equivalent of the swan's lake and the negress's sunlit palm-trees, but rather the confusion of the rebuilding: and this is very vividly presented in [III, VIII] by apparently random enumeration. General concepts such as *palais neufs* [30] and *vieux faubourgs* [31] go together with minutely observed detail—the cut-stone capitals [10], grass growing on the building sites [11], ashlar lying in the rain accumulating a covering of green lichen [11], and the jumbled contents of shop-windows [12]. It will be noted that Paris is presented as a city of rain [11] and fog [44] contrasted with the warm tropics [43] which are so often used by Baudelaire as an expression of 'l'Idéal'.

Sentences are often long and complex. After *Ce petit fleuve* in [1] the syntactical sequence is suspended until we reach the verb *a fécondé* in [5], and in the meantime the image of the river has been developed. Similarly in [14] *là je vis* is left without an object until the poet has given us his description of the early-morning scene in Paris. In [24] *ce malheureux* is left in suspense until completed by *tendant sa tête* in [27B]. This is the result of the lack of chronological development in the poem: the poet throughout is expressing more or less simultaneously associated ideas.

VERSIFICATION AND SOUND

GENERAL DESCRIPTION

Le Cygne consists of thirteen quatrains of alexandrines. The division into two parts affects versification only by introducing a longer pause than normal after the seventh stanza. This division, together with the use of stanzas rather than an unbroken sequence of lines, is related to the manner of presentation of the material, which involves the linking of a number of themes—three in Part One—and the recapitulation and development of them, with appropriate extensions, in Part Two. Stanzas are related to themes as follows: (*a*) Andromache—[I] and [X]; (*b*) Paris and the poet's feelings concerning its transformation, [II-IV] and [VIII]; (*c*) the swan [V-VII] and [IX]; (*d*) further illustrations of exile, [XI-XIII]. Allusions to the act of creation of the poem occur in [II] and [XIII].

The sentences, often long and complex, are not necessarily co-terminous with the stanzas. They overrun between [I/II],[IV/V/ VI/VII], and [IX/X], and this is likely to have the effect of reducing the pause between the stanzas. In [II], [VI], and [XIII] sentences begin in mid-stanza, and in [V], [VI], [IX], and [XII], in the fourth line; some of the latter cases producing an effect of enjambement with the stanza following. The general effect is free and discursive. The stanza-form is, however, on occasions used to advantage by placing either stressed words [I, IV, V, VII, X] or rhetorical repetition [IV, VII] in an initial position.

The rime-scheme is *rimes croisées* which, by creating regular alternation throughout the poem, favours continuity between stanzas and is therefore better adapted to the poet's syntactical form than would have been the alternative *abba*, which would reinforce the stanza-form. Only three of the twenty-six rimes are weak [26/28, 29/31, 34/36] and in two of these cases an approximate *consonne d'appui* is used—[f/v, l/r]. Eight rimes are rich, and the remaining eleven sufficient. But in nine cases only is the *consonne d'appui* assimilated into the rime, and richness or sufficiency is in most cases due to the use of blocked vowels in the rimes. In [14/16, 29/31] the quality of the rime is much enhanced by associated phonetic patterns, and the matching of [l/r] in six cases may also be felt to strengthen them. Rime-words are not used more than once and contiguous rimes are always very strongly contrasted (e.g. *Afrique| brouillard*). Rime-vowels are varied, though [i] predominates, occurring in eight stanzas, while [ü], often associated with it in phonetic patterns, occurs in two more. The possible significance of these sounds in the poem will be discussed again. There are no cliché rimes, and the words used are always of importance to the poem. In general, we may say that the riming is strong without giving an impression of extreme virtuosity. It stresses form and variety rather than repetition, and does not, as is sometimes the case with Baudelaire, introduce a strong lyrical or hypnotic quality.

The alexandrine metre used throughout is appropriate to both style and matter: philosophical reflection, description, anecdote, and rhetoric. Regular rhythm is sometimes varied by enjambement on the caesura or, more rarely, the line-ending to express an accumulation of emotional force [1, 36, 44, 45/46] or to achieve strong premature stress [13, 17, 29, 30, 38]. It is also used to weaken the line, particularly in evoking the confusion of the rebuilding of Paris [10, 30-1] and in one case, by introducing a variation of rhythm, it suggests the busy movement of city life [15]. It is associated throughout with rich phonetic patterning, both linear and interlinear, but nowhere with greater power than in the opening stanza recalling, in fine, imaginative rhetoric, the sufferings of Andromache. It is this more than anything else which establishes the emotional tone of the poem. Apart from producing a rich phonetic texture, clusters tend to reinforce regular metre and in some cases rhythmic variations. In some cases they have a clear onomatopoeic function and they are often closely associated with emotion. In this latter respect, [i] is the vowel most commonly used. One of the most unusual phonetic features of the poem is the ubiquity of the consonant [k] which occurs fifty-seven times, often in strong patterns. Although in some cases it is used to a very definite effect, it is difficult to specify an overall function, and it may possibly result from an association in the poet's mind of the words *Andromaque* and *Carrousel*.

Of the features we have mentioned, some tend to weaken formal unity: uneven movement between disparate themes, uncertain relationship between syntax and stanza, and considerable rhythmic variation within the line. Others reinforce it: strong riming, masterly control of the alexandrine, a firmly maintained emotional tone and rich phonetic patterning. While this may result in some weaknesses, the general effect is dynamic, and consistent with the sense of the infinite potential of its theme for expansion which is implied in the closing line.

EXAMPLES

   (*a*) *Overrunning the stanza*
Continuity of sense between stanzas is reinforced by phonetic

copulas. Between [I/II] we have 'grand*it* [] a fécondé soud*ain* ...'
Between [IV/V]:

> Pousse un sombre ouragan dans l'air silencieux, []
> s   s   si si
>
> Un cygně qui s'était ...
> si   s

and between [V/VI]:

> ... la bête ouvrant le bec []
>   bè   bè
>
> Baignait nerveusěment ses ailěs...
> bè è è   è

Between [IX/X] we hear the echo of *vous|époux*, made effective by the strong syntactical break which isolates *tombée* at the end of [37].

(*b*) *Rimes*

Although technically the riming of *mélancolie* with *allégorie* in [VIII] is weak, the approximation between [l kò li|l gò ri] is surely significant. The matching of [l] with [r] is a characteristic of the poem, and occurs in the following rimes: *resplendit|grandit* [2/4], *baraques|flaques* [9/11], *mélancolie|allégorie* [29/31], *blocs|rocs* [30/32], *opprime|sublime* [33/35], *retrouve|louve* [45/47]. In [14/16] the rime is enhanced by an extended phonetic cluster common to both lines:

> ... à l'heure où sous les cieux
>   l   r   s   l sÿœ
> ... dans l'air silencieux [,]
>   l   r s l siœ̀

The statement that all contiguous rimes are strongly contrasting is not true of [II], where all the rime-words end in [l]. This seems to result from phonetic association of the words *fertile, forme* and *mortel*. There are in the poem other examples of free phonetic association which do not affect the rime. In [II] we have *vieux, ville,* and *vite*, and in [X] *vil* and *vide*. This latter is supported by further phonetic associations, heard in *vil bétail| tombeau vide* [ví b t| tb ví]. In [VIII] we note the sequence *bougé, faubourgs, lourds*, somewhat akin to rime. The association between *vous* and *époux* in [36/37] has already been mentioned.

Two examples of internal rime involve the word *pleurs*. In [4] we hear

Ce Simoïs menteu.r | qui par vos pleu.rs grandit [,]

made effective by the syntactical break after *pleurs* which results from the inversion of the sentence. In [46-47] the rime on the line-ending is answered on the caesura:

... à ceux qui s'abreu.vĕnt de pleu.rs
Et te˙ttĕnt la Douleu.r ...

There are two further rimes which, like *vous|époux*, are at the discretion of the reader. In [12] *bric-à-brac* answers *flaques* at the end of the previous line, though in this case there is no syntactical justification for a rime. There is every such justification in [13/14]:

Là s'étalait jadis unĕ ménageri˙e;
Là je vis ....

Here *vis* is isolated from the clause following and must remain in the mind until its complement, *un cygne*, is heard in the next stanza. It gains an appropriate importance if heard as an echo of the previous line-ending.

(*c*) *Enjambement*

The use of enjambement on the caesura to build up an accumulation of emotional force is exemplified in [36]:

Commĕ les exilés, | ridicule et sublime,
Et rongé d'un dési.r sans trê./ve!...
   r   r   r
é   é d   dé   è

Here the phonetic patterning reinforces the effect by also over-running the caesura. There is enjambement on the line-ending to similar effect in [45-46], resulting in further enjambement on the caesura in [46]:

Jamais, jamais! à ceux qui s'abreu./vĕnt de pleurs
       sœ   s   rœ̀   œ̀r

Et te˙ttĕnt la Douleu.r ....
        œ̀r

And in [44] a long phrase overrunning the caesura is used to suggest the overwhelming physical power of the fog to blot out the vision of sunlit Africa:

Derriè.rĕ la mura. ille immen./sĕ du brouillar.d [;]
   .   .   ..   ..

In this case too the enjambement is strongly supported by phonetic patterning.

However, the case of [10] is somewhat different. Here too we have a long opening phrase and a phonetic cluster spanning the eroded caesura:

> Ces tas de chapiteaux ébauchés/et de fûts [,]
>
> ch   p   ó   bó ch

But here the word *ébauchés* has little intrinsic importance and does not represent a climax. As a result, the only effect of enjambement is to weaken the rhythm. It is part of the poet's general tendency to disturb his metre in lines describing the confusion of Paris during the rebuilding. This effect is particularly striking in the stanza following, where two *contre-rejets* are used in succession:

> Là je vis, un matin, | à l'heure où sous les cieux
>
> Froids et clai.rs le Trava.il s'éve./ille, où la voirie
>
> Pousse un sombre ouragan | dans l'ai.r silenci:eux [,]

Here the disturbed rhythm suggests agitation and movement. Erosion of the caesura in [15] is strongly supported by phonetic patterning heard in *le Trava.il s'éve.ille* [v ў| v ў], the [v] being picked up again on the line-ending by *voirie*. Stress on the first *contre-reject (sous les cieux)* is reduced to a minimum by the close syntactical link with the line following, whereas stress on *où la voirie*, much less closely linked, is likely to be normal.

The same tendency to disturb rhythm is apparent in [VIII], the last stanza devoted to Paris. The effect of enjambement on the line-ending in [29/30] is of course to stress *n'a bougé*. Although there is no enjambement at the end of [30], the rhythmically confusing list of items is continued on into the next line with *Vieux faubourgs*. This results in erosion of the caesura:

> Vieux faubourgs,/tout pour moi devient allégorie [,]

and again, since *Vieux faubourgs* has no great intrinsic interest and does not bring the enumeration to a climax, the result is a weakening of rhythm. It will be noted however that in both [IV] and [VIII] Baudelaire concludes his stanza with a firm regular line.

Erosion of the caesura as a result of a strong premature stress is also apparent in [17] and [38]. However, there are cases in which the isolation of the opening phrase by punctuation should not necessarily be regarded as stressing it. One such is [22], where *plein* surely merits the major stress rather than *disait*. Another, I think, is [37]. There is certainly a case for stressing *Andromaque* and reading the line as

Androma./quĕ, des bras ' d'un grand époux tombée [,]
     ..   .   .   ..

but there is an even stronger case for exploiting the stress which the caesura can give to *des bras*. For this phrase, with its implications of love and protection, is in strong contrast with *sous la main*, suggesting tyranny, in the next line. I would therefore read the line as

Androma.quĕ, des bras | d'un grand époux tombée
    .   ..   .   ..

I also prefer a regular reading in [50]. It may be tempting to erode the caesura and put the main stresses on *Souvenir* and *souffle*. But apart from the awkwardness of a line opening with a five-syllable segment, we effectively lose *sonne*, a word which in terms of meaning and of sound is crucial to the line. The only vowel in the line capable of suggesting loud musical sound is [ò], for [u] is too closed: and a regular reading has the great merit of giving prominence to the [ò] doublet:

Un vieux Souveni.r so|nne à plein sou.fflĕ du co.r [!]
        . ..   .   ..

            ò   ò
  s u   s   su

(d) *Long vowels*

It is not surprising that long vowels are particularly associated with solemn and rhetorical language, since they tend to slow up the line and enhance its musical quality. The maximum number of any such vowels in a stanza is sixteen, since only a stressed vowel can be long: the minimum is two, produced by the feminine rimes. In [I] we have no less than ten long vowels. In [II] the number of drops to six, limited to *mémoi.rĕ ferti.le* and the elegiac closing phrase

(la fo ˙ rmĕ d'unĕ vi.lle
Chan.gĕ plus vite, hélas! que le cœu.r d'un mortel [;]

In subsequent stanzas devoted to Paris and the swan their occurrence is minimal. They are heard again in [VIII]:

> Et mes che.rs souveni.rs | sont plus lou.rds que des rocs [.]

In [IX] they contribute to the solemnity of

> ´Aussi devant ce Lou.|vre une ima.gĕ m'oppri˙me:
> Je pen.se à mon grand cy.|gne avec ses ge˙stĕs fous

and to the powerful enjambement of the last line:

> Et rongé d'un dési.r ' sans trê./ve .....

In [X] they are strategically placed: *béta.il, supe˙rbe, en exta.sĕ, veu.vĕ.* In [XI] they have great importance in reinforcing the enjambement of the closing line:

> Derriè.rĕ la mura '.ille immen./sĕ du brouilla.rd [;]
>   ў   ў   ў

and here they are further lengthened by association with the semi-consonant *yod* which occurs in a powerful triplet. And they occur again, with high emotional associations, in [XII]:

> ... à ceux ' qui s'abreu./vĕnt de pleu.rs
> Et te˙ttĕnt la Douleu.r | comme unĕ bo˙nnĕ lou.ve!
> Aux mai˙grĕs orphelins | séchant commĕ des fleu.rs.

Finally, they are heard in

> Un vieux Souveni.r so|nne à plein sou˙fflĕ du co.r [.!]

It may be noted that all the rimes of the last stanzas of the poem are on long vowels, the masculine ones in each case being lengthened by a terminal [r]. This vibrant can itself be extended to lengthen the last syllable, and the reader will doubtless take advantage of this possibility at the end of each stanza.

(e) Reinforcement

Any phonetic patterning which is characteristic of the line as a whole will have the effect of reinforcing the metre. This is often achieved by a strong doublet or triplet accompanied by a more subdued effect running throughout the line:

Pauvre et tri.stĕ miroi.r | où jadis resplendit
      is   i   is s   i
   r   r   r r   r

Et, brillant aux carreaux, | le bric-à-brac confus [.]
   bri   bri   br
       k   k   k

Et, de ses pieds palmés | frottant le pavé sec [,]
       p   pa   pa
    s
é   é é   é   é è

Derriè.rĕ la mura.'ille immen./sĕ du brouilla.rd [;]
      m   m
   ў   ў   ў
  r r   r   r   r

Phonetic reinforcement may be helpful in giving a degree of symmetry to lines weakened by metrical and syntactical imbalance:

Froids et clai.rs le Trava.'il s'éve/ille, où la voiri`e
f rwà   vwàr
             v ў v ў

N'a bougé!/palais neufs, échafauda.gĕs, blocs,
      b j l   f   f   j bl
  á   á   á à
             f   f

In the first case, there is a pivotal cluster around the weakened caesura and the line is enclosed in a defining cluster. In the second case, the pivotal cluster [f | f] is less strongly heard, and is probably best regarded as part of the prevailing doublet [bjlf | fjbl] which combine with the cluster in [a] to give a general unity of tone to the line.

Sometimes the two hemistichs may have strongly contrasting phonetic colouring, which again emphasizes the metrical units. In [3-4]

L'immen.sĕ majesté | de vos doubleu.rs de veu.ve
   m s m j s   d v d   d v v
                œ   œ

Ce Simoïs menteu.r | qui par vos pleu.rs grandit [,]
 s s m s m   p r   p   r
   i   i   i   i
         œ r   œ

the [A] hemistich has an [s m] pattern which is absent from [B]. (It may be noted that Baudelaire increased this effect by changing his original *Le Simoïs* ... to *Ce Simoïs* ...) We are similarly aware of contrast in [25]

> Vers la ciel quelquefois, | commĕ l'ho.mmĕ d'Ovi.de [,]
> è l è el   ò   l ò   ò
>   k k   k
> v   m   m   v

and

> Sur son cou convulsif | tendant sa tête avi˙de
> s s k k   s   s
>   t d   t t   d

Effects such as this occur commonly in the poem. But even more frequent is the use of a terminal cluster to reinforce the ending of line or hemistich. A simple doublet will suffice, as in [14] *sous les cieux*, or [32] *que des rocs*. But generally the effect is more complex, and we have clusters such as *jadis resplendit* [dís|s dí], [22] *lac natal* [lá á ál] [33] *imagĕ m'opprime* [ím m mí], or [38] *superbĕ Pyrrhus* [süp r|pürüs]. There are more than thirty such clusters on the caesura or line-ending, though some such as [12] *aux carreaux* [ó|ó] or [52] *d'autres encor* [ó r|òr] may not be immediately obvious. A rather similar effect is the terminal echo, in which the ending of one hemistich is matched phonetically with that of the next:

> Les he˙rbĕs, les gros blocs | verdis par l'eau des fla˙ques,
>   l k   l k
>
> Là s'étalait jadis | unĕ ménagerie [;]
>   já i   aj i
>
> Sur son cou convulsif | tendant sa tête avi.de [,]
>   v í   ví
>
> Aux mai.grĕs orphelins | séchant commĕ des fleu.rs [!]
>   rf l   fl   r

When the corresponding elements of the doublet are situated at the beginning and end of the metrical unit we have a defining cluster such as is heard in [5/6]:

> A fécondé soudain | ma mémoirĕ fertile
>   fé   fè
>
> Commĕ je traversais | le nouveau Carrousel [.]
> k   k

This effect is not common. But it does deserve to be noted if only for the very striking use made of it in [20] to set off the [B] hemistich:

> Près d'un ruisseau sans eau | la bête ouvrant le bec [   ]
>   l bè   l bè

In this case it is particularly useful as a means of keeping the form of the line in view of the strong syntactical link with the stanza following. As we have already seen, effects such as these may be married to rhythmic variations just as readily as to regular metre. Thus in [10] *chapiteaux ébauchés* [ch p ó|bó ʤ] and in [15] *le Travail s'éveille* [v ỹ|v ỹ] are terminal doublets to an extended metrical phrase. They may also extend beyond the line, particularly in cases where a terminal echo links the line-ending with the caesura following:

> Aussi devant ce Lou.|vre une ima.gĕ m'opprime:
>   i   i
>
> Je pen.se à mon grand cy.|gnĕ ......
>   i
>
> ... à ceux'qui s'abreu./vĕnt de pleu.rs
>   rœ̀   lœ̀.r
>
> Et te˙ttĕnt la Douleu.r | ...
>   lœ̀.

(f) Phonetic texture

When many clusters interlock, the reader naturally draws attention in his reading to those which are of significance in supporting his metrical or syntactical interpretation of a line or stanza. However, the coexistence of patterns produces a certain phonetic 'texture' which is independent of rhythm. In this way phonemes may be effective which do not form part of any linear cluster but are prominent in adjacent lines. This is particularly true of [I], where the phonetic texture is so dense that we might change our metaphor and speak of 'orchestration'. We may begin by identifying the linear patterns:

> Androma.que, je pen.se à vous! / Ce petit fleu.ve,
>   p s v   s p   v
>   à   à
>
> Pauvre et tri.stĕ miroi.|r où jadis resplendit
>   i s   i   dis   di
>   r   r   r   r   r
>
> L'immen.sĕ majesté | de vos doubleu.rs de veu.ve
>   m   s m   s   d v d   d v   v
>   œ̀   œ̀

```
Ce Simoïs menteu.r | qui par vos pleu.rs grandit [,]
 s   m sm    r        p r   p  r r
    i  i              i                   i
           œ              œ
         à              à
```

These are the most significant phonetic patterns. But they alone do not account for the over-all texture of the stanza. They do not reveal that the [psv|spv] cluster in [1] is continued, together with the *ti* of *petit*, in *Pauvre et triste*... Nor do they show that the rather minor [à] cluster of [1A] extends throughout the stanza, and is in fact the only nasal vowel in it. One cannot read this stanza properly without being aware of interlinear affinities. While it is impossible to isolate such effects, it may be worth studying the degree of phonetic overlap of the words, and for this reason I have arranged them below in groups sharing a common phoneme. It is interesting to note that rarely indeed do they have only this phoneme in common.

à   menteur—immense—pense—resplendit—grandit—Andromaque
        mà   *mà* s   *à*s   r s   *à*di   r *à*di   *à*dr m

p   petit—resplendit—pense—par—pleurs—pauvre
       p   i   sp*à*   i   p*à*s   p   r   p   r   p   r

i   petit—triste—Simoïs—immense—miroir—grandit—resplendit—
       p   ti   trist   sim is   i   m*à*   mir   r   r*à* di   r sp *à* di
       jadis—qui
        di   i

s   ce—pense—immense—Simoïs—resplendit—triste—majesté—jadis
       s   *à*s   i m*à* s   sim is   r s   *à* di   trist   aj st   ja i

v   pauvre—vos—vous—veuve—fleuve
       ó v   vó   v   vœ v   œ v

d   de—douleur—grandit—jadis—resplendit—Andromaque
       d   d   r   r*à* di   dis   r s   *à* di   *à* dr

œ   veuve—fleuve—pleurs—douleurs—menteur
       vœ v   lœ v   lœr   lœr   œr

m   miroir—Simoïs—immense—menteur—majesté—Andromaque
       mir   r   sim is   im *à* s   m*à* t r   ma st   à   r ma

It is this degree of phonetic affinity between words that accounts for the extreme richness of texture of [I].

A number of these phonemes are continued in [II], the most effective interlinear pattern being formed by [vr], with some assistance from [f], and by [m]:

A fécondé soudain | ma mémoi.rĕ ferti˙le,
  f   r f r
          m m m

Commĕ je traversais | le nouveau Carrousel.
    v r   v   r

Le vieux Paris n'est plus (la fo˙rmĕ d'unĕ vi˙lle
  v   r   f r   v
                      m

Changĕ plus vite, hélas! | que le cœu.r d'un mortel) [;]
    v   r   r
                               m

while in [III] the stanza is coloured not only by the forceful [k] but also by the more subdued [o]:

Je ne vois qu'en esprit | tout ce camp de bara˙ques,
      k   k   k

Ces tas de chapiteaux ébauchés/et de fûts,
          ó   ó

Les herbĕs, les gros blocs | verdis par l'eau des fla˙ques,
        ó   ò   ó
           k   k

Et, brillant aux carreaux, | le bric-à-brac confus [.]
  ó   ó
     k   k   k

The most striking textural feature of the poem is the ubiquity of [k]. This occurs frequently in clusters and in a significant number of rimes. It seems to flaunt its presence in such words as *bric-à-brac*, *cocotiers* and even *quiconque*. Its abundance is not the result of rhetorical repetition, for words are very rarely repeated; nor in general is it consciously organized to produce effects *à la* Poe. It is just there. In some cases a specific effect may be attributed to it, but in others not. I have suggested the possibility that it arises in the poet's mind from an association of the words *Andromaque* and *Carrousel*.

(g) *Onomatopoeic Interpretations*

In both [I] and [XIII] the vowel [œ] is specifically associated with sorrow. This arises in both cases from the building of extended clusters on the words *douleur* and *pleurs* and therefore it is unnecessary to look for any onomatopoeic explanation. There is no such clear explanation of the sequence *bougé*, *faubourgs* and *lourds* in [VIII], supported as they are by *tout pour moi* and *souvenirs*. This sound is much used by Romantics and Symbolists (and, of course, by Baudelaire himself) to suggest a mood of melancholy. It recurs, in this poem, in [50]. Its association with feelings of melancholy may be related to the fact that it is a closed sound (i.e. with implications of repression) and rounded (i.e. approximating closely to a musical sound). It does not occur significantly in *Le Cygne* with any other associations.

Conspicuous by its rarity in the poem is the sound [è], which, particularly in the combination [è, r], is much used in nineteenth-century poetry to suggest a musical sadness. Despite the fact that words such as *cher*, *cherchant* and *perdu* offer ample opportunity for the building of clusters, in this poem Baudelaire uses it effectively only twice: in *la négresse amaigrie* [grè|ègr] and in the longer and very impressive sequence:

> ... la bête ouvrant le bec
> Baignait nerveusĕment ses ailes ...

This sparse use of the sound in which so many poets luxuriate is presumably related to the poet's wish to minimize the lachrymose and pathetic aspects of his theme and to present it as a human drama, richly varied, without too much self-indulgence. If the poet's feelings dominate the poem, they do so only indirectly and are not in themselves the spectacle towards which the reader's attention is directed.

However, [i], that other stand-by of the nineteenth-century poet, is abundantly present. It accounts for an appreciable number of rimes and is present in many clusters. It is a thin, closed sound which seems to suggest a frustrated discontent, in Baudelaire as in others. We hear it in [2]:

> Pauvre et tri˙stĕ miroi.|r où jadis resplendit [,]

and in *ironique* [26], *convulsif/avide* [27], *melancolie* [29], *une imagĕ m'opprime* [33], *vil* [38], *vide* [39], *amaigrie et phtisique* [4], and *où mon esprit s'exile* [49]. The word *convulsif* reminds us of the close association of this sound with [ü], which we also hear in [35]:

> Commĕ les exilés, | ridicule et sublime [,]

in which even *sublime* (and *immense* in [3]) takes on some of its colouring from their presence in clusters with words of a contrary sense. There can be very little doubt that, for whatever reasons, this sound is closely associated with discontent. The reader will recall the extensive use made of it by Mallarmé in his *sonnet du Cygne* (doubtless suggested by Baudelaire's poem). Here, too, it carries similar implications. A further reason for the predominance of the sound in both poems is the presence in the poet's mind of the word *cygne*.

We have suggested a similar explanation for the ubiquitous presence of [k]. When we examine the actual use of the sound, we find that it dominates [III] and [VII], though these stanzas are quite different in tone. In the latter, as in [35], it will be pronounced harshly, but in [43]

> Les cocotiers absents | de la superbe Afrique [ ]

it will have a soft sound. Only in

> Sur son cou convulsif | tendant sa téte avide [,]

can we attribute a definite function to it, for there, together with the other voiceless stop [t], it suggests the jerky movements implied in the word *convulsif*.

We can also, I think, say something about its use in [43]. This line and the one that follows it present two images, the latter of which annihilates the former.

> Les cocotiers absents | de la superbe Afrique,
>   k k   ps   sp   k
>
> Derriè.rĕ la mura.'ille immen./se du brouilla.rd [;]
>   m   m
> r r   r   r   r
>   ÿ   ÿ   ÿ

We have already referred to the use of enjambement and long vowels to strengthen [44]. To this I think we may add a further point. [43] consists largely of voiceless stops, light in sound; [44] of nasal consonants, vibrants, and voiced consonants, which carry much greater resonance, and also the strong triplet in *yod* which suggests force because it does in fact require a certain effort to pronounce. In reading these lines aloud, one is aware of the much greater degree of effort which is required to pronounce the second in comparison with the first. This, then, I think is a true onomatopoeic effect.

Finally, two examples of imitative onomatopoeia. In [16]

> Pousse un som.bre ouragan | dans l'air silencieux [,]
>   s   s   si   si
>   r   r   r
>   ò   à   à

the [s] in [A], together with the vibrants, evokes the idea of wind associated with *ouragan* and will be strongly pronounced, whereas in [B] it will be much softer as it derives its only significance from *silencieux*. The nasal vowels of [A] contribute the idea of sound, that of [B] being insignificant. Baudelaire originally wrote 'un sale ouragan', which gives the [s] cluster but not the nasals, and the need to supply these was probably one of the reasons for the change. This line is a particularly interesting example of the degree to which onomatopoeic sounds derive their force from the meaning of the words to which they belong.

Our last example is [50], to which we have already referred:

> Un vieux Souveni.r so|nne à plein sou.fflĕ du co.r [!]
>   ò   ò
>   su   s   su
> v   v   f

The lack of nasals, the most effective way of suggesting resonant sound, is striking. Only the doublet in [ò] suggests strong sound. The poet is *dans la forêt*, and the sound is perhaps muffled. But the main cluster expands the word *souffle*, and its sibilants, together with the other fricatives, suggest breathing, and, it seems to me, effort. I would not attempt to interpret this, but would suggest that it is one of the factors which contribute to the mystery of the line.

INDEX AND SUMMARY
OF DEFINITIONS USED
IN THE TEXT

Terms which have been devised specifically for this book are indicated by an asterisk. Numerical references are to pages. They refer only to Chapters 1-7 and do not include the Commentaries, where further examples may in some cases be found.

alexandrine: A line of twelve syllables which in the regular *binary form* (46, 66) has a *major stress** on the sixth syllable, called the *caesura* (47-50, 56-9), which divides the line into two equal *hemistichs* (21, 44, 47). There is usually one *subsidiary stress* (44, 47, 50-1) in each hemistich, though there may be more, or none. The subsidiary stress may fall on any syllable, and divides the hemistich into two *stress groups** which are called the *segments** of the line (24, 43, 47, 50, 51). The syllabic placing of segments and caesura in a binary alexandrine may be expressed symbolically in a form such as 2:4|3:3 (see RHYTHM). The alexandrine sometimes has a *ternary* rhythm (66-8, 86). The true ternary alexandrine has two evenly spaced caesuras and a rhythm of 4|4|4. An irregular ternary rhythm may sometimes result from enjambement on the caesura (see ENJAMBEMENT). The binary alexandrine is sometimes termed *classical* and the ternary form *Romantic* (but see 66). The alexandrine was the standard line used in classical drama, but has also been widely used for lyric verse.

alliteration: the obtrusive use of a prevailing cluster of consonants (98-9).

assonance: a correspondence heard between vowels in circumstances which do not constitute rime (99, 128, 133).

consonants: 154, 160-70. For definition, see PHONEMES. A consonant differs from a vowel by being a noise rather than a musical sound, and results from interruption or obstruction of the flow of air from the throat through the lips. A brief but total interruption produces a *stop*; an obstruction, which constricts the air-passage sufficiently to interrupt the vowel sequence, produces a *fricative* (162). A consonant pronounced with the vocal cords relaxed is said to be *voiceless*, and as it represents a complete suspension of the vowel sequence, it is obtrusive; if the vocal cords are tensed the consonant is *voiced*, and as this causes the vowel-sequence to be to some degree sustained, the interruption is less obtrusive. Stops are [p/b], [t/d] and [k/g], the first of each pair being voiceless and the second voiced. Fricatives, which produce a degree of hiss, are [f/v], [s/z], and [ʤ/j] (164-6, 169). [r] is also a fricative but is in a class by itself and is called a *vibrant* (162, 166, 169, 175-81) and [l] is a *liquid* (166-7, 169, 175-81). [m] and [n] are nasal consonants in which the air-flow is interrupted in the mouth but escapes through the nose (168-9). Voiceless stops may strongly colour a line, as may the fricatives [f/v] and the *sibilants* [s/z], [ʤ/j] — i.e. fricatives with a high degree of hiss (162, 183-6). So may [m] and [n] and also [l] and [r], all of which produce effects of great musicality. For qualities of consonants, see (169-70), and for significance of initial consonants, (98). See also SEMI-CONSONANTS.

diction: the manner in which verse is spoken (6, 12-14, 19-20, 22).

echo*: an echo* (90-3) is the repetition of a phoneme or a group of phonemes from one segment, hemistich or line to the next, in such a way that one is heard to answer the other. It is *contrapuntal** (91) if it runs counter to the normal rhythm of the line by linking a stressed with an unstressed syllable; and *liminal** or *terminal** (90) if it establishes a correspondence between, respectively, the beginning and the end of consecutive metrical units. In an asymmetric triplet* (see PHONETIC CLUSTERS) that element of the triplet which is separated by some distance from the doublet (usually occurring in the other hemistich of an alexandrine) is termed an echo if it follows and a pre-echo if it precedes: thus [pp| -p] includes an echo and [p|pp] a pre-echo.

enjambement: this occurs when the syntactical structure of a line causes a major stress, on the caesura or line-ending, to be *delayed**, thus producing a modification of rhythm (56-65). This happens when a phrase overruns the line-ending in such a way that a few syllables (called the *rejet*) encroach on the line following. In this case, major stress is transferred from the line-ending to the last syllable of the *rejet*. Enjambement is recognized by the fact that the second line (or its first hemistich, in the case of the alexandrine) is *dislocated**: i.e. the segments of which it is composed are syntactically incoherent, since the *rejet* carries on the sense of the previous line and is to a greater or less degree isolated from what follows. The irregular stress produced by enjambement is particularly strong, and its function is normally to give greater imaginative impact to the *rejet*. Enjambement is sometimes produced by a *contre-rejet*: i.e. a small group of syllables isolated syntactically at the end of one line and leading on to the line following. Enjambement between short lines causes the terminal stress of one line to be transferred to the subsidiary stress position of the line following. In the case of the *alexandrine*, enjambement may also occur on the caesura (often as a result of enjambement on the line-ending, which disturbs the accustomed stresses of the line). A phrase may overrun the caesura (which is then *eroded** or *vestigial**) so as to form a *rejet* which dislocates [B]. This brings the *rejet* into prominence and the major stress of the line is *delayed**, whereas enjambement on the line-ending will normally produce *premature** stress in the line following.

feminine endings: a word which ends in a fossilized [e], or a syllable containing a fossilized [e], is said to have a *feminine ending*, and at the end of a line produces a *feminine rime* (31, 140, 145). In this position, the fossilized [e] is mute and not counted in scansion; but it does have the effect of lengthening the preceding stressed vowel. It is likewise mute if the first hemistich of an alexandrine has a feminine ending, in which case the second hemistich must begin with a vowel in order to cause elision of the superfluous [e] (49-50). If an upright stress-bar is used to indicate the caesura, this must be written immediately after the vowel so as to cut off the consonant following (e.g. bran| che), and this consonant then attaches itself to the second hemistich.

fossilized* sound: standard French spelling includes many letters which are written because they were sounded at earlier stages of the development of the language, but are now mute in verse as in ordinary speech. These are described as *fossilized sound** (140-143), and when they occur at the end of a line may affect the validity of a rime. (See RIME.) Fossilized sound becomes actual sound when it makes liaison with a vowel following, though the sound is often considerably modified (e.g. *x* is heard as [z]).

line: the line is the fundamental rhythmic unit of verse, and is indicated in print by spacial separation of one line from another and by the use of a capital initial letter for the first word (though the latter custom is often ignored in modern times). When spoken, lines are separated from each other by a pause of variable length (21 *et seq*).

In French verse the main stress always falls on the last syllable (except in the case of enjambement, q.v.) and in regular verse it must be reinforced by rime (101). If the line has a *feminine ending* (q.v.), the fossilized syllable does not count in scansion. (For third person plural verbs, see 37.) The metre depends upon the number of its syllables. Short lines of two or three syllables occasionally occur (usually in conjunction with longer ones), but 6, 8, 10 or 12 syllables is normal: the *impair* line, with an odd number of syllables, is exceptional, and used to produce an effect of greater fluidity. All lines except the shortest will contain at least one subsidiary stress of varying position (see RHYTHM). They will normally be of constant length throughout a poem, but in lyric verse shorter lines may be introduced among longer ones in a regular pattern (21, 41, 44, 121-5). When this occurs, there will often be a simple ratio between the number of syllables in the longer and shorter lines. Most lines end in punctuation, i.e. are *end-stopped* (109). If there is no punctuation the line is *open-ended* or *run-on* (18, 56, 62): in that case it is always *unstable** and ends at *middle* or *high pitch** (16-17, 55) so as to suggest that the sense is not yet complete. But the fact that the line is run-on does not eliminate the pause on the line-ending. (See PUNCTUATION.) Long lines are suitable for narrative, rhetoric, and the exposition of complex thought: short lines are lighter, give greater prominence to rhythm and rime, are more easily sung, and in consequence suited to lyric verse (100).

lyric: the term originally applied to verse intended to be sung to musical accompaniment, but now applies to all verse which retains song-like qualities and is directed primarily to the emotions (3, 11, 43, 111).

masculine endings: words and lines which do not have *feminine endings* (q.v.) are described as masculine. They end either in a free vowel or in a consonant. The stressed vowel is not lengthened as in the case of a feminine rime, but may be either naturally short, or naturally long if followed by [r] and no other consonant, or by a voiced fricative, and in certain other circumstances (171-2).

melodic line or pattern*: the term is used to describe the variations of pitch of the voice during the reading of a line verse. This is to some extent at the reader's discretion, but is influenced by punctuation, and the positioning of the stresses within the line, as well as the imaginative and emotional force of the words (13-19, 26, 42, 48, 54-7). For *neutral, low, middle*, and *high pitch**, see 14. The line will normally reach high (or sometimes low) pitch on its major stress. In the regular binary alexandrine there is a tendency for the voice to slope upwards through the first hemistich and downwards through the second, to reach neutral or low pitch on the rime-word if the line is *stable**: if it is *unstable*, the voice turns upwards at the line-ending. The stability of a line is indicated by its punctuation (q.v.). Where there is enjambement the voice will normally run in a continuous slope through the eroded stress and reach high or low on the displaced stress: so the melody of the line will depend on whether this is premature or delayed (see ENJAMBEMENT).

neutral [e]: a rounded middle vowel which owing to its self-effacing nature has ceased to be pronounced in current usage except where strongly supported by consonants. In regular verse, this deterioration has not gone so far as in ordinary speech, and [ĕ] counts as a full syllable in scansion except where elided by a vowel or non-aspirate *h* following, or on the line-ending, where it is mute. In verse it never bears stress and is appreciably shortened if the vowel of the syllable preceding it is stressed, in which case that vowel is correspondingly lengthened to compensate for the shortening of the [ĕ] (29-34).

onomatopoeia: the suggestion of non-linguistic sounds or of imagined qualities by the use of linguistic sound. In ordinary speech, this is a feature of certain individual words whose sound is associated by the hearer with their meaning; in verse the effect may be extended by associating phonemes from adjacent words with those of the word itself. Certain phonemes lend themselves readily to the suggestion of specific qualities: e.g. constricted vowels may suggest frustration and melancholy, nasal ones may suggest musical or resonant sound, liquids may suggest a flowing effect, back nasal vowels may suggest depth and darkness: but such association is entirely dependent upon our knowing the meaning of the words and our readiness to associate the sound with it. See 149 and Chapter Seven *passim*.

orthography (French): French orthography is only partially based on the representation of sound, and retains many features surviving from earlier forms of the words or from conscious effort to suggest etymology. Many phonemes which now have identical sound evolved from a variety of forms, and retain evidence of this in their spelling. Any consideration of the sound of verse should be limited to heard phonemes, and it may often be convenient to represent these by a phonetic transcript in which silent letters are ignored and ambiguous symbols (e.g. *c* in *place, corps, château* or *ai* in *fait, vain*) eliminated and replaced by ones having a constant value (27).

phoneme: a phoneme is a single sound characteristic of a language, the presence of which is necessary for the correct pronunciation of a word (155). Each phoneme is regarded as a constant, though it may in speech vary in ways which do not affect the form and significance of the word. Phonemes in French are classed as *vowels, semiconsonants*, and *consonants* (all of which q.v.). All phonemes result from modification, generally by movement of the tongue, teeth, and/or lips, of a flow of breath passing through the cavity of the mouth (and sometimes the nose) which is caused to vibrate and so given resonance by contact with the vocal cords in the larynx. The number of phonemes in a line of verse is variable, though the number of vowels is fixed by metre. The degree of stress attributed to a phoneme may be varied at the will of the speaker (though metrical stress falls only on vowels), so also may be the effective length of all vowels (subject to certain rules of convention) and of some consonants. The poet's art involves the appropriate grouping of phonemes to achieve musicality or to encourage imaginative or emotional response, and the reading of verse requires the sensitive interpretation of such effects (see Chapter Seven *passim*).

phonetic abstract*: a phonetic abstract is prepared by writing underneath a line of verse, in positions corresponding to their occurrence in the line, symbols to represent those phonemes which form *phonetic clusters** (q.v.). The purpose is to indicate visually the degree of balance or imbalance produced by sound-groupings, the degree to which they are *linked** or run counter to each other, and the richness of the total effect. Only effects felt to be significant will be included and to this degree the phonetic abstract represents a subjective interpretation. The sense of that interpretation should be indicated as clearly as possible by the groupings, but will usually need some comment or explanation. Individual clusters are set out each on its own line (though they may be blended when they are felt to be closely integrated). Dominant clusters are normally placed first and linked clusters kept as close together as possible so as to suggest their relationship. The same phoneme may be incorporated in more than one cluster if it is felt to contribute to different patterns (74).

phonetic cluster*: a phonetic cluster is a recognizable correspondence of sounds which is not explicable by the requirements of metre (75, 79). It is a free effect which may be associated with either metrical or syntactical rhythm (85, 87). It is normally heard as a *doublet** which involves two occurrences of a phoneme, or a *triplet** which involves three (75). When only one phoneme is involved the cluster is *simple**, whereas if two or more phonemes are repeated it is *compound** (75). A simple doublet will normally be effective only if the phonemes occur close to each other or are associated with metrical stress or with important words related by syntactical function or correspondence or contrast of meaning. These factors will always reinforce any cluster. A triplet* may be either *symmetrical**, in which case the elements which compose it are evenly spaced, or more commonly *asymmetric** (75), in which a doublet (the *nucleus**) is answered from a distance by an *echo** or *pre-echo** often situated in the other hemistich of an alexandrine (see ECHO*). The recurring phonemes or groups of phonemes are known as the *elements** of the cluster. Where phonemes are repeated frequently but with no obvious rhythmic distribution, the result is a *prevailing cluster**. A cluster may be *dominant** or *subsidiary**. Specific terms may be used to identity the position of a cluster within a line, these being: (*a*) the *defining cluster** in which there is a phonetic correspondence between the beginning and end of a hemistich or line (87); (*b*) the *pivotal cluster** which is balanced around the caesura (88); (*c*) the *liminal cluster** which reinforces the beginning of a line; (*d*) the *terminal cluster** (89) which reinforces its closing syllables; (*e*) the *liminal** and *terminal echo** and the *contrapuntal echo** (see ECHO*). Clusters of this kind are said to be *linked** if they follow a similar order and rhythm and are thus heard to reinforce each other (perhaps blending in one or more important words of the line) and *cumulative** when the elements of several clusters are gathered up in one word or phrase situated late in the line. Clusters which occur within the limits of the line are *linear**; those which extend over the line-ending are *run-on** (77, 93), a particular case being the *phonetic copula** often associated with enjambement (93); and those which run through a number of lines or a stanza are *interlinear** (93-5). A cluster may be said to be *used** when it is recognized by the reader as a significant element in the line or verse, and to be *brought out** when it is emphasized in reading. (See Chapter Four *passim.*)

punctuation: the function of punctuation in written language is to group words in syntactically significant relationships and in some cases to modify their stress and emotional significance. In speech these effects are achieved by modification of pitch and tone of voice. Punctuation should therefore be carefully interpreted by the reader and expressed as sound. Punctuation within a line will not necessarily be followed by a pause (23, 28), but punctuation on the line-ending will normally reinforce the pause at that point. On the line-ending the comma, semicolon, and full stop normally produce a *stable** line; the colon, exclamation mark and question mark produce an *unstable** one (16). If the line ends without punctuation it is *run-on* and unstable, but this does not annul the pause which follows (see LINE). At any point in a line punctuation generates a certain degree of stress, and so is an important feature of rhythm (q.v.).

rhetoric: the use of cadenced language and carefully-chosen vocabulary in order to produce a desired emotional response in the hearer. Rhetoric is akin to verse and in France, from the sixteenth to the nineteenth century, was regarded as one of the major resources of poetry, particularly as a result of its cultivation in the Latin literature on which was based the education of cultured men. Since the middle of the nineteenth century it has fallen into some disrepute, since it can, at its worst, involve the mere manipulation of words: but it nevertheless remains a prime feature of much of the greatest French verse. It involves the use of many verbal devices such as apostrophe, personification, metaphor, antithesis, etc., which long experience has shown can be effective when coupled with significant thought and emotion, but can sometimes be used as a substitute for either of these, and even in the greatest of poets can lead to a form of verbal intoxication. The reader should not dismiss effects as 'mere rhetoric' since much of the most powerful language the world has known is rhetorical; he should rather seek to assess its effect, its significance, and its justification, and so come to a conclusion in any particular case as to its poetic worth. Rhetoric, like grammar, involves the systematized study of human expression, and when properly used can give to words great emotional force which otherwise they would not possess; and in lighter verse can often serve as a pleasing ornament (70).

rhythm: the rhythm of a line results from the distribution of stresses, which in French occur on the final syllable of a *sense-group** or syntactical phrase. In speech, such phrases are usually separated by a pause, and any such pause generates stress. In verse, the pause at the line-ending causes the main stress to fall on the last syllable of the line; in the alexandrine there is similar stress on the caesura; and in any line subsidiary stresses occur wherever is required by syntax. Rhythm is represented symbolically by figures representing the number of syllables in each *stress-group** or *segment**, each subsidiary stress being represented by a colon: thus 3:5 indicates an eight-syllable line with a stress falling on the third syllable. In the case of the alexandrine, the caesura occuring on the sixth syllable (or on the fourth and eighth in the case of the ternary alexandrine) is represented by an upright stress-bar: so that 4:2|2:4, 3:3|3:3 and 4|4|4 are symbolic representations of the rhythm of alexandrines, with the major metrical stress indicated by the bar. When the major stress is displaced by enjambement, the caesura becomes a subsidiary stress and the displaced stress is shown by a sloping stress-bar, thus: 3:3:2/4 or 2/4:3:3. In such cases the figure immediately preceding the stress-bar represents the *rejet*. In some cases when the second hemistich is *dislocated** the final figure may represent a *contre-rejet*, and this may be shown by the addition of a hyphen or an arrow. Thus 3:3:4/2–indicates a line in which there is enjambement on both the caesura and the line-ending, and that the latter effect involves the use of a *contre-rejet*.

The word *rhythm* is also used in all the arts, including poetry, with much wider implications than those of metrical rhythm as discussed above. Some reference to this point is made in Chapter One.

rime or rhyme: see Chapter Seven *passim*: also 7, 100-3.

Rime has the same form and function as a *phonetic echo*, but differs from it in being a metrical feature governed (in French verse) by strict conventions. It is an obligatory feature of the line-ending in regular verse, and normally should not occur elsewhere (though the term may sometimes be used for free effects). At times (though rarely) rime on the caesura has been used as a metrical feature.

A rime is said to be *proposed** when the poet places a word in a position which leads us to expect an *answer**: i.e. a matching word which satisfies the conditions of rime (104, 126). These are: (*a*) the answer must have exactly the same stressed vowel (approximations are not permitted, save that occasionally differences of vowel-length may be ignored, and an open vowel may match a closed one); (*b*) it must be completely different in meaning and not be so closely related in etymology as to be felt to be merely a variant of the proposal; (*c*) any sounded consonant or consonants which may follow the stressed vowel must be identical; (*d*) any fossilized sound at the end of the rime-words must match within limits set by convention (140-3). Rime is entirely based on difference of meaning associated with similarity of sound: therefore fossilized sound is not felt to make any positive contribution to it, but is merely a necessary feature. There are however certain exceptional cases (of which *rime normande* is the best-known) in which convention allows the poet to use fossilized sound as an active feature of the rime either in the proposal or in the answer (141, 143). (An *active feature** of a rime is any sounded phoneme which helps to validate it.) The answer to a rime normally bears greater stress than the proposal. A rime which ends in a fossilized [e] or a syllable containing one is termed *feminine* (31, 140, 145), all other rimes being masculine: and the convention of *alternance des rimes*, which has been strictly observed from the sixteenth to the twentieth century, requires that a rime of one gender must be followed by a rime of the other (145).

Rime is usually felt to be most effective if it is contrasting: i.e. if the stressed vowel changes from rime to rime and also the consonants, and if the *consonne d'appui* (i.e. the consonant preceding the stressed vowel) is an active feature of the rime. It is felt to be weakened if two similar parts of speech are rimed together, in which case it is called a *rime banale*. But considerations such as these are in practice often ignored.

French rimes are distinguished in terms of quality. If only the stressed vowel matches, the rime is *faible* or *pauvre*; if two phonemes match it is *suffisante*; if three or more match it is *riche* (128-31). In each case, one of the phonemes must be the stressed vowel. A very rich rime, matching more than three elements, may be described as *sumptuous**, *acrobatic*, or *millionaire* (131). An amplified *rime** is one in which the rimewords, in addition to satisfying the normal requirements of rime, contain phonetic correspondences which technically do not form part of the rime (134-136). A *punning rime** is one in which both proposal and answer consist of words identical in form but different in meaning: the effect of this is felt to be rich (132, 138). A rime is usually proposed by one word and answered by another: but in cases of rich rime it is not unusual for the active elements to involve more than one word (132). The richness of a rime is not in any way affected by the fossilized phonemes, but only by the sounded or active ones.

A *rime-scheme* represents the order in which rimes occur and are answered. For this purpose both proposal and answer may be represented symbolically by the same lower-case italic letter (107), *a* standing for the first rime, *b* for the second and so on. Gender is not normally shown, but if it is wished to do so, a capital may be used to indicate a feminine rime; and where short lines are used with long ones, the short line may be shown by a letter enclosed in square brackets, thus: AbA[b], which shows that the short line has a masculine rime. The commonest rime-schemes are: *aabbccdd* etc., called *rimes suivies* or *rimes plates* (these are *couplets*, and may also be used as separate stanzas: *aa bb cc*) (109-11); *abab*, called *rimes croisées*, in which the rimewords of two rimes alternate within every four lines; or *abba*, called *rimes embrassées*, in which two rimes are proposed one after the other and answered in inverse order (112-15). Occasionally, in a block of lines, rimes are answered in varying order, this effect being called *rimes mêlées*: an example might be *ababccdede*.

When verse is divided into stanzas, the rimes will normally be answered in the same order in each stanza, though there are occasional exceptions (113); and there will be a complete change of rime with each stanza. In certain traditional verse-forms such as the *terza rima*, the *sonnet*, the *rondeau*, and the *pantoum* (117-20) rimes and even whole lines may be repeated or answered from one stanza to the next. In the medieval *chanson de geste* assonance was used instead of rime, and this effect may sometimes be found in modern free verse; and in lyric verse a *refrain* may sometimes be used, repeating a word or phrase with complete disregard for the rules of rime.

semi-consonant: a *semi-consonant* is a constricted vowel which, when occurring immediately before another vowel, is shortened into the equivalent of a consonant, this effect being known as *synaeresis*. (When the vowel does not so change but remains in hiatus, the result is *diaeresis*.) One semi-consonant, the shortened [i] known as *yod*, may also occur at the end of a syllable: the others, [ŭ] and [w̆], can only occur at the beginning (39).

syllable: a syllable is a sounded vowel either by itself or accompanied by one or more consonants (25-9). A consonant will always attach itself to a following vowel if one is available, with the result that most syllables in French begin with a consonant, and will end with a consonant only if there is no following vowel to take it over. Certain groups of consonants involving [s], [l] or [r] are indivisible and so will occur together at the beginning and sometimes at the end of a syllable (the latter only on the line-ending).

vowels: for definition, see PHONEMES. Vowels may be *rounded* or *unrounded*, *open* or *closed* (155) according to the shape and position of the lips; *front, middle,* or *back* (156) according to the position in the mouth in which they are formed. Those which are formed in the mouth alone are *oral*; those which require the nasal cavity to be joined to that of the mouth are *nasal*. The vowels [i], [ü], and [u] are *constricted**, the first two being frontal and thin in sound, the latter being a back vowel and richer: they are much used in clusters together. Middle vowels have no marked character in verse, and may be called *neutral* or *toneless* (159). Back vowels tend to be *strong* and *sonorous** (172). Nasal vowels are *resonant* and often suggest musical sounds. A vowel is *free* when it ends a word, and *blocked* when followed by a sounded consonant in the same syllable (171). Most vowels in French are short, and may be *naturally long* (i.e. long in normal usage) only when stressed and blocked by certain consonants (27, 35, 171-2). They may be *lengthened** in verse when stressed and followed by a syllable containing a neutral [e]. When two vowels come into immediate contact with each other the effect is known as *hiatus*: according to classical theory this should never happen between words, and it is in fact generally avoided (39). See also SEMI-CONSONANTS.

INDEX OF LINES QUOTED
IN THE TEXT

References are to the numbers attached to the quotations in the body of the text, with the exception of a few lines from which only incomplete and un-numbered quotations have been used. In these cases, page references are given. Lines quoted in the Commentaries have not been included.

The names of poets are abbreviated as follows: